PASTORAL PSYCHOLOGY

PASTORAL PSYCHOLOGY

By KARL R. STOLZ

DEAN OF THE HARTFORD SCHOOL OF RELIGIOUS EDUCATION
AUTHOR OF "THE PSYCHOLOGY OF PRAYER," "EVOLUTION AND GENESIS"

COKESBURY PRESS
NASHVILLE, TENN.

SET UP, ELECTROTYPED, PRINTED, AND BOUND
BY THE PARTHENON PRESS AT NASHVILLE
TENNESSEE, UNITED STATES OF AMERICA

O

44658

THE MEMORY OF MY MOTHER

CONTENTS

CHAPTER XVIII

FOREWORD

THIS book is a product of my work as a teacher and student adviser and as a pastor. It is designed primarily for the use of pastors who seek further guidance in their work with individuals, and of candidates for the Christian ministry.

Many a minister of the Gospel who is able to preach effectively to an audience of five hundred persons is tragically impotent when face to face with one individual involved in a crisis. Although trained in the science and art of public ministration, many have assumed the responsibilities of the pastoral relation without adequate preparation. Pastoral psychology was not taught in theological seminaries when the majority of pastors now in active service were students. Practical experience in the field apart from specific training is a costly and often a futile teacher. A love of mankind, a desire to serve a broken human spirit, a native tact and winsomeness, however essential to pastoral helpfulness such attributes may be, cannot compensate for ignorance of the fundamental principles of personality growth and adjustment and for lack of skill in their direct application. To meet the needs of pastors who desire to enrich their pastoral functions was an objective which governed the writing of the present treatise.

This book has not been written specifically for the benefit of the favored pastor whose professional resources include a staff of educational, social service, and psychiatric specialists. It is possible for such a pastor to refer to the appropriate associates the cases of personality immaturity or disorganization and social maladjustment which he encounters in his constituency. The specialists at his command undertake forms of highly specialized work the description of which is beyond the scope of this treatise. He may, to be sure, derive a measure of stimulation and direction from such an introductory volume as this in the work of personality development and reconstruction which he himself may attempt. The interests and needs of the alert pastor of the local church of ordinary means have conditioned the selection of the types of personal service herein

11

presented. It has been my dominant purpose to assist the pastor who is thrown upon his own personal resources in his ministrations to undeveloped, depressed, harassed, and divided individuals in his parish.

It is hoped that this volume will introduce the prospective minister, in the course of his formal professional preparation, to a variety of typical major pastoral problems and duties. Pastoral psychology is a newcomer among the disciplines included in the curriculum of the theological seminary. The literature available to both the teacher and student in this promising branch of practical theology is not yet so plentiful and complete that an additional treatise, if it possesses any merit, is superfluous. It is conceded that the mastery of the contents of a book like this does not fully qualify one for effective pastoral service. To theory there must be added actual experience as a pastor. Books are not adequate substitutes for life. Fortunately the theological student is in many instances able to test and verify his knowledge and to develop skill in personality guidance under seminary supervision.

Implications of mental hygiene and clinical psychology for the service of the pastor to individuals have been developed in the following pages. Divergent psychological theories, while not described in detail, have not been ignored. It appears that the scientific explanations of some varieties of personality adjustments are more subtle and baffling than the effective hygienic or clinical procedure which practical experience has developed. Since many pastors have some knowledge of them, the variant fundamental conceptions of psychologists like Freud, Jung, and Adler are here and there introduced and my own attitudes indicated. I have adopted the eclectic method. Theories and practices which the results of experimentation and the facts of observation support and which prove of service in pastoral work have been appropriated from several schools of psychology.

Concrete cases of various types of personality defects, conflicts, and adjustments have been cited. An apt illustration or case study has a pedagogical value which is its own justification. The illustrative material has been drawn from various sources. Contributions of clinical psychologists, cases introduced by writers of psychological treatises for the use of pastors, as well as my own observations and experiences, have been laid under tribute. In addition, valuable case material has been provided by my own students, many of whom are pastors of mature judgment. Of course personal identities have been disguised with fictitious names and with the elimination or change of such other details as might be embarrassingly revealing.

It is assumed that the majority of pastors have no disposition to encroach upon the special field of the psychiatrist. The average pastor, however conversant he may be with personality singularities and successful in his treatment of the same, is not competent to outline and direct therapeutic courses for individuals of the extremely defective group. He is not a mental pathologist. The feeble-minded, the idiots, the imbeciles, the epileptics, and such sexual perverts as the nymphomaniacs he will be content to entrust to the care of the psychiatrist. At best the pastor can minister to very seriously or chronically diseased minds through prayer, confession, religious instruction, and other instruments of his office only under the directions of the specialist in charge. This treatise, accordingly, for the most part presents only those types of personality problems with which the pastor of intelligence may hope to cope with justifiable confidence. He who aspires to more technical compentency in rebuilding personality is referred to the more technical and exhaustive works of a pastoral specialist like Pfister. The pastor is to respect his limitations as well as to exploit his abilities.

The function of the Christian religion as a personal experience with social consequences has been emphasized throughout the treatise. Many references to the use of religious motives, attitudes, and practices in developing or rehabilitating personality have been made. In addition, two chapters have been entirely devoted to the subject. So far from assuming that religion is a delusion and at best an opiate or an escape mechanism, it is maintained that it should be the central experience of the individual, an inspiring, organizing, and unifying experience, an experience grounded in the nature of the universe, supported by reason, and justified by its fruits and emotional satisfactions. The Christian religion is the progressive integration of personality with a dynamic sense of ultimate reality, as manifested and interpreted by Jesus Christ, as the constant center of reference. Many personality disorders are primarily the outcome of an ineffective mobilization and use of the resources at the command of the individual. It is the special province of the pastor to make available and determining moral and religious forces for the enrichment of those to whom he ministers. I offer no apologies for occasional exhorting and preaching in my zeal to describe and illustrate the significance of Christian faith and conduct for the enlargement of personality.

It is fitting that I acknowledge the debt of gratitude I owe my colleague, Professor Plato E. Shaw, for reading sections of this work in manuscript form and all the proof sheets, and for many constructive suggestions which he offered.

K. R. S.

CHAPTER I

THE PSYCHOLOGICAL APPROACH TO PASTORAL WORK

THE higher integration and expansion of personality is the governing objective of modern Christian education and pastoral care. The centrality of personality in the program of the Church is being proclaimed and realized with intelligent zeal. Pastors in rapidly increasing numbers are turning to mental, social, and allied sciences for light and guidance in their work with individuals. A new pastoral technique is being evolved and the expression "the cure of souls" is assuming a significance hitherto unknown.

Not that throughout the history of the Christian Church there have not always been pastors who have given the individual face to face with a crisis wise counsel and practical assistance. The application of common sense by pastors in bygone days has in a multitude of cases delivered the individual from doubt, fear, error, delusion, waywardness, and other obstacles to the fulness of life. Many responded to the life-needs of the individual to the measure of their ability. In their pastoral service they utilized such instruments of their office as prayer, confession, instruction, exhortation, and assurance. Nevertheless, a more scientific knowledge of personality and its social setting, in the light of which the needs and conflicts of men are more accurately understood and effectively met or resolved, is an achievement of recent times.

A revival of pastoral service comparable to the revival which has been thriving in the field of religious education within the local church is now well under way. The movement is principally the outcome of two factors: first, the recognition that in the past and present preoccupations of the Church the private concerns of men have been slighted; second, the development and formulation of a more scientific pastoral approach. To these producing influences may be added one or two others, namely, the protesting attitude of some of the neglected and

15

the fact that many have sought the help of counselors good and
bad available outside the Church.

Preoccupations of the Church

The Protestant Church in America, to restrict our discussion to one branch of organized Christianity, has not as a
whole always made the enrichment of the individual personality
an immediate major charge. Private adjustment problems have
been altogether too frequently obscured by the preoccupations
of the Church. Theological reconstruction or disputation,
mass evangelism, and the application of the social teachings of
Jesus to the institutional life of the nation have held the attention and absorbed the energies of large parts of the Church.
The special engrossment which during a given period has
dominated a local church or denomination has tended to
determine the quality and extent of the pastoral care which the
individual has received.

In the second half of the previous century a theological upheaval was produced by the invasion of the field of religion by
modern science. The theories and findings of science challenged
certain long-accepted doctrines and practices of the Church.
In some quarters aspects of the Christian faith were rein-
terpreted and restated in the light of the methods, the spirit,
the hypotheses, and the results of the physical and social
sciences. The leaders of the liberal party assumed that a
process of progressive theological adjustment will be imperative so long as our knowledge of the world continues to increase. The historical approach to the study of the Bible
gained ground, to specify but a single positive consequence of
the scientific attitude in the field of theology. In other sections
of the Church the inherited tenets and customs questioned
by science were stoutly defended and retained. The leaders
refused to come to terms with scientific thought. For example,
they combated the theory of evolution with zealous acerbity.
Furthermore, they attacked those religious leaders who were
making their peace with science, branding all such as heretics.
The so-called liberals retaliated.

There was scant nourishment in the theological controversies
in which branches of the Church were embroiled for most

individuals hungering for comfort in sorrow, for freedom from delinquency, and for inward peace. Of the laymen who were doctrinally inclined some were dismayed, others were confirmed in their opinions, and still others were theologically reconstructed. The theologically-minded laity constitute a minority. The majority of men are burdened with cares, vexations, and obligations which are far removed from abstract argumentation and debate. The issues of their lives are not met in a crosswork of theological disputation or adaptation. When the warfare between theology and science as well as the warfare between opposing systems of theology was raging the individual could not be given sufficient pastoral service. To say the least pastoral work was secondary, theological preoccupation was primary.

At the same time mass evangelism was by some evangelical denominations recognized as the means of propagating the Christian faith and delivering persons from skepticism and iniquity. The popular evangelist attracted large crowds. There was intensive preaching with an urgent appeal for an immediate surrender to Christ. Most churches annually conducted what was called a protracted meeting; every night for a few weeks of each year an evangelistic service was held in which the call to repentance, conversion, and regeneration was sounded. Pastors with redemptive passion utilized the Sunday evening service throughout the year as a special evangelistic opportunity. Personal workers, laymen as a rule, were trained to bring to the conscience of the individual the evangelistic message, either privately or in the congregation after the exhortation of the preacher. Many who were redeemed from sloth or evil were added to the membership of the churches. Although the indifferent were roused to a new ardor, the erring and wayward reclaimed, and the faithful rededicated to a godly life and the salvation of the sinful, men were on the whole dealt with *en masse*.

To be sure, the saying, "a house-going pastor makes a church-going people," was frequently quoted and sometimes adopted as a maxim by pastors. The precept affirmed the purpose of the pastoral ministration, which was to persuade people to attend church services. The unchurched were personally solicited.

The conscientious pastor made periodic calls in the homes of the members of his flock. The bereaved were consoled and the sick visited. The essence of pastoral visitation was the reading of a Bible passage and the offering of prayer. These pastoral procedures did make for the enlargement of the individual, although vast areas of personality difficulties were untouched. On the whole the gauge by which the effort of pastoral work was measured was the number of persons who were induced to attend church. That many pastors developed proficiency within the restricted scope of work undertaken should be gratefully acknowledged.

The emphasis in the program of an influential part of the Church was shifted. For a generation extending to recent times a section of the Protestant Church in America has made a heroic effort to Christianize the institutions of society. Abuses in industry, commerce, and politics stirred the conscience of religious leadership. The Church proceeded to humanize religion. In seeking to meet the competition for the allegiance of the people and to cope with powerful antisocial organizations it created new arms of service and increased its support of the agencies already active in behalf of the underprivileged. Mission chapels were established in industrial centers, and settlement houses designed to bring together the prosperous cultured and the uneducated poor were founded. The Y. M. C. A. and the Y. W. C. A. received additional aid. Religious leaders studied afresh the messages of the Old Testament prophets and the teachings of Jesus for their application to the corporate life of America. Men like Washington Gladden, Josiah Strong, and Walter Rauschenbusch interpreted and enforced social religion with a clarity and vigor which reminded men of the glorious succession of the Hebrew prophets.

The accent on the social application of the Christian religion has no doubt resulted in the temporal and moral welfare of a host of persons. The measure of social justice which has been established has released the private possibilities and resources of multitudes. But as somebody has sagely remarked, we Americans never have enough of anything unless we have too much. In many quarters the social implications of the Gospel were developed to the almost complete neglect of the peculiar inward needs of the individual. Frequently the fact was lost sight of that the Christian life has its conscious inception in an interior illumination of the individual and a personal experience of the Father as ultimate Reality. The message of Jesus is personal in its direct application although many of its intended consequences may be social.

Discriminating individuals have sensed the absurdity of enlisting in crusades to make the institutional life of the nation Christian, save as an escape or diversion, apart from the dynamic of personalities religiously unified and inspired. A woman of discernment is reported to have withdrawn from the membership and fellowship of a prominent city church, giving as her reason her pastor's absorption in the social implications of religion. She explained that she was among those whose private necessities received no pastoral care. She referred, for example, to a brilliant and convincing series of sermons which the minister had recently preached, the burden of which was the waste, the futility, and the brutality of war among the nations. Throughout the series he incessantly exhorted his constituency to labor and pray for a warless world. She was in hearty accord with the movement to rid humanity of the scourge of war but felt that she herself was at the time personally incapable of active participation in the campaign. She remarked: "How can I adequately co-operate in a project to abolish war so long as I myself am the battle ground of conflicting emotions and contrasting desires? Only after I have achieved peace in my own soul can I strive with a whole heart for international peace." Cases of this kind may furnish an inkling of why the social message has not been more enthusiastically received by many intelligent people.

The neglected individual has here and there summoned courage to protest against the preoccupations of the Church. He has ventured openly to deplore the fact that when he has needed the bread of pastoral counsel and aid in his private distress he has been offered the stone of an irrelevant theological abstraction. He has resented the inference that if he has not been responsive to an evangelistic mass appeal which ignored individual differences he is necessarily a lost soul. Although actually in accord with the social principles of the teachings of

Jesus, he has on occasion voiced his disapproval of organized religion altogether obsessed by a utopian urge.

The implications of the pronouncements of Jesus, "I am come that they might have life, and have it more abundantly," are, the discerning layman maintains, to be developed in personal as well as social values. He craves the abundant life. He wants guidance in progressive integrations of freedom from personal defects, from internal conflicts, from fears and hatreds; he desires intelligence, health, enjoyment, power, self-expression, and a chance to create. Involved in a civilization of unusual tension, he is seeking the inward spirit of tranquillity and balance.

In their extremity many have turned to the lawyer or physician or clinical psychologist or social case worker for advice and help. Others have appealed for aid to the palmist, the clairvoyant, the astrologer, and the spiritualistic medium. It has been assumed that the pastor is either indifferent or incompetent, or both. Many earnest, harassed people no longer look to the pastor for light and direction.

The engrossments of the Church, although they have in large measure overlooked individuals floundering in their private crises, must not be altogether abandoned. The substance of the emphasis each incorporates must be retained. A philosophy of religion, a cogent system of Christian doctrine, is an educational and intellectual necessity, and as such should be reformulated and restated in the language of each successive cultural period. There is, moreover, a place in the life and work of the Church for group meetings. Mass evangelism, if the signs of the times are correctly discerned, will be replaced by educational evangelism, by protracted series of expositions of the Bible, by popular lectures on church history, and the meaning and obligations of church membership, by intensive instruction in the methods and materials of Christian nurture, the building of the Christian family, and responsible citizenship in a democracy. Furthermore, to silence the social note would be a calamity. The reclamation of the institutions of society must go forward. Such giant iniquities as war, economic oppression, and civic pollution must be opposed and exterminated. The Church must not fail to cry out against such abuses and to give aid and comfort to every agency which makes for the reconstruction of the social fabric. These emphases and pastoral care so far from being indubitably incompatible may all contribute to the development or reconstruction of the individual.

The More Scientific Approach

The mere acknowledgment that the preoccupations of the Church have overshadowed the individual might have led to more extended but hardly to more effective pastoral service. The improvement of pastoral method and procedure as well as the emergence of the individual into the consciousness of the Church was urgent. Psychology in its several branches is being exploited for what it may contribute to the pastor's intimate work with individuals. It has been repeatedly demonstrated that many personality problems which the pastor encounters are not fundamentally theological but psychological in origin and nature. Many personality issues when adequately understood are lifted from the realm of theology and transferred to the field of psychology, in which area of reality they are then attacked.

Pastoral psychology seeks to make effective the principles which undergird the mental health of the individual. It implies an intelligent familiarity with the complexities of personality throughout the range of its successive stages of development and with the social setting in which the individual lives and has his being. It discovers and appeals to the motives which determine constructive behavior. It fosters the progressive personal and social adjustments which preserve the self from devastating emotional or other conflicts, and which liberate the competencies and enrich the outlook of the individual. It furthers the organization of stabilized personality.

Pastoral psychology is remedial as well as preventive. It makes use of the gathered knowledge of clinical psychology and employs its tested methods in the correction of minor mental pathologies and anomalies. It seeks to deliver the individual from crippling anxieties, from a sense of debilitating inferiority, from character defects, and from social maladjustments. Like that of medical science, the ministration of pastoral psychology to the confused or divided personality passes through the successive stages of diagnosis, treatment, and prognosis.

The new pastoral approach must have breadth and depth as well as clinical competency. It must not sacrifice the inculcation and utilization of an adequate philosophy of life to technical proficiency. Pastoral psychology makes use of religious values in personality organization and rehabilitation. It appropriates the outlook and dynamic of the Christian faith. It offers guidance in the progressive integrations of the various functions of personality with personal committal to the Determiner of destiny disclosed and expounded by Jesus as the unifying center.

Our people may be divided into four groups. The first to be mentioned consists of those who are normal, of those who are able to live in our complex social order without debilitating personality defects or irritating unsolved adjustment problems. They have a clearly defined objective toward the attainment of which they direct their energies; they cultivate an avocational outlet, perhaps a hobby, which serves as a tension reducer or safety valve; they achieve emotional gratification through identification with husband, wife, child, or friend; they are sustained by a philosophy of life or form of religion by which the conduct of their lives is sanctioned and which is at least one of sufficiency; they accept with courage the common lot of mankind, expecting no special concessions from life. They are socially adjusted and although not necessarily self-satisfied are patient with themselves. It is evident that the number of persons who constitute this group is relatively small.

The second group is composed of those who are somewhat personally dislocated or socially maladjusted or both, but who somehow contrive to accept life's second-bests and its compensations for deprivations with more or less grace. Outward circumstances or inward conflicts reduce their possibilities for abundant living. They may be overworked, or fail to realize their legitimate vocational expectations, or subsist on an insufficient income, or be distressed by the lack of education, or if married be mismated, or be handicapped by a bodily defect, or be socially inept, but they do actually rise in some degree above their limitations and achieve a measure of satisfaction.

The third group consists of those who are so submerged by privation or incapacitated that they are undone and defeated. They are overborne by poverty, or loneliness, or disease and misery, or ignorance, or moral depravity, or by a combination of these elements. Some of these persons are almost sub-human; the contrast between what is and what should be has not created an unsatisfied desire for betterment; they are unconsciously submissive to the pressure of devastating conditions; they merely exist day by day, taking their misfortunes for granted. Others of the same group, while acutely aware of their predicament and of their inability to extricate themselves, have no philosophy which makes their lives tolerable; they exist in a state of resentful hopelessness.

The fourth group consists of those who are so mentally arrested or deranged that they cannot provide for their own temporal support and in many cases must be confined in institutions. Idiots, imbeciles, and the insane are included in this group. Drug addicts and moral morons come under the same category. Psychiatric treatment can restore some of these to mental health, others are chronically disordered.

The classification of humanity suggested is of course not absolute; there is overlapping; it would in all probability be impossible to assign every person in whom the pastor is interested to one of the four above groups. Nevertheless, the classification will serve to indicate areas of specialized pastoral ministration. The pastor's obligation to the first group, which consists of normal persons, is essentially preventive and educational; to the second and third groups, which are respectively composed of moderately and seriously disordered individuals, it is primarily corrective and re-educational; the only personal service he can wisely render to those of the fourth group is under the direct supervision of the psychiatrist in charge.

Too much should not be expected of the newer pastoral approach and procedure. No doubt much that today passes for well-grounded theory and sound practice will retreat before the advancement of more scientifically based principles and methods. If pastoral psychology justifies itself by its works, so far from being a fad and as such speedily overtaking itself, it will gradually multiply and deepen its insights into human nature and refine its methods. Religious leaders, although well trained and experienced in clinical pastoral psychology, will discover cases of personality adjustment which are beyond their comprehension and skill. They may extract a measure of comfort from the fact that the psychiatrist, however wise and successful, does not profess to be competent to restore all the disordered personalities that come to him for professional treatment. Even the specialist often fails.

It is not implied that the application of psychological principles to pastoral work will retire the office of preaching. On the contrary, intensive work with individuals will enrich the pulpit ministration. It will be a fruitful source of homiletical suggestions. It will help to keep preaching within the realm of the life-needs of the people. Judiciously exploited, it will transfuse the public message with a wealth of human fascinations. Above all, it will deliver the preacher from the tyranny of his own outlook and experience; it will keep him from the errors which result from an unconscious use of his own religious life as a standard by which to measure the genuineness and validity of the experiences of all others. So far from being antithetical, preaching and personal work are complementary and mutually stimulating. Good preaching so searches and finds the individual that he is moved to appeal to the pastor for private aid.

CHAPTER II

THE ORGANIZATION OF PERSONALITY

WHAT sort of being is Thomas Simpson or Mary Williams or any other person whom the pastor by virtue of his office or as a man is called upon to assist in a crisis? How does anybody become what he is? Under what conditions does one develop personality? What are the principal constituents of personality, and how are they acquired and combined? What is a normal human being?

It must be confessed that the process of taking a person apart, of analyzing the various elements, and of discovering what holds him together is exceedingly baffling. No complete answer to the above questions can be submitted until our present knowledge of human nature shall have advanced far beyond its present stage. Partial answers are, however, suggestive and stimulating. Biologists, psychologists, and sociologists have gleaned insights into the growth and formation of personality which are of practical value to the pastor. We know enough about the subject to guide us in the work of cultivating gracious and wholesome personality. In the present connection all that can be attempted is a survey of some of the essentials of personality organization which seem to be scientifically established and of special importance to the pastor.

Personality as an Organization

Let us begin by assuming that Thomas Simpson is an organization. What does that assumption imply? In general an organization is an entity which consists of related parts. It is a union of parts, each one of which performs a function, the whole being inclusive and self-dependent. An organization is more and other than the sum of its various parts; it is a new creation with a special characteristic or activity. A pen is an organization the essentials of which are a penholder and a pen point which serve a purpose. An inkwell is another organization, one which is composed of a bowl and a cover

25

designed to meet a need. It occurred to somebody to unite these two organizations in such a manner as to combine their functions and thus to eliminate effort and waste in writing. He placed the inkwell inside the pen and produced a more complicated organization known as a fountain pen. It is conceivable that an inventive person will evolve a hierarchy of organization in which a further refinement or elaboration of the structure and function of the fountain pen will appear. The fountain pen which I am at present using is a mechanical contrivance in which the several parts are intimately related to the whole, and that whole by eliminating the frequent dipping of the pen point and thus conserving time and energy, and by being conveniently carried from place to place in my waistcoat pocket, and serving me at will, possesses utilities peculiar to itself.

Personality is an organization of all that constitutes a human being of experience. Personality is that which a man as such is in the totality of impulses, attitudes, habits, abilities, and ideas. As thus summarized personality is more than the combination of qualities which make Mary Williams attractive, winsome, and charming, and more than the association of characteristics which distinguished her from another human being. It is more than individuality in itself. Organized personality may be regarded as the systematized and integrated whole of such driving forces as impulses whether native or acquired, and of such processes as feeling, thinking, remembering, imagining, self-conscious reflecting, and evaluating. The completely organized personality is free from disturbing internal conflicts which remain unresolved, free from increments existing and functioning apart from or contrary to the rest of the personality, and adjusts itself to novel or critical situations bravely and effectively. It operates with a minimum of emotional friction. Each aspect of personality contributes to the whole, and the stabilized whole possesses a unique character and power. The subsidiary selves are embraced and harmonized in one all-inclusive self.

Personality adjustment should be coextensive with the ongoing life of the individual. Paradoxical as it may seem to some, the unification of the individual depends on the continuous reconstruction of personality. It is safe to infer that but few personalities are always perfectly organized or in the process of becoming so. In most of us there are areas of experience which are not in subjection to the dominant interests of the person, areas which we ignore or condone, areas which if or when they do disturb our tranquillity are repressed without serious disruption of the personality as a whole. Even in cases which pass as normal, organization is as a rule relative.

The Development of Personality

It should be evident that no one is born into the world with more than the beginnings or the active possibilities of personality. It is a misuse of language to insist that the new-born child is a personality. The infant is an energetic candidate for personality. The capacity for personality development is realized through expanding experience in a social order. Personality is not acquired in complete solitude or isolation. It is not a biological inheritance, nor a gift imposed upon one wholly from without, but the perpetual achievement of a human being continuously adjusting himself to the exigencies of life in a group.

Even if an infant could survive apart from other people, he would not develop what should be called human personality. In isolation he probably would not learn to speak an articulate language. His thinking would hardly pass beyond the boundaries of the simplest relations. His talents would, for the most part, be undeveloped. Budding personality is nurtured, enlarged, and enriched in a social matrix. Society as represented by parents and other members of the intimate group stimulates the child by example and precept, directs his energies, and gives him an opportunity to realize his potentialities. In certain countries a person learns to sit on a rug, in our land he sits on the chair fitted to the human frame; as a member of an orthodox Jewish family he worships wearing a hat, as one of a Christian household he prays with bared head. If the child grows up to be a social radical, his very opposition to the established order is based on a transmitted and environing culture. Personality, although possessed of a biological foundation, is the outcome of social interaction.

The infant is a living organism. The basic property of any vital organism is its responsiveness to appropriate stimuli. Its primary feature is reaction. Energy is captured, stored, and released through action, reaction, and interaction. When the organism includes supplies of unexpended energy an unstable condition called restlessness is the result. The qualities of personality depend on the nature of the ideals and objects in the interests of which the energy of the organism is applied. Various terms have been used to designate organic energy. The energy with which human beings adapt themselves to their environments is by the physiologist called the irritability or excitability of the protoplasm. The Freudians refer to stores of libido which may be granted free expression, or repressed, or sublimated. Other workers in the field of psychology speak of impulses. Still others, taking their cue from Bergson, call the organic impetus *Élan Vital*. Whatever we may call this restless human energy, its utilization and organization for definite purposes is the corner stone of personality.

According to the findings of some reliable biologists, the continuity of life from its lowest to its highest forms is in terms of purposive activity. Protozoa such as the amoeba or the paramecium, humble as they are in structure and function, exhibit marks of purposive behavior. Their reaction to stimuli is persistent until the end aimed at has been actually gained. Cessation of effort follows the attainment of the objective. Even micro-organisms behave as units. Vital organisms grow, restore themselves, and mold a part of their environment to their purposes. Man is the most complex and refined organism to which science can point. Man is inventive and opposes his will to unfavorable circumstances. Is the assumption that ordered and disciplined personality is the chief end of man an unregulated flight of the imagination?

Let us return to our consideration of the behavior of the infant in order that we may observe more closely how restless energy is utilized in the early formation of personality. Sprawled in his little bed, the baby kicks his legs and waves his arms, striking his feet and hands against both hard and soft substances. His early movements are the random consequences of the internal pressure of surplus organic energy.

Little by little there emerge from the undifferentiated mass which surrounds him persons and objects. He begins to associate his mother with hunger satisfaction and warmth. He learns that she reacts to his cries with desired responses. Other persons become separated from the rest of his little world and are recognized as loving entities. His father, for example, is gradually individualized, and since he seems to be a benevolent being is appropriated. Meanwhile the baby has been an investigator of the many objects within sight and reach. He appears to be obsessed with the notion that everything he grasps is to be carried to his mouth. His exploits induce the agreeable feeling of power. When he learns to walk and to talk his world expands with remarkable rapidity and a consequent increase of the feeling of conquest occurs.

He develops in a frame of social reference. The attitudes and preferences of the intimate group profoundly affect the growing child. He learns to love his mother because she first loved him. He makes the startling discovery that some of his doings are acceptable in the sight of his elders, and that others arouse their displeasure. The consequences of some of his actions are agreeable and those of others painful. He wants to live on good terms with his parents and friends, since their approval affords him various satisfactions. At an early stage in his life society transmits to him its standards and customs, its taboos and inhibitions, and confers its rewards and exacts its penalties.

The little child is beginning to achieve personality. His experiences are somewhat systematized. The subjective phases of his life become more or less correlated. Gradually he discovers himself to be the center of his experiences. An organizing something emerges. Self-consciousness dawns. At first, perhaps because he is able to assume the rôle of his elders toward himself, he calls himself "Baby," or refers to himself by name. "Henry wants a drink." "Let Henry see." Self-realization occurs when he distinguishes himself from all other persons within the scope of his world. Self-feeling matures. Its quality is largely determined by the responses he arouses in others. The attitude of the young child toward himself is conditioned by the attitude others take toward him. When, for example, in the case of the preferred or the only child the attitude of admiration is accentuated he is likely to become an egocentric type individual. A different attitude toward the child will give rise to a corresponding form of self-consciousness. The most momentous adventure of his growing and exciting life is the achievement of conscious selfhood.

The Rôle of Suggestion

As the years pass, the child's personality continues the delicate and complex process of enlargement and organization. New interests, habits, and attitudes emerge. Social psychology teaches that the specific forms which restless energy takes depend on such factors as suggestion, imitation, imagination, and fundamental urges or wishes. Innumerable incitements proceed from the complex culture which envelops the individual. It is obviously impossible for any person to react to all the promptings of the social environment. It follows that not a person's entire environment but only the part of it to which he responds contributes to his personality.

Suggestion may, for present purposes, be regarded as a social overture. It is an incitement to action or to consideration. Susceptibility to an environmental prompting is called suggestibility. Stimuli that attract and fascinate the attention are likely to receive appropriate responses. The restriction of the field of consciousness to an impression is the core of the state of suggestibility. The object of attention becomes vivid, colored with emotion, and compelling. We select from the resources which experience has placed at our disposal those possibilities which seem important and desirable. This explains why two people, say brothers or sisters, may grow up together but develop different tastes and standards of conduct. They do not respond to the same sets of stimuli deriving from a common environment. Imitation may be considered the form of suggestion which reinstates a copy. If the suggestion involves the past, a picture constructed from experience is thrown upon the mental screen. If the suggestion is unrelated to the past, the imagination tries to produce a picture of its own.

Of all persons little children are the most suggestible. They exercise but little control over the impressions made upon them, for they are inclined to accept whatever is uncontradicted by their limited experience. They have no adequate fund of ideas to serve as a basis for discrimination. Their resistance to stimuli which are intensive is negligible. They are readily swayed by proposals which are associated with bodily appetites and the emotions, or which promise immediate and gratifying results. They are relatively indifferent to far-off considerations and postponed contingencies. The wise educator in so far as it is possible exposes them to those social stimuli the responses to which further constructive personality development.

To praise a child is to put him on his mettle, to belittle him is to engender in him a sense of inferiority. He is disposed to accommodate his life to social expectation. It is easy to plant a suggestion of success or failure in the fertile subsoil of the young mind. "Whatsoever a man soweth, that shall he also reap." James when eleven years old obtained a horoscope which informed him that he was proud, stubborn, shrewd, slow to anger and equally slow to calm down, sometimes fickle and jealous, straightforward, and fond of choice foods. When he read this depressing list of attributes to his mother her only comment was, "That hits you off." His belief in the astrologer's report was confirmed by his mother's statement. Ever since then James has been making special efforts to shape his life in accordance with the specifications of the horoscope.[1]

The dominant ambition of the adolescent is to enter the world of adults, to find himself there, and to function as an accepted adult. As an adolescent, a person is still sensitive to the promptings of the social order, but he displays increased independence in the selection of possible courses of activity. Interesting adults, especially those who have outstanding achievements to their credit, cast a spell upon him. He does more than admire his hero, he identifies himself with him through imagination and imitation. He assumes the rôle of his hero. He exhibits a tendency to idealize the opposite sex and is likely to fall in love. At any cost he wants to live and move and have his being in the world of adult interests, occupa-

[1] Boorman, W. Ryland, *Developing Personality in Boys,* p. 46 (New York: The Macmillan Company, 1929).

tions, amusements, and responsibilities. He values the opinions
and standards of the adult group with which he is connected.
He reacts eagerly and positively to the social incitements which
give promise of qualifying him for admission to adulthood. It
is the solemn obligation of society to give him a correct impression of what constitutes desirable and wholesome adult life.

The adult as well as the child or youth is suggestible. Imagination, imitation, and suggestion outline ways and means for
the release of restless energy so long as the individual lives.
They influence the entire gamut of adult experience. To be
sure, when the individual has lost self-control and is at the
mercy of the external forces impinging upon the mind the
effects of suggestion are debilitating and deleterious. The
balanced personality, emotionally stable and exercising discretion, subordinates the process of suggestion to its own welfare.
It adopts suggestions which minister in conformity with its
tastes and ideals. Professor George A. Coe refers to a college
president who occasionally remarked to a rich man, "If I were
in your place, I would build myself a monument." Time and
again the hint was dropped. One day the affluent man reported, "Doctor, I have decided to build myself a monument,
namely a building on your campus." [2] Of course this was
exactly what the college president had been trying to bring to
pass through suggestion. Imagination played its part in the
decision of the man of wealth; such a one desires to perpetuate
his personality and power, and imaginally tests out the various
possibilities. When he decided to contribute a building to a
college he was following the example of many others; imitation gave his desire for an earthly immortality approved by
society an appropriate outlet.

Dominant Wishes

As we have already suspected, wishes or desires have much
to do with the determining of the manner in which organic
energy is discharged. Wishes should be studied both objectively and subjectively, both as objects of desire and as states
of mind. The two constitute a single situation. Wishes have

[2] Coe, George, A., *Motives of Men,* p. 125 (New York: Charles Scribner's Sons, 1928).

a psychological and biological basis, but most if not all of them derive their form and content from environmental conditions. So long as a desire is ungratified a turbulent state with an unpleasant feeling tone persists. Once the wish has been fulfilled and expectations have been met, the personality recovers its equilibrium. If the attainment of the desire falls below the level of anticipation, an emotional disturbance follows.

Dr. William I. Thomas has submitted a classification of wishes which consists of four groups, as follows: the desire for recognition, the desire for response, the desire for new experience, and the desire for security.[3] This grouping and the analysis on which it rests have proved of value to the student of human nature in the social setting. Professor Ellsworth Faris, in unpublished lectures, on the basis of his critical examination of the work of Thomas and others, suggests a modified and expanded division of desires into five groups, with special emphasis on the content and definiteness given restlessness by the cultural environment.

The first group of desires Faris lists consists of appetites centered in physiological conditions, such as hunger, the sexual urge, and the craving for bodily sensations for their own sake. Because the sexual impulse figures so extensively in personality problems, a later chapter will be devoted to a discussion of its nature and significance.

Another set of wishes has to do with allegiance to the social group. Loyalty, altruism, and patriotism are typical forms of this urge. Desires of this kind express themselves in two ways, namely, in a readiness to submerge or eradicate the self for welfare of the group, and in participation in the activities of the group.

A third set of impulses includes such opposing wishes as the desire for excitement and the desire for security. The craving for excitement leads to new experience, to adventure, daring deeds, explorations, athletics, and scientific research. The wish for thrills, novelty, and new sensations often attaches itself to injurious objects and enterprises. For example, a

[3] Thomas, W. I., *The Unadjusted Girl*, p. 1 ff. (Boston: Little, Brown & Company, 1924).

certain woman who was nursing a dope fiend became almost morbidly curious about the effects of opium. Not content with observing its consequences in the life of her patient, she finally experimented on herself and soon became an addict. On the other hand, the desire for security makes one cautious, conservative, industrious, and thrifty. Moved and directed by this impulse, one may secure an education or make the acquiring and saving of money the major life-purpose. Those who seek protection in its various forms are likely to cling to the assurances of religious faith.

The fourth group of urges is characterized by the negative quality of avoidance or disgust. Most of us have a feeling of repugnance for such things as the filthy or the malodorous. In so far as possible we avoid or evade the dull, the irksome, and the monotonous. We are disposed to withdraw from situations which arouse dread, hatred, or anger. Conduct which we consider vile or indecent nauseates us. The sight of a married woman flirting with a young man evokes disgust in the person of good taste and elevated moral standards.

The fifth set of wishes embraces the desire for intimacy and the desire for recognition. The craving for response or intimacy seeks outlets in friendship, courtship, romance, companionship, and marriage. The religious consciousness cultivates intimacy with the spirit of the universe. The warmer type of personality longs for fellowship with God not only for moral inspiration but also for the sake of the experience of the intimacy itself.

The desire for recognition or distinction is such a dynamic factor in the formation and organization of personality that it merits more than a passing reference. The thirst for recognition is gratified by attention, approval, appreciation, applause, popularity, reputation, and social standing. A person whose desire for recognition has been unfulfilled in actual life sometimes pictures himself as the successful and appreciated leader of an imaginary adoring group. Daydreaming is often the outcome of the frustration of the wish for recognition by one's associates. There are individuals who migrate from group to group until they discover a group which accords them the coveted attention and standing. The urge for excitement is frequently expressed in an exploit which wins applause and popularity.

Adler, the famous psychologist and educator, maintains that the wish for superiority, which is akin to the desire for recognition or distinction, is the central and primary impulse of human nature.[4] According to this authority the restless energy of the child takes the basic form of the will to power. Adler holds that children feel inferior to more mature persons and forces which surround them, and naturally expend energy in the direction of presumed superiority, security, and totality. The infant in arms soon learns that he exercises power over his mother. Gradually it dawns upon him that he has toys under his own control. He continues the attempt to dominate objects and persons. The boy may decide to become a chauffeur in order that he may manipulate a machine and lord it over pedestrians. The little girl may resolve to be a teacher when she is old enough in order that she may dominate children. The urge to overcome inferiority and to achieve power expands and organizes personality. In order to subdue the earth and to have dominion it is necessary to foster and cherish such robust qualities as courage, self-confidence, and independence. The child who lacks these attributes shirks or avoids his responsibilities and in so doing tacitly accepts and continues the state of inferiority.

Adler goes on to explain that the most important task of the educator is the inculcation of a sense of social responsibility in the growing personality. The degree of social feeling which the child has determines the manner in which the will to power is expressed. If the cultivation of social sympathy is neglected the child becomes a menace to the group of which he is a member. A boy who was asked what profession he intended to learn replied that he was going to be a physician in order that he might conquer death. He had social feeling. Another lad who lacked this ingredient said that he wanted to become a grave digger in order that he might bury people. The first mentioned, realizing his ambition, became a physician and throughout his distinguished career did all within his power

[4] Adler, Alfred, *Education of Children* (New York: Greenburg, Inc., 1930).

to combat and overcome death. The second became an un-scrupulous merchant who, figuratively speaking, dug graves for his competitors. Criminals, neurotics, and suicides in so far as they are devoid of a consciousness of social obligation are self-centered and selfish. The unwanted child, the spoiled child, and the child hampered by physical disability, unless they are reorganized, grow up seeking only their own advantage and striving to reach a goal of personal superiority at the cost of others. To arouse and nurture social feeling in such children is a delicate but by no means hopeless project. Exposure of such to the contagious influence of socialized persons will accomplish more than formal instruction.

The Hierarchy of Interests

No pretense has been made in this discussion to offer an exhaustive and detailed account of personality growth, but what has been presented should afford serviceable insights into this fascinating developmental process. Attention has been called to the origin and significance of restless human energy. Restlessness was considered the store of unapplied energy of the human being. A statement has been made of the dynamic nature of suggestion, imagination, and imitation and their function in the selection and appropriation of the possible outlets for restless energy. Adopting the analysis of Faris and others, the forms which restlessness assumes have been briefly described in terms of physiological needs, fidelity to the social group, the cravings for excitement and security, the negative urges of disgust, dread, hate, anger, and monotony, and the desires for intimacy and distinction. The interaction and interpenetration of these drives and impulses have been implied. It remains to show that these and other volitions and emotional dispositions and urges are organized in relation to a hierarchy of interests.

An interest may be described as a system of active and emotional dispositions centered in the concept of an object, personality, or quality. The measure of personality is the number, variety, and nature of the interests which it embraces. Art, friendship, truth, goodness, material prosperity, good health, social progress, and religion are typical interests of normal people. Not one of these interests is reducible to a single or simple principle or element, but each is a complexity of factors correlated by a dominant idea. The interests as a whole constitute a hierarchy in which each occupies its proper place and is subordinated to a central control.

Religion is a regulative interest. It embraces all other interests in one all-inclusive interest. The religious interest demands that personality be governed by an interpretation of the nature and purpose of ultimate Reality, the prevailing emotional tone being one of wonder, reverence, and worship. It is the special task of the pastor to motivate life by the compulsion of a deliberately cultivated idealism.

When the various impulses and interests are integrated with the dominant value as the point of reference a condition of stabilization or balance occurs. Balanced personality is characterized by emotional stability. The disorganized or unorganized personality stages a conflict of emotions. The majority of the personality problems with which the pastor copes are heavily charged with emotion. In fact, many cases of personality maladjustment are purely emotional in nature. Few personalities are emotionally serene and without areas not in captivity to the central organizing compulsion. Nevertheless, so long as the inconsistencies or anomalies do not engender severe emotional tensions, the poise and tranquillity of personality remain relatively undisturbed. To be sure, many persons who continue in a state of emotional equilibrium should be disturbed in order that a higher synthesis of personality may be formed. One should normally and constantly make an effort to bring conflicting elements, created by daily changes in circumstances, into adjustment with one's growing sense of ultimate value.

CHAPTER III

THE DEVELOPMENT OF EMANCIPATED PERSONALITY IN CHILDREN

PSYCHOLOGY has made important contributions to our understanding of the nature and function of education. It has shed light upon parental responsibility. It has placed at the service of parents and teachers valuable insights into the nature of childhood, and has suggested reasonable goals for the educational process together with methods for their attainment. Applied psychology offers guidance in the development of personality which is wholesome and happy, self-reliant and resourceful, at home in God's world, and a contributor to the stock of social welfare.

If it be objected that psychology in cultivating the area of child life has rushed in where angels fear to tread, one may in justification of the venture refer to the substantial body of information it has gleaned and to the practical results it has achieved. Not that all the aspects of childhood have been minutely studied and all the implications for education developed, tested, and validated. In fact, to date no one who appreciates the intricate and elusive functions of the human mind will presume to volunteer a detailed description of normal personality. Nevertheless, to postpone the supervised process of personality development until all areas of human nature have been explored, all educational goals established, and all methods refined would be to shirk parental and pedagogical responsibility. The general task of the educator is the guidance of the child in a quest for balanced personality.

Much of the responsibility of the parent moves within the area of mental hygiene. Much of the work which mental hygiene attempts to do is precautionary, anticipatory, and preventive. It would forestall the development of mental disorders which disrupt personality. It seeks to discover and to correct personality defects and social maladjustments in their incipient stages. It endeavors to discover, formulate, and make

38

effective the principles which undergird the process of wholesome personality development.   To employ the well-grounded findings of psychology and its better established theories, and meanwhile to be ready to revise or reject our practices in the light of scientific progress, is obviously the course which wisdom commends.

The Continuity of Experience

Psychology makes prominent the strategic importance of the individual's period of immaturity.   Freud, for example, insists that neurotic disturbances which proceed from mental causes invariably have an infantile history.   He contends that every neurotic symptom, originating in a nonorganic condition, traced to its secret source brings to light a critical incident of the first four years of life.   We may not agree with Freud that such is always the case.   There is no doubt a continuity in the life of the individual from birth to maturity, but as life proceeds new interests and forces are established which are among the several determinants of outlook and conduct.   It is of course hard in every instance to distinguish childhood proclivities from the governing developments established later.

Nevertheless, the intimate relation which exists between childhood experience and adult reaction is significant.   It is impossible for the adult altogether to transcend the child he was. It is a matter of common observation that old people, persons seriously ill, and those who are hopeless and thwarted in their endeavors and ambitions occupy themselves much with the early years of life, seeking a solace and compensation in the hallowed memories of childhood days.   It is not to be denied that the life of childhood is preserved in an active state in the adult disposition.   For example, the religious forces which impinge upon the child may be adopted and developed later by choice.   Horace Bushnell anticipated the psychological interpretation of religious experience when he wrote that Christian conversions or transformations are the restored activities and more developed products of the properties and associations of childhood.   Psychology has given the bearing of early religious impressions upon adult religious experience a deeper meaning and value.

Analytical psychology discloses the underground connections which unite the present with the past and outline the future. Professor John G. Mackenzie relates that he used to have a peculiar feeling at the close of a happy day that some evil was likely to overtake him. The irrational feeling was sufficiently unpleasant to make him miserable. One day when he attempted to analyze it memory carried him back to a happy day spent at home with other children. He could recall the laughter of himself and his playmates, and then there emerged into remembrance the incident which was the causal factor of the irrational and depressing feeling. He distinctly remembered that his mother interrupted the hilarious laughter with the remark that she wondered what would happen as a result of the high spirits. She became so downcast that the fun of the children was ended. Fortunately, Professor Mackenzie was able to associate the feeling of misery with the original experience with such vitality that he was delivered from the irrational fear of distressing endings to happy days.[1]

The continuity of human experience suggests the value of preventive and precautionary measures in education. For example, the child should be guarded as much as possible against nervous shocks. Neurotic behavior in adults is often attributable to emotional shocks sustained in childhood. A man forty years old reports an abnormal dread of snakes although he realizes that no poisonous serpents infest the region in which he lives. The mere mention of a snake fills him with horror and terror. At night he is often visited by dreams in which he is frightened and attacked by serpents. Most men have a feeling of repugnance for snakes, but this man's aversion is abnormal. Fortunately he is able to account for his phobia. When he was a small boy an older schoolmate threw a rubber snake over his shoulder, which prank so frightened him that he was ill for several hours. Often such a disturbance occurs when the child is too young to remember it, but the shock holds the child in remembrance and to an amazing extent shapes and colors his life to the end of his days.

[1] See Mackenzie, John G., *Souls in the Making*, p. 163 (New York: The Macmillan Company, 1929).

The Self-Reliant Personality

The goal of home training is emancipated, happy, and socially invested personality. The child who is pampered with debilitating tenderness becomes a self-centered personality. When everything is done for him and nothing demanded of him he is likely to assume that his every whim is a law which others are obliged to obey. He presupposes that he is the absolute monarch of his world and that nothing or nobody can dethrone him. The only God he will recognize is one whose function it is to come to his aid on demand. The slightest restraint results in a paroxysm of rage. When he is an adult he will react to frustrations with the same outbursts of tantrums. The college girl who has been pampered as a child will indulge in a mixture of weeping and laughing when she is restrained from doing anything upon which she has set her heart. As a wife she will insist that it is her husband's privilege to give her everything she craves and to expect nothing in return. The husband who as a child developed the egocentric consciousness becomes wrathful when his wife does not give him all the attention he desires. Pampered children are sold into bondage to themselves, and when grown up make others miserable.

The dominated child, on the other hand, grows up without a will of his own. He is the product of authority. Punished when he dares to deviate from parental restrictions and mandates, he grows up devoid of courage to assume initiative and responsibility. He is the product of authority. If he does not rebel and assert himself, he will go through life dependent on others. A youth in whom the attitude of dependence had been established by parental control, having left home in order to attend college, actually committed suicide in a fit of helplessness and despondency. A married woman recently remarked that she had never made an important decision herself. When she was a child her mother told her that she was too young to decide matters, and when she became a wife she still relied on her mother. "Mother knows best, and if she does make a mistake it is all for my own good," is the young woman's explanation and defense. That she has deserted her husband and returned to her mother's home should occasion no surprise. A small boy in the church school studied the Bible record of the pilgrimage of the boy Jesus to Jerusalem. He was amazed to learn that the parents of Jesus missed him on the homeward journey only after three days. "Three days!" exclaimed the church school pupil. "My mother would have missed me in less than thirty minutes and begun the search for me!"

Nor is the neglected child likely to develop a wholesome and capable personality. He may be neglected because he is an unwanted child or an ugly child or an intellectually deficient child. The refusal of the parental affection and recognition which he naturally craves may lay the foundations of a neurotic disposition. He feels that the world is unfair to him. He is likely to grow up a cynic, if not a criminal. Juvenile delinquency is in many instances the outcome of parental neglect.

When the child is emotionally overstimulated, personality disorders are probable. When parents are in conflict the emotional life of the child is likely to become abnormal. The child feels obliged to take sides in the state of friction which exists between his parents and to his own injury experiences excessive hatred, love, and jealousy. Again, parental partiality is as detrimental as lack of devotion. No decided preference for the child of one sex over the child of the other sex should be shown by either parent. The extreme preference of the mother for the son or that of the father for the daughter may eventuate in an unwholesome attachment. Furthermore, children should not be employed as convenient avenues of relief for parental irritations and inhibitions. And fear as a persuasive to good conduct should be cast out by creative love. To add one more admonition to this list, the weak rather than the strong child should be encouraged by praise. To deprecate and dispraise the child whose attainments are a disappointment to his parents breeds a sense of inferiority in him. It has been estimated that fully eighty per cent of adult inferiority complexes have been induced by faultfinding, scolding parents. To be sure the commendation of the parent should be truthful, for only when it is such will it act as a tonic the consequences of which will be substantial and gratifying.

The good home is an institution where the child is prepared for hearty and effective participation in his world. The child does not belong to his parents but to himself. The respect and affection of the child are not to be demanded as rights but earned as privileges and awards. Home is the place where the child is to be taught to stand on his own feet and to take his own part. So far from being home-bound the child should be gradually emancipated from his parents. He is to be weaned psychologically as well as physically. As the relation of dependency on the parents is progressively relinquished the associations of the child with other persons, especially with those outside the home, should be increased and enriched, in order that in due time he may become a self-reliant and contributing member of society. The good parent like the good physician makes himself unnecessary as soon as possible.

The emancipated child is reared in a home atmosphere of affection and obligation. He is not treated as an asset to be exploited. He is not debilitated with attention, nor crushed by domination, nor embittered by parental habitual negligence, nor rendered unstable by emotional tensions, but is directed and advised, thrown upon his own resources, taught to fight his own battles, and is morally sensitized and socially inspired. It is the task of the parent to set conditions, to suggest profitable areas of inquiry and experimentation, and to stimulate rather than to domineer. There should be no attempt to superimpose upon our children the ideas and experiences of a previous generation which have no connection with the currents of the modern world. The major aim of the parent-teacher is to obtain an adequate response to the present. The developing personality is to be encouraged to analyze conditions, to exercise discrimination, and to cultivate good taste, rather than to force itself into a parental pattern of thought and practice. The wise parent helps the child to help himself and hopes that he will transcend his father and mother in character and usefulness. The risks of such a procedure are conceded and frankly assumed, but the conviction governs that only he who faces the necessary perils of life can learn how successfully to contend with them.

The Transformation of Crude Forces

The principle of sublimation should receive intelligent application in personality development. Human nature includes raw materials both inherited and acquired which can and should be refined and socialized. From wild animals and plants man has derived types which minister to human need and comfort. Dogs are reclaimed wolves or jackals, and cabbages and carrots are cultivated weeds. Left to themselves or relegated to the state of nature, domesticated types of animals and plants either perish or revert to the original stock. By that supervised process of the revision of experience which we call religious education primitive human impulses and instincts are converted into social forces.

The impulse to fight should be expressed in such constructive activities as the conquest of nature for human ends, the elimination of ignorance, disease, and poverty, and the reduction of the manifold evils which hamper and debase mankind. Hunger should assert itself not only as a desire for needful food for the body but also as a desire for wisdom, goodness, and beauty. Fear in the religious attitude is to be converted into awe of and reverence for the sacred and morally exalted. Anger, so far from being permitted to discharge itself in the wanton destruction of property or life, is to be socialized, to be transformed into ethical fervor and zeal for justice. Self-regard is by a process of direct refinement to manifest itself as self-respect which is above the petty and sordid. These and other fundamental human functions and drives, whether parts of our organic inheritance or the resultants of social interaction, should be neither suppressed nor eradicated but disciplined and directed in accordance with the precepts of Christianity.

A boy whose deportment had been exemplary suddenly displayed a pugnacious disposition which brought him into collision with the school authorities. Investigation revealed that he had failed in arithmetic and as a consequence was placed in a class generally regarded by the older boys as consisting of subnormal pupils. These boys taunted him with his loss of status, which aroused his ire and impelled him to fight with one after the other. A social worker who understood the case in its various bearings suggested that the boy battle with the unsolved problems in arithmetic and subdue them. The worker volunteered to tutor the lad. He accepted the challenge and attacked the problems with such vigor and intelligence that he made satisfactory progress in arithmetic. After three months his delinquency practically ended. He did have one notable lapse. He engaged in a fight with his persecutors, afterward explaining that a "licking" was the only language they understood and respected.[2]

The Administration of Discipline

Corporal punishment generally fails to accomplish the purpose for which it is administered and frequently succeeds only in embittering the child and arousing in him a secret but violent antagonism against his tormentor. Furthermore, the unexplained application of physical force is likely to entrench evil tendencies the more deeply and firmly. Discipline by violence is irrational, for goodness is never the product of force, and should be administered only as a last desperate measure to protect the child from himself or to conserve the imperiled rights of society. It is a confession of parental failure. A lover of horses once remarked that he had never seen a balky horse which had not been maltreated as a colt. Was St. Paul moved by depressing memories of his own childhood when he exhorted fathers not to provoke their children to wrath? Unintelligible discipline is likely to erect barriers of opposition between parent and child.

A complimentary word should be spoken to the child about to be restrained or disciplined. The reference to the commendable helps the child to preserve his self-respect throughout the difficult period of discipline. The parent should express disappointment rather than rage. The sorrow of the parent may beget a change of heart in the child, but rage breeds only rage.

The child's own explanation of a fault or misdeed should be heard and considered by the parent. An effort should be made to discover the motive of the offense. The parent who is persuaded that the case in hand demands discipline, once he understands what prompted the child to act, may conclude that the child needs instruction rather than punishment. The parent

[2] Cf. Burgess, E. W., *American Journal of Sociology*, Volume 28, pp. 663, 664.

should give due weight to the fact that the young child does not pause to reflect before he acts but is moved by impulse or the urge of immediate desire. He does not anticipate consequences. It sometimes happens that an intimate conference with the young culprit brings to light the embarrassing fact that he has been actuated by the bad example of father or mother. In such an instance it is the parent rather than the child who stands condemned before the tribunal of social judgment. The child's immaturity and the blundering which attends the coming of age rather than moral perversity account for much conduct which seems reprehensible to the adult.

Reasons for restrictions should be submitted to the child. To proceed upon the assumption that the child ought to refrain from this or that on the ground of mere parental authority is to violate the fundamental rights of the child as a person. For example, the wise father who is anxious lest his son become addicted to cigarette smoking will lay before the youth the reasons why such bondage is deleterious. A mere prohibition is likely to arouse in the boy an irresistible Freudian wish for that which is forbidden. The teaching of the consequences of wrongdoing, together with the offering of a reward for abstinence for the critical period of immaturity, will accomplish more than the assertion of parental authority or threats of violence. The possibility of unethical choice as a necessary peril of living should likewise be recognized and accepted by parents and teachers.

The oversensitive child is in need of skilfully supervised self-discipline.[3] Such a child is likely to weep or laugh, to blanch or blush, on the slightest provocation. His behavior, whether good or bad, is prone to exaggeration. He is much too dependent on praise and recognition. He reacts too intensely to disapproval, censure, and correction. His oversensitiveness may manifest itself in one or more of the various forms of fear. He may be afraid of the dark. The considerate parent so far from compelling the child to go into a dark but familiar room may enter it himself and thus demonstrate the harmlessness of

[3] See Riggs, Austen Fox, *Just Nerves,* pp. 55 ff. (New York: Houghton Mifflin Company, 1922).

the child's object of dread. The child will be advised not to ignore his fear altogether nor yet to occupy himself unduly with it. He will be encouraged to conquer the disagreeable attitude by action of his own. Whatever the specific expressions of oversensitiveness may be, the emotional equilibration of the growing personality can be brought about only by the positive processes of instruction, assurance, co-operation, and self-control.

Security, strength, ethical achievement, and mental health are all involved in the theory and practice of the Christian faith. The Christian religion would preserve the growing self from undue anxiety, melancholia, and other neurotic symptoms, Psychoanalysts refer to the increase in neurosis which follows a general decline in religion. Christianity exalts love. It teaches that love should move in three directions—toward God, toward one's self, and toward one's fellow-man. In loving God the child clings to the heart of the universe. A God of love as the world-orderer is both a theoretical and practical necessity. He is not austere and fearsome. The child should be taught to consider Him as father, friend, and protector. Again, the child should be taught and trained to love his neighbor as himself. As he matures he is to apply to himself the gospel of self-respect. He can develop no adequate appreciation of his fellow-men if he fails to learn to recognize his own intrinsic worth as a person. He is not to love others less than he ought to love himself. In addition, Christianity is a religion of social obligations. It regards the fraternal attitudes of justice and mercy as the divine will and command. Such a type of religion which expands and completes itself in these various modes of creative love preserves the self from one-sidedness and morbidness and keeps it balanced and wholesome.

CHAPTER IV

THE MENTAL HYGIENE OF ADOLESCENCE

ADOLESCENCE is a complication of youthful experiences, some of which are physiological, some psychological, and still others social. In general it is a process of change in the points of view and the conduct of life from those which govern the boy and the girl to those which are characteristic of the adult. The course of adolescent social adjustment is accompanied or immediately followed by definite physiological developments. The reorganization of personality is profoundly influenced by both the physiological and social increments. The interaction of the physiological and the social gives rise and direction to diversified psychological processes.

Adolescence, roughly speaking, begins with the teens and ends in the early twenties. The length of the period varies with the nature of the circumstances with which the individual copes. The process is prolonged by such elements as school life, leisure, and freedom from economic cares. It is shortened by such experiences as the pinch of poverty, the necessity to earn one's daily bread, and the assumption of the responsibilities and burdens of adults. The adolescence of the girl who leads the sheltered life of a college student financially supported by parents is far more extended than that of the girl who is obliged by grim circumstances to work for a living in a shop or factory or in case of the death of her mother to serve as housekeeper at home. Social and economic conditions may not materially delay or hasten such a physiological phenomenon as puberty, which occurs during adolescence, but they do to an amazing degree extend or abbreviate the process of converting the boy or girl into an adult.

The present consideration of adolescence moves within the domain of mental hygiene rather than within the realm of clinical psychology. It is the purpose of mental hygiene to surround youth with the positive influences which relieve emotional distress, tend to stabilize the personality, and guide it in the process of achieving adulthood. It would preserve the adolescent from experiences which seriously impair or permanently disrupt the self. Mental hygiene strives to correct or eradicate pernicious habits or attitudes in their early stages and before they have done irreparable harm. It seeks not to dictate but to counsel, not to coerce but to suggest, not to impose a system of thought and conduct from without but to stimulate the growth of inward convictions and control. It aims to reveal the adolescent to himself in order that self-knowledge may deliver him from needless fears, anxiety, and confusion.

The Reduction of Emotional Tension

The adolescent period as a whole is exceedingly difficult to describe, involving as it does so many contradictory tendencies, functions, and competencies. Almost anything one may ascribe to it is at least partly true and at the same time at least partly offset by opposing increments. The high school boy, for example, is such a bundle of contradictions that he is in rapid succession dependable and irresponsible, dignified and unrestrained, bold and timid, modest and boastful, idealistic and lax. He is at odds with himself. Nevertheless, running through the maze of conflicting forces and attitudes one may trace lines of development which determine the reintegration of personality in terms of adulthood.

Adolescence is a time of intense and even morbid emotional disturbance. An outstanding attribute of the adolescent is his emotional instability. Forces are active within and without him which generate a tumult of conflicting emotions. Much has been made of the fever and ferment, the yeasty-mindedness of the adolescent. It has been well said that emotionally he is like a cone trying to balance itself on its apex. He runs the gamut of the emotions, experiencing reverence, awe, admiration, gratitude, contempt, hatred, anger, disgust, scorn, affection, pity, joy, grief, shame. The areas of adolescent interest and difficulty to which special attention will presently be directed, such as the release of surplus energy, sex attraction, vocational adaptation, and idealism, are all suffused with intense emotional states. Even under the most favorable conditions the process of being converted into an adult is accompanied by a measure of worry, confusion, and disillusionment.

Organic changes, for example, call the attention of the youth to himself and make him painfully self-conscious. Muscles and bones in their growth do not always keep pace. Sometimes the handwriting goes to pieces as a result of the unequal development of the bones and muscles of the arm and hand. He lurches from side to side when he walks because the bones and muscles involved in locomotion lack co-ordination. An enlargement of the larynx and a lengthening of the vocal chords are incidents in his bodily growth. During the transition the voice of the adolescent boy breaks and often ranges from bass to tenor in a single sentence. He cannot control these organic factors, but is rendered humiliatingly self-aware by them. Thoughtless and unsympathetic adults who make his awkwardness a subject of disparaging and facetious remarks increase his confusion and agony. On the other hand, a tactful explanation of the physiological sources of his perplexities will reduce the emotional tension. Self-knowledge will give the assurance that he is sharing an experience common to boys of his age, and that nothing pathological or singular attaches to his temporary state of body and mind.

Again, the youth views the prospect of beginning to shave with mingled emotions of pride and dread. Others who see in his predicament only an occasion for merriment injure his pride and augment his dread. The necessity for periodically removing the growth of hair on the face in the customary manner should be taken for granted. Instruction in shaving will be appreciated. One father presented his son with a razor and taught him how to shave himself, an act of consideration which the lad will always remember with profound gratitude There are many ways in which discreet adults can prevent or reduce the perplexities of youth.

The Release of Excess Physical Energy

Both sexes achieve the maximum height during adolescence Despite rapid and uneven bodily growth, the power to with stand illness now reaches its culmination. Health is excellent The stores of physical vitality seem unbounded. The girl i

equal to the demands of a calendar of social engagements extensive enough to stagger her mother.   The restless energy of the
privileged boy is discharged in physical feats of strength, en-
durance, and skill.   The majority of athletes are youths, or
young men who have recently emerged from adolescence.   The
capacity for the consumption and digestion of large quantities
of food arouses in the parent a feeling compounded of admiration and anxiety.   An abundance of nourishing food is actually
required to sustain growth and activity.

The recreational life of the adolescent is accompanied by
potential or actual perils.   Recreation as a necessary part of the
program of youth may be either a creative or a destructive
activity.   The girl may dissipate her energies in parties and
dances.   The outcome of such feverish activity is not recreation
but excitement.   The youthful wage-earner, bored by daily monotonous toil, may expend a disproportionate amount of his
time in commercialized amusements.   Furthermore, many
adolescents who work for a livelihood have developed no capacity for recreation involving mental effort or muscular skill
and are therefore dependent on amusements appealing to sight,
hearing, and taste.   Such may be ignorant of or wilfully disregard the fact that genuine recreation refreshes the toil-worn
personality.   On the other hand, the high school or college
student may exhibit a marked tendency to overindulge in athletics, or to overexert himself, which may result in bodily injury, undermine health, and shorten life.

Participation in athletic games properly controlled is highly
beneficial although not without its peculiar moral dangers.
In the intense desire to win in a competitive game such possible
character values as fair play, honesty, and self-control may be
sacrificed.   Betting on games, engendered by cupidity, reckless-
ness, and love of excitement, is a temptation to which many
succumb.   In many cases sports usurp the resources of the
student so that instead of being a means of keeping the body fit
and relaxing the mind they become the chief end of life.

Youth should be given instruction in the wise use of excess
physical energy.   Goals which are body-building and character-
forming should be brought to the attention of young people.

An arrangement of life in which work and play in proper proportions alternate may be suggested.

The Mating Impulse

The reproductive system becomes pronouncedly active during middle adolescence.   Puberty, or the biological ability to contribute to the reproduction of the human species, marks a new departure.   Organic changes accompany the process of sexual maturing.   Previously somatic cells have been building the body; now, in addition, the reproductive cells function.   Sex qualities are not restricted to the specialized reproductive functions but permeate the entire organism.   The activity of the gonads induces secondary sex developments.   The body of the girl gradually acquires a graceful roundness, her skin becomes velvety, her hair silken, and her laugh rippling.   On the other hand, the boy runs to angles.   His body is rebuilt for strength rather than for grace.   Down, which later gives way to bristly hair, covers the upper lip, chin, and cheeks.   Hair appears also on the chest and limbs.   His voice deepens.

The adolescent girl experiences a strange restlessness and discovers in herself a mounting and romantic interest in the once indifferently regarded or barely tolerated male sex.   Secondary sex characteristics enhance her own charms.   The biological significance of her attractiveness may not be suspected by the girl herself, although it may exhilarate her and give pleasure to others.   The dissolute as well as the honorable are captivated by girlish charm, freshness, vivacity, and beauty. In love with love, reveling in the luxury of being loved, the girl may abandon herself to the conviction that she has found her predestined lover.   The pretty girl with a knack of dressing attractively and a jolly disposition sometimes has her head turned by the masculine attentions shown her and becomes the calculating flirt who takes as keen delight in numbering her male conquests as the Indian warrior of a former day took in collecting scalps.   It is natural for a girl to exercise the particular power she possesses.   Her competency should not be suppressed but redirected, refined, and socialized.

The passion for love, action, and beauty is stimulated by reading in the fields of romance, adventure, poetry, and biog-

raphy. Nearly all high school girls, whether studiously inclined or not, spend the major portion of their leisure time
reading. As she reads the girl emotionally identifies herself
with the heroine and imaginally experiences the thrill of being
distinguished or the object of ardent love.

The reading of current magazine fiction is largely responsible for the sordid view of love which sways so many young
women. Erotic literature makes the sexual element appear to
be the sum of life. Atrociously and repellently immoral reading material is not the most deleterious. The most debilitating
type of book or magazine is the one in which the characters are
physically and outwardly attractive but morally irresponsible
and reprehensible. The author miraculously saves such characters from the normal consequences of their infamy and confers upon them material success, happiness, and social popularity. Government censorship of literature is a negative
remedy and as such only partially effective. The cultivation of
literary taste and moral discrimination is an efficacious preventive.

The lad dreams of a love which will be life's choicest experience and possession. He would like to fall in love with someone who will return his love in order that the two may cultivate
an intimacy which neither would want another to invade. He
would like to have this relationship publicly recognized and
religiously sanctioned in marriage. He would have all the
world know that they belonged to one another. He wants children in the course of time, for children sanctify the union and
complete his identification with his life-partner and society.
This is the dream which he cherishes and nourishes and which
to a greater degree than even he may suspect colors his outlook and motivates the conduct of his life.

The home and the church should provide opportunities conducive to the wholesome intermingling of adolescents of both
sexes. The selection of a mate is frequently made in later
adolescence, a choice which is too often prompted by a wave of
emotion which gilds its object, no matter how palpably defective
it may be in the eyes of others, with glamour and charm. After
the honeymoon he may learn that his wife cannot prepare a
simple palatable meal, nor restrict her expenditures to his in-

come, is emotionally immature and demands excessive personal attention. On the other hand, the young woman who blindly plunges into matrimony may come to grief. The emotion of love should be the outcome of friendship and mutual understanding and appreciation, a relationship which takes time to cultivate and mature. To keep the sexes apart is only to drive them together under conditions which may be debilitating. If the girl is not allowed to entertain her boy admirer in her home, she may meet him at the corner drug store under pretense of going to a friend's house to study algebra.

There is a definite correlation between the program of the local church and the moral quality of the adolescent life in the community. The young people of the church should constitute a fellowship in which friendship, love, courtship, and marriage are normal expectations. Many churches in the city are making wise provision for the social life of youth living in rooming houses. There should be places other than the dance hall and the excursion steamer where young people who have left home can make contact with one another and others. The church's program of mental hygiene for youth should include education for marriage and parenthood, unless such instruction is already adequately provided by another community agency. The welfare of domestic relationships should not be intrusted to chance.

Problems relating to sex so far from being simpler and more easily solved in our day than formerly become more and more complex and baffling with advancing civilization. Sexual desire is one of the most deeply rooted urges. Procreation must needs have strong emotional support if the human race is to be perpetuated, but man cannot live on a purely biological level alone and remain an acceptable member of society. The reproductive impulse must be balanced by social restraint.[1]

Vocational Adjustment

Modern youth is enmeshed in a type of civilization to which an adjustment which will further the abundant life is exceedingly difficult. Youth is in no way the creator of the present age, but rather the legatee of it. Our age is the most scientific

[1] Sexual conflicts of adolescence are specified and discussed in Chapter XII.

and mechanically inventive of all history.   Youth is overwhelmed by the flood of new powers and devices which applied science has released.   It is not easy to subordinate the resources of modern invention to the enrichment of personality.

It is well to bear in mind that the majority of the older adolescents with whom most pastors come into contact are not college students but workers in industry or business.   The young wage-earner of either sex is in most cases reduced to a piece of human mechanism.   Individuality is sacrificed to an impersonal standard of efficiency.   The youthful factory employee is depersonalized.   There is little scope for self-expression or craftsmanship in performing a single operation with a machine day by day.   Routinized obedience to superiors in the business world is no less stultifying.   The functions that are most distinctively human, such as appreciation, choice, voluntary co-operation, reflection, and initiation, are repressed.

Our industrial civilization itself is at fault, a fact for which no one person is responsible.   The final objective of industry is not a finished product for the consumption of the public, much less the development of wholesome personality, but the making of money.   Young people are helplessly involved in an industrial system which is not organized and conducted for personality values but for profits, income, and spending.   Is it possible to balance the economic drive of industry or business and the welfare of the individual?   Are the two mutually antagonistic and destructive?   Have not some industrial and commercial experiments which have guarded the rights of persons been economically profitable?

One net result, not already mentioned, of the prevailing mechanization of personality is the creation of a gulf between work and leisure, a gulf that moves youth to seek excitement to offset deadening routine.   Another is the drifting of young people from one job to another in order to break the monotony of industrial routine.   Still another outcome is the baiting of foremen and other superiors, the wasting of materials through carelessness or wilfulness, and the playing of rude or rough pranks on one another.   Sometimes the youth in his reaction against a depressing vocational situation turns to an adventurous life of violence and crime.   A definite correlation can often be traced between frustrated and impoverished personality and adolescent delinquency.

Fortunately the church under wise and alert leadership can do much to ameliorate the lot of the young toiler and to realize his personal potentialities. It can promote a program for youth in business and industry, which will include lectures, musical concerts, dramatics, reading courses, systematic supervised study, athletics, entertainments, and parties. In making provision for self-development and the improvement of the vocational status, intelligent church leadership will proceed on the level of the actual needs and conflicts of employed youth. Many a well-intentioned effort to minister to toiling adolescents has come to a speedy and unhappy end because its educational and cultural presuppositions were too lofty.

The adolescents who are in the upper classes of the high school and in college constitute a privileged group. As members of a preferred class they are in special need of expert vocational guidance. Fortunately this service, more and more scientifically refined, is being offered them in an increasing number of educational institutions. Educators are systematically attempting to determine the vocational tastes and aptitudes of students of both sexes. Mental tests of various kinds are applied, special gifts are discovered, vocational counsel is given.

To be sure, a given ability may function in almost numberless ways. For example, the young man who has executive and administrative gifts may become the head of a college, or a factory, or a religious denomination, or the underworld of a metropolis. It is recognized that character and opportunity will determine the specific application of the discovered vocational aptitude.

Guiding principles for the selection of a life-work have been formulated and are being brought to the attention of youth. Questions designed to assist the young in the process of self-discovery are raised. Is the proposed business or professional career actually supported and prompted by native capacity? Is it socially valuable? Is the youth cognizant of its importance? What are its financial returns? Are the social and personal motives balanced? Is the youth intelligently planning to prepare himself for the best possible investment of himself in the chosen vocation?

The church can provide adolescent boys and girls with opportunities for the understanding of the various vocations, the tastes and aptitudes which each demands, and the Christian service each renders. A group of boys in a church school decided to make a study of vocations in which they were individually interested. The project was called "What We Boys Will Do." Each boy received suggestions and assignments from the teacher, made a careful investigation of the advantages, the disadvantages, and the opportunities for personal growth and service the contemplated professional choice involves, and gathered pictures, clippings, quotations, and cartoons which illustrated his study. Each boy spent hours examining the materials which the others had accumulated. Law, medicine, farming, the ministry, electrical engineering, and mechanical engineering were investigated and evaluated. Approximately a period of six months was devoted to the project. Each boy took charge of the class two Sundays and in his own way tried to make clear to the others why he proposed to enter the profession of his choice.[2]

An Adequate Philosophy of Life

Adolescence brings about not only a more intense interest in self as an individual but also as a member of society. The social horizon expands. The world of the little child is the home, the world of the boy or girl is the school, the world of the older adolescent is the social order. New social forces play upon the adolescent, and in a very real sense he becomes a new creature.

The adolescent hungers and thirsts for recognition and appreciation. He may long for friends but not know how to make them. He may appear indifferent to those who love him most. He may be shy and embarrassed just because he so keenly desires status in the eyes of others, or he may assume an air of boldness in order to conceal his real feelings. He may, however, be openly and genuinely sociable. The desire for the ap-

[2] Shaver, Erwin L., *The Project Principle in Religious Education*, pp. 225, 226 (Chicago: University of Chicago Press, 1924).

proval of others, secretly entertained or frankly avowed, is a powerful determinant of conduct and outlook. If the adolescent, moved by the dictates of conscience, acts in the face of the disapproval of his group, he may do so with the expectation or hope of winning the approbation of those whose commendation he actually prizes.

Rebelliousness arises when parents seem unaware that their adolescent sons and daughters are no longer children. Parents are astonished and hurt when their authority is questioned and when the expected implicit obedience is not forthcoming. The docile adolescent may assume that the judgment of older people is best and accept their declarations that it is not right to break this or that rule of conduct. To the adolescent with the usual degree of self-assertiveness, the forbidden is a challenge. The mother may undertake to censor the reading of her daughter and object to the borrowing of so many novels at the library, but the girl may read more romantic literature than ever—but secretly. She wants to do things in her own way. She wants to choose her own friends and to live her own life. She has a passion for freedom. To hedge the adolescent about with a complication of prohibition only incites him the more to follow his own inclinations and to assert what he supposes to be his rights and privileges as a personality. Control from within, control which is an expression of a chosen way of life, rather than coercion from without reduces the conflict between immaturity and maturity, and establishes a balance of competing forces.

The spirit of youthful independence often manifests itself in unexpected changes and attitudes. The day comes when the adolescent by some word or act notifies his elders that he is no longer a boy and that he desires them to recognize his new status. One father vividly recalls how the consciousness of the self-assertation of his son of thirteen dawned upon him one evening when he attempted to enter the boy's room without knocking and found the door locked. A dignified youth unlocked the door and invited the father to enter the room and to be seated. The episode symbolized to the surprised father a step taken by the boy in the making of a man.

The adolescent is face to face with the necessity of construct-
ing an adequate philosophy of life. The moral integrity of the
self, the altruistic obligation to society, and the catching of the
spirit of the universe are the most important phases of idealism
which demand recognition, clarification, and unification. Be it
said to the credit of the adolescent that he has the courage to
cope with stupendous issues of life.

A new sense of moral values develops with an increased
understanding of social situations and the consequences of conduct. The younger adolescent erects ideal moral standards.
He exhibits a pronounced tendency to objectify his ideals, to
attribute qualities of perfection to someone who is the object
of his admiration, to revere and honor him, and to expect an
exclusive affection in return. The model of perfection may be
a fictional or historical character as well as a living person. The
character so idealized may warp or elevate the life of the
adolescent.

The idealism of the older adolescent is practical. His altruism, for example, seeks expression in definite forms of social
betterment. His sympathy and co-operation are enlisted by
concrete situations which demand prompt and heroic action.
In his attempt to better the world he is generally rebuffed. The
first contact with reality is likely to impart a shock and a sense
of bewildering loss. The world is not so responsive to his efforts to improve it as he had anticipated. The world seems to
know no law save that of the survival of those who are strong
enough to take and hold all they can grasp. The youth does not
foresee how rocky and steep is the road to the realization of his
ideals. Disillusioned and discouraged, he is tempted to abandon
altogether the altruistic purpose which hitherto has given direction and value to his life.

Intellectual growth keeps pace with bodily development and
experience as a member of a group. Relations which exist between facts are perceived, the normal consequences of contemplated action are foreseen, data are interpreted, reason as a
guide begins to assert itself. The critical functions are brought
to bear upon the traditional moral standards. A period of
moral bravado may follow, a period of self-indulgence, de-

fiance of conventions, and ethical experimentation.   The fact
is often overlooked that in order to be truly critical one must
recognize a canon of judgment, a norm of reference.   Youth
may clamor for a new morality, but nobody has yet indicated
what this new morality is expected to grant that the inherited
ethical values withhold.   Youth that demands the freest self-
determination may have nothing but primitive impulses to release.   Well for youth if it learns, before moral decay has set in,
that liberty is achieved through the voluntary exercise of self-
discipline.

The radicalism of youth is in many cases a serious attempt
to discover reality.   Social customs, no matter how ancient and
honored, are viewed with skepticism until a reason can be advanced for their continuance and observance.   Youth must
know whether we can get along better with or without the
transmitted culture.   The adolescent is dominated by a passion
for actuality grounded in verifiable experience.   Youth will
break away from the old restraints if they fail to justify themselves.   Adolescence is a new wine of revolt which bursts the
old skins of outworn convention.   The adolescent is, however,
often betrayed by his own immaturity, for he is not always
competent adequately to evaluate the restrictions and customs
which society has imposed upon him.

In most respects modern youth is as a whole decidedly conventional.   It is by no means as socially radical as it thinks it
is.   It accepts the opinions and prejudices of the group to
which it belongs.   After all our youth has been trained not for
independence of thought but for conformity.   It is unimagina-
tive in its political, social, and economic attitudes, orthodox in
its conceptions of patriotism, nationalism, and militarism, and
obedient to the dictates of current fashions in ideas and manners.   Exceptions are notable.   There are vast areas of our
social order in which youth like the older generation exercises
no appreciable critical intelligence.

The newly awakened or expanded social consciousness is,
however, intimately associated with a fresh and increasing
sensitiveness to religious values.   During the teens most boys
and girls pass through a period of religious storm and stress.

Critical and analytical youth seeks a religion which is equal to the demands of contemporary life. Inherited religious doctrines and requirements are cast into the crucible of the adolescent's zeal for reality and reaffirmed or rejected in accordance with his sense of values. Those whose religious nurture has been adequate from childhood seem to experience this transitional stage without great personal upheaval. Those who have grown up in an atmosphere charged with constructive religious elements, who have been kept reasonably free from dogmas which are incompatible with the demonstrable teachings of science, and whose life-needs have been met as they have emerged in the course of advancing experience, make the transition with minimal confusion and loss. For such the period is one of testing, inquiry, and confirmation.

Defective early religious training breeds destructive doubt. Later educational influences are the most frequent occasions of religious questioning and uncertainty. A science course taken in high school may arouse doubt as to the value and validity of religious concepts once uncritically held. Ill health or calamity may induce skepticism. Unanswered prayer in a personal crisis may shatter the whole structure of the religious life. The misconduct of Christians is often the causal factor. The existence of God, the inspiration of the Bible, the authority of traditional religious customs and obligations, the deity of Jesus, the operation of a special Providence, and the doctrine of personal immortality are among the more prominent specific objects of doubt. Not that doubt is necessarily a calamity, for doubt resolutely faced clarifies ideas and ideals, is an indication that the critical powers are functioning, and is a step in the process of self-maturing. Honest doubt leads to positive religious experience.

The usual procedure is to berate the doubter and to read him out of the Kingdom as an unbeliever, or to heap ridicule upon him and to belittle his intelligence. It is more helpful to listen to the recital of his doubts with patience and sympathy, to answer to the best of one's ability the questions which he raises, to refer him to books which throw light upon himself and his perplexities, and to teach him that he can be a Christian

without being competent to solve theological problems which
have puzzled the wisest and best minds. Fellowship with consistently loyal followers of Christ will dissipate many of the
youth's fears and uncertainties and encourage him to put religious faith to the pragmatic test.

One should not overlook the possibility that the doubter is
to some extent assuming a pose. He has a penchant for argumentation and controversy. He likes to create a sensation, to
play to the galleries as it were, and if his heresies scandalize
his parents and teachers and the pastor he may yield to the
temptation to pretend that he is far more radical and heterodox
than he actually is. An inordinate fondness for dramatic effects in the production of which he plays the stellar rôle may
confuse fact and fancy in the mind of the youthful debater
and skeptic. He as well as his counselor may be deceived.

Religion as a way of life which refines, regulates, and co-
ordinates the functions of personality is not a luxury but an
indispensability. It enables the adolescent to throw all of himself into the enterprise of the good life. There is no source of
moral energy and inward peace comparable to the conviction
that the universe is the outcome of purpose, that every individual has a place in the total scheme of things, and that the
search for truth and beauty is a fundamental attribute of human nature. The foundations for a philosophy of life which
relates the individual to a functioning whole should be laid in
the home and the church.

CHAPTER V

PERSONALITY TYPES AND RELIGIOUS EXPERIENCE

It does not take the young pastor long to discover that his following includes a variety of people. No two persons have exactly the same conception of and attitude toward the Bible, the church, or God, although they may belong to the same local church. The law of individual variation operates in the domain of religious experience as well as elsewhere. The Christian religion as Jesus lived and taught it, so far from demanding uniformity of religious experience, encourages the self-realization of the individual.

Psychologists teach us that despite individual differences persons may be classified in accordance with the dominant characteristics which groups of them share. When the organization of personality has advanced to such a degree that a state of constancy exists, one may be classified as a more or less well-defined representative of a group or type. Everybody recognizes such personality varieties as "the dude," "the rube," "the bully," "the flapper," "the high-brow," "the low-brow," "the go-getter," and "the sheik." Of the more comprehensive schemes of classification which scientists have outlined at least one or two of special value to the pastor will be described.

In the trend of the historical development of the Christian Church at least six different recognizable varieties of religious personality have emerged. They may be found in local churches of today. Some Christians appreciate and appropriate religion in terms of a personal experience of God as an actual, illuminating, and satisfying Presence. They are the mystics. Others have an aptitude for the administration of the temporal affairs of the local church and prefer to raise funds, provide for the relief of the poor, support hospitals, and to develop other social implications of religion. They are the practical Christians. Still others with an intellectual turn of mind formulate the doctrines of the Church, and expound, teach, and defend them. They are the rationalists. Many rely on some one in whom they have complete confidence and whose beliefs, policies, and standards of conduct and service they accept as authoritative. They are traditionalists. A large number are incurably hopeful under adverse circumstances; their intellectual processes are superficial, they are incapable of persistent effort. They are the optimists. Some incorporate dynamic characteristics of the mystical, the rationalistical, and the practical varieties, and select from the past what can function effectively in the present and break new paths of thought and service. They are the prophets. To be sure, it is impossible to bring all persons who embrace the Christian faith under six categories, but the pastor in the course of his work will discover that the suggested grouping does actually classify the majority of the flock.[1]

What concepts of psychology interpret the various forms of religious personality? What are the particular excellencies and what the defects, if there be such, of each variety indicated? What does each contribute to the life and work of the church? Should local churches or denominations include the several varieties or should the membership of each religious organization consist of a company of persons who individually share the same combinations of mental functions? Should temperament

[1] A comprehensive and exceedingly useful classification of all sorts of personalities has been presented by Dr. William S. Sadler in an unpublished manuscript. He recognizes twelve main types of groups of personalities: the deficient, the perverted, the criminal, the stupid, the lonely, the cheerful, the well-balanced, the neurotic, the queer, the moody, the insane, and the disabled. The deficient group embraces all who are unable to take care of themselves —the paupers, the epileptics, and the feeble-minded. The perverted group consists of vicious, depraved, and demoralized personalities. The antisocial form the criminal group. The individuals of the stupid group are retarded and dull, but self-supporting. The lonely group is composed of isolated people, those who are self-conscious introverts and the victims of a sense of inferiority. Those who belong to the cheerful group are the typical optimists. The more ideally integrated, the dominant and self-reliant personalities form the group of the well-balanced. The neurotic group includes anxiously introspective, perplexed, and frustrated personalities. Egoists, cranks, radicals, and the eccentric are members of the queer group. The melancholic and dejected personalities constitute the moody group. The insane group is a tragic assortment of broken, disintegrated, and demented personalities. The disabled group embraces the diseased, the crippled, the deformed, the aged and infirm. It is hard to think of any individual who has been excluded from this comprehensive outline.

rather than doctrine or polity determine the constituency of each of the different denominations? Is it possible to modify a personality type? Furthermore, what is the bearing of a given personality type on the form in which religion is experienced? Is religious belief, manner of worship, and specific service to humanity independent of native predispositions and general mental conformation? Such questions outline the present analysis and evaluation of the varieties of religious personality.

Extroverted Religious Types

Dr. Jung, the distinguished psychologist, has suggested a grouping of personalities which is of help in interpreting religious types.[2] Personalities according to Jung are either extroverts or introverts. Nothing morbid or pathological necessarily attaches to these designations. The classification grows out of the tendency of some individuals to occupy themselves almost exclusively with external affairs and of others to lead sedentary lives, lives devoted to their own thoughts and feelings. To these two types may be added a third, the ambivert, which combines characteristics of the extrovert and introvert.

The older grouping, according to temperament, while open to objections, is still serviceable. Refined and judiciously used it supplements Jung's classification and thus throws light upon specific religious varieties. Temperament may be described as the relative proportion of personality qualities which precondition one's behavior as a whole. A whim is a passing notion and is often unreasonable. A mood is an emotional tone which often persists for hours and even for days. Temperament is both more complex and more enduring than either a whim or a mood. It was Galen, often called the father of modern medicine, who gave the four temperaments which have held the field the names by which they are still known—namely, the sanguine, the choleric, the phlegmatic, and the melancholic.[3] Generally

[2] Jung, C. G., *Psychological Types* (New York: Harcourt, Brace & Co., 1923). For a refinement of Jung's classification see Hinkle, B. M., *The Re-creating of the Individual* (New York: Harcourt, Brace & Co., 1923).

[3] The names of the four temperaments are reminiscent of the ancient conception of the relative preponderance of the four liquids or "humors" of the body—blood, yellow bile, phlegm, and black bile. This conception foreshadows the modern chemical interpretation of personality which has captured

speaking, they are subdivisions of the more inclusive extrovert
and introvert types.   The sanguine and choleric temperaments
are predominantly extroverted, the melancholic and phlegmatic
are introverted.

The extrovert is, then, an individual the conformation of
whose personality is such that he is attracted and held primarily
by objective circumstances.   He has formed attitudes which
predispose him to lose himself in the objective world.   The
external order sways him.   His interests move outward toward
business, politics, sports, and other practical affairs.   He does
not deeply appreciate the fine arts and is likely to suppose that
the man who delights in symphony concerts and art galleries is
effeminate.   It must not be inferred that the extrovert is incapable of incisive and creative thought, for he has the ability
to analyze an external situation, to understand the interrelation
of its parts and to draw sound inferences from his data.   As a
man of action his ideas are ideas of action.   Washington was
an extrovert.   He was not a brilliant military strategist nor an
inventive statesman.   His strength lay in his industry, objectivity, executive ability, and moral integrity.

The choleric temperament, which is extroverted, is characterized by quick thinking, strong feeling, and vigorous activity.   Although intelligence and feeling are marked, the
activity of the will predominates.   The person of choleric disposition thinks rapidly and accurately, feels deeply and sincerely, and incited by thought and emotion passes into decisive
action without delay.   He seems to have an inexhaustible supply of restless energy which gets him out of bed early in the
morning, drives him at top speed all day and until late at
night, and makes him plan the work of the next day after he

the popular imagination.   The chemical affinity of individuals is by some
supposed to underlie compatible personal and social relations.   Those who
are contemplating matrimony are advised to consult the chemist before obey
ing the promptings of romantic love.   We are told that when a man and a
woman form the proper chemical combination domestic felicity is assured
For example, a carbon woman is urged to seek a calcium mate, while
an oxygen man is advised to select a sodium bride.   Such admonition
rests on the assumption that despite the fact that they have much in com
mon, persons are not all alike in physiological composition and in dis
position.   The possibility of chemical classification is, of course, taken for
granted rather than scientifically demonstrated.

has retired. In the parlance of business he is a "live wire."
He is an extrovert.

The practical or socialized Christian may be considered a
choleric extrovert. He is ethical, motor-minded, energetic, and
urgently aware of the social implications of the Christian religion. He is persuaded that real religion is not a system of doctrine nor an emotional attitude, but a summons to the will and
a program of activities. He thinks in terms of surveys, cam-
paigns, crusades, settlement houses, institutional churches, welfare leagues, and political reforms. He has an active passion
for Christianizing the institutions of society. With commendable zeal he strives to better the temporal lot of the underprivileged, the poor, the ignorant, the outcast, and the oppressed. In the words of St. James he maintains that "to visit
the fatherless and the widows in their affliction, and to keep
one's self unspotted from the world" is religion pure and unde-
filed. Resourceful, self-reliant, and socially sensitized, the
major movement of his personality is toward the tangible and
concrete mission of religion. It is difficult if not impossible
to induce him to conduct a prayer meeting, but he functions
with gusto and success as the leader of the annual financial
campaign of the local church. The subtle meanings of religious
movements escape him, the intangibles and imponderables of
religion as interior experiences or possessions elude him.

Many a traditionalist is an emotional extrovert. The authority of the Church, of the Scriptures, and of a specific form
of religious experience is firmly entrenched in his mind.
Change and nonconformity are regarded as a deliberate assault upon true religion and as such are to be stoutly resisted
and overcome. The mere suggestion of deviation from what
has come down from the revered past is labeled blasphemy.
When aesthetic appreciation has been developed, worship takes
the form of an elaborate and embroidered liturgy. The un-
questioning acceptance of the inherited beliefs, rites, and institutions of the Church is reminiscent of the credulity of childhood. The traditionalist has never undergone the stimulating
process of religious weaning. He is controlled by religious
dependency. He shares the spirit of those who take refuge in
the motto, "Rome never changes." His attitude is not a rea-

soned but an emotional one. Many extroverted traditionalists belong to the ranks of those whose secular employments are so numerous, insistent, and taxing that neither time nor strength is available for the process of emancipation from the tyranny of the superimposed past. The phlegmatic traditionalist is, on the other hand, rather introverted and will presently be described as such.

The sanguine temperament is marked by quick thinking, weak feeling, and a cheerful outlook on life. The thought processes while rapid are superficial. Inferences based on insufficient evidences are likely to be drawn. The emotions, although bright and airy, are unstable. The man of sanguine temperament is lively, excitable, optimistic, and socially popular. In all matters he takes the most hopeful view. Slight incentives incline him to act. He is an extrovert who is swayed by changeable and exhilarating emotions.

The extroverted sanguine temperament is well represented in our churches. Parishioners whose temperaments are preponderantly sanguine may be called religious optimists. They are incapable of making unique intellectual patterns; they are possessed of no overmastering theological urge. They comprehend only what is obvious or apparent. If a tragedy occurs within the household of faith, they assure the bereaved that "all is for the best." Their faith in human nature is unshaken by perfidy or delinquency, for their attitude toward others is preponderantly one of implicit credulity. Their religious faith is so hopefully expectant that so far from being crushed by misfortune they quickly recover the dispositional uncritical attitude. Micawber-like they rest assured that favorable circumstances will speedily overtake and outweigh any temporary failure or loss. They are friendly, sprightly, cordial, generous, and likable. They like to greet and welcome strangers in the congregation, visit the sick, and cheer the burdened. They cannot wisely be entrusted with church projects which demand sustained and tenacious effort, although they are capable of lending a hand in the less taxing affairs of the parish.

Introverted Religious Types

The introvert, as has been hinted, is one whose interests

move from the object to himself and his own psychological processes. His life is ruled by abstractions and principles, theories and interpretations, meanings and values. He deliberates much before he acts, and therefore hesitates to act. He likes to read, study, write, and to cultivate the fine arts. He is somewhat shy and retiring, and prefers solitude to the company of others, especially that of the extroverts. He is for the most part calm and collected unless he is forced into a situation which demands decisive action.

The melancholic temperament is an introverted disposition characterized by slow thinking and feeling. The emotional coloring is markedly dark and depressing. The melancholic person is ponderous but self-reliant and dependable. His reactions to situations are cautious but intensive. He thinks deliberately but clearly; he takes time to reason with a transparent clarity. He is inclined to regard the world and what it contains in an unfavorable light. He lives in a world of imagination and gloom. Many of these introverts, but by no means all, are indifferent to practical affairs. They are musical, poetical, artistic, and sentimental. Abraham Lincoln and George Bernard Shaw are typical representatives of the melancholic group.

The Christian mystic is as a rule a melancholic introvert who seeks the immediate awareness of God. He studies the Bible devotionally rather than critically, spends much time in prayer and meditation, and identifies himself with religious truth. His true self is integrated in a personal and intense experience of the God of forgiveness, inward illumination, and moral victory. The subjective and personal aspects of religion capture his attention and appropriate his energies. Entrenched in his inner world of religious certainty, he is not much disturbed by the turmoil and the clash of external affairs. He agrees that "to know God and to enjoy him forever" is "the chief end of man." The mystic is generally a brooding, introspective, and gloomy personality.

The Christian rationalist, while diverging from his mystical brother, belongs to the same general type. The two are varieties of the introverted group. The mystic relies on faith, on processes below the level of awareness; the rationalist on cognition and logic. The one seeks to apprehend Reality, the other to comprehend Reality. The rationalist has an almost unlimited confidence in his ability to construct a consistent body of ideas and principles. He declares that in order to appreciate he must first understand. He derives satisfaction from his intellectual independence, and refuses to surrender the right to think for himself. The objective and critical approach to religion tends to reduce religion to an intellectual adventure rather than to a personal integrative experience.

The phlegmatic temperament is marked by slow thinking and weak feeling. It is another variety of the introverted type, although thought is sluggish and feeling for the most part almost neutral. The person of phlegmatic disposition is impassive, heavy, dull, dilatory, and disinclined to exert himself. His responses are both slow and weak. Because he is apathetic he remains cool, calm, and composed in situations which agitate and distract people of other temperaments. He lacks initiative and courage and is, therefore, at a disadvantage in the face of the exigencies of life. He is negatively introverted.

Many traditionalists in the churches are phlegmatically dis-positioned. Some are too inert and dull to think for them-selves, to analyze the vast heritage of religious tradition, and to arrive at independent conclusions and to espouse them. Their uncritical acceptance of the authority of the church is the joint product of intellectual indolence and incompetency. They are disposed to shirk their church responsibilities. Causes and crusades which arouse the enthusiasm and enlist the co-opera-tive participation of others are regarded with indifference. They are submerged in their own confused and inadequate ideas of the mission and doctrines of the church. They are too apathetic to appreciate the significance of a personal crisis.

The Ambiverted Religious Type

Theodore Roosevelt, the hunter, warrior, and political re-former, was warmly responsive to the call of practical affairs. He was an extrovert. Woodrow Wilson, capable of formu-lating an international political philosophy, was crippled by what he himself called his "single-track" mind and by his reluctance to act with promptness and vigor. He was an introvert. Many people, uniting in themselves the characteristics of both the extrovert and the introvert, are like Roosevelt one day and like Wilson the next. One and the same individual can, as observation teaches, be an extrovert at one time and an introvert at another. One may for weeks be almost entirely absorbed by an abstract consideration such as the writing of an essay and later be as completely absorbed by the external events of a fishing expedition. It all depends on the content of the focal point of attention. As the attention is gripped by an objective or subjective circumstance, the same person may be an extrovert or introvert for more or less prolonged periods. Such a one has been called an ambivert.[4]

[4] The foundations of character and temperament have been identified with the action of the ductless glands in the human body or the endocrines as they are called. These include the pituitary, the adrenal, and the thymus glands, together with the gonads and thyroids. The ductless glands are structures of internal secretion; they discharge chemicals. The active agents in the secretions are known as hormones. The ductless glands constitute an interlocking system the general function of which seems to be to accelerate or retard the vital processes of the organism. The effects of the hormones are somewhat comparable to those induced by drugs. For example, they stimulate or check the growth of the bones, the muscles, the skin and hair, help or hinder the work of the nerves, and decrease or increase the action of the heart, lungs, and digestive organs. Some endocrinologists maintain that personality types are determined by the dominance of the glandular organization by one or the other of the glands or by a combination of them. (See Berman, Louis, *Glands Regulating Personality*, New York: The Macmillan Company, 1921.) The individual of the choleric temperament, for example, is said to be a thyroid personality. The thyroid gland consists of two maroon-colored cell masses bridged by an isthmus of the same tissue and is situated at the base of the throat and near the larynx. The normal thyroid personality is supposedly marked by rapid perception, strong volition, and abundance of energy and persistency. The pathological swelling of the thyroid gland is a condition known as goiter. The product of the gland is called thyroxin. The secretion, the active ingredient of which is iodine seems to be a regulator of all the vital processes of the body. It controls the speed of living. When thyroxin is liberated food materials are more rapidly burned or oxidized, the rate of metabolism is increased and an excess of energy is released, and as a result the person thinks, feels, and acts with greater rapidity and intensity. An insufficient supply of thyroxin is said to arrest the bodily growth of children and to account for the small stature of midgets. The underfunctioning of the thyroid gland in other persons brings about dryness and brittleness of the skin, nails, and hair, and a general retardation of both physical and psychological processes. On the other hand, an overplus of thyroxin, or hyperthyroidism, is accompanied by such symptoms as the loss of bodily weight, moist skin, rapid pulse rate, protrusion of the eyes, and extreme nervous irritability. That man is the creature of his glands of internal secretion, as has been claimed, is a contention which the majority of physiologists and psychologists, to say nothing of the sociologists, are as yet unprepared to subscribe to and sponsor. Such a solution of the riddles of

The creative or prophetic religious personality belongs to the class of ambiverts, including as it does mystical, pragmatic, and rationalistic functions. The creative variety discovers truth which enriches personality, in moral striving and socialized living as well as in the promptings of the emotions and the processes of reasoning. It is neither enslaved by tradition nor entirely severed from the past. Balanced personality critically examines and evaluates the religious and moral bequests of the fathers, and accepts, conserves, and applies only what possesses significance for the contingencies in which it is entangled. It seeks not to destroy the law and the prophets, nor to perpetuate them as they are, but to grasp their inwardness and to complete them. It engages in social experimentation, not for the purpose of discrediting and retiring inherited precepts, but for the purpose of applying tested religious principles to fresh circumstances. It assumes that revelation in terms of religious discovery and rediscovery is progressive and will not come to an end so long as the world contains men and women of prophetic insight and passion. The members of the creative group are few in number, generally misunderstood, and often vilified and persecuted by their contemporaries, but they revitalize religion, clarify and redefine its verities, and develop and apply its germinal truths. Fortunate is the local church the membership of which embraces representatives of the balanced, prophetic group.

It is exceedingly fortunate that the membership and constituency of the majority of Protestant churches include more

personality seems to involve more than our present knowledge of the endocrine system warrants. To date, the evidence that has come from the laboratory and the dissecting room does not make the conclusion inexorable that the ductless glands secrete the essence of personality. There appears to be much justifiable criticism of the technical procedure of endocrine research and of the interpretations of the experimental data. That the endocrine system plays a strategic part as a groundwork for emotion, as predisposition for habit formation, and as a regulator of the vigor of reactions, must be conceded, but social experience rather than glandular secretions as such forms specific habits, attitudes, and ideas, and gives to healthy personality its definite content and quality. It is, however, scientifically established that many personality difficulties and moral lapses are the outcome of disordered endocrine activity. For instance, neurotic, nervous, irritable, and unstable conditions which are associated with hyperthyroidism are prolific breeders of personality problems which can be solved only by the correction of the physical cause through surgical or other means. Religious counsel alone is insufficient in such cases.

than one personality type or variety. In a denomination or local church the membership of which has been recruited for the most part from a single group or class the process of religious cross-fertilization cannot occur, and the potential defects of a one-sided emphasis are made manifest. The points of similarity as well as those of contrast between such varieties of religious personality as the rationalist and the traditionalist and the practical Christian and the mystic should be recognized, understood, and taken into account not only by the pastor but also by the rank and file of the church.

Each temperament or personality type needs the corrective and constructive impetus which the others can give. Close contact with a rationalist should keep the traditionalist from becoming so formal, static, and reactionary as to be intellectually dwarfed and morally inert; and association with a traditionalist should keep the rationalist from the sin of captiousness and the rejection of the creative values bequeathed by the past. Fellowship with a mystic should incline the socialized personality to respect if not to emulate him who discovers in the practice of the presence of God the dynamic and inspiration for his tasks; fellowship with a practical Christian should give the mystic pause and induce him to validate some of his subjective certainties objectively and to harness a generous measure of his spiritual energies to social purposes. The ambivert should find the impact of other types stimulating.

Psychologists and sociologists are by no means agreed as to exactly which elements in each of the personality types are biologically inherited and which acquired, but it is safe to say that no type is absolutely rigid and unalterable. The prophetic or ambivert type is no doubt impelled by a creative urge which is native but which exercises itself in an environmental opportunity. Extroverts and introverts should arouse and challenge the latent powers of the ambivert. Each variety of extrovert is flexible and modifiable enough to make dangerous extremes avoidable and to incorporate within itself excellencies of the others. In most cases self-criticism and self-discipline can do much to further the balanced religious outlook and practice. The interaction of the rationalistic, the mystical, and the practical functions within the individual is a precondition to balanced personality of the highest order.

Fundamentalist Psychology

Of the conflicts which are dividing the Church of Christ none is more deplorable than the warfare between the extroverted traditionalists and the introverted rationalists, between the ultra-conservatives and the extreme liberals. Each of these parties has formulated a system of theology which is enthusiastically disseminated and tenaciously defended. Liberalism like conservatism, rationalism like traditionalism, includes a characteristic theology, approach, and spirit. A psychological study is not primarily concerned with the historical setting, consistency, and reliability of the theological tenets of each of the opposing factions. Attention is here directed to an attitude, to a certain temper and disposition, characteristic of both. Fundamentalist psychology is distinguished from fundamentalism as a doctrinal scheme.

A prominent increment in fundamentalist psychology is an emotional cast of mind in terms of an attitude of dogmatism. The liberal accuses the conservative of espousing his beliefs with a tone of finality which is irritatingly offensive but seems not to be aware that he himself is often prejudiced and static, if not actually stagnant, in his thinking. In so far as he exhibits this spirit the liberal is affected by the virus of emotional fundamentalism. Both liberals and conservatives are inclined to cling to some wrong things in a presumptuous temper and to cleave to some right things in the wrong spirit. Both parties demand unconditional acceptance of what each proclaims as the cardinal faith. The fundamentalist attitude is, wherever present, a matter of how as well as what one believes.

Both lack vision and brotherliness. A well-known and respected spokesman for the liberals says that the conservative lacks charity and the liberal lacks clarity. The statement is clever and epigrammatic, but is the lack of charity restricted to either? Are we not at this juncture dealing with a pot and a kettle? Is it any more reprehensible for a conservative to call a liberal a heretic than it is for a liberal to call a conservative an intellectual moron? Failure to accord the values of manifold types of religious faith cordial recognition occurs on both sides. The liberal, in fact, more often than the conservative is unwilling to give a dissenter a chance to state his case.

One recalls the problem of personal liberty in Corinth, which engaged the attention of St. Paul. The liberal party in the church argued that the eating of animals sacrificed to idols was of no consequence, but the conservative party maintained that such a practice constitutes idolatry and as such was contrary to the obligation to worship only the God of Jesus. The liberals evidently treated their less mature brethren with scorn and contempt. It is significant that St. Paul launches his reproofs against the liberals rather than against the conservatives. The liberal is exhorted to practice the principle that the Christian is to forgo his freedom and his rights when the welfare of the conservative is at stake. The liberal is to do nothing which his less enlightened brother cannot imitate without offending his conscience. The reactionary is not the only one who displays the intolerant spirit; the liberal also is guilty of the moral priggery and religious snobbery which mark the fundamentalist disposition. The man who stands apart from men of contrary beliefs when he prays and thanks God that he is not like other people is just as likely to be a liberal as a conservative.

In the second place, the fundamentalist attitude is often characterized by a morally sterile intellectualism. Representatives of both the liberal and conservative groups are consumed by an appetite for controversy. To be sure, there is satisfaction in demolishing the thought system of another and in establishing one's own. The process as an exhibition of human nature is readily understood. The fundamentalist absolute approach is espoused by militant champions who challenge their opponents to a contest over intellectual interpretations of which many are ethically barren. Multitudes in both camps are guilty of captiousness which would remove from the circle of respectability all who dare to dissent. They are likely to entangle themselves in abstractions and to ignore the rich currents of contemporary life. Many of their ideas are defensible.

It is to be regretted that some of the perfectly sound conceptions of the liberal are so emotionally lifeless that they are morally impotent. A logically consistent formula is no substitute for transforming experience.

One of the foremost thinkers of Europe said of the teaching of a leader of American liberalism: "His philosophy is penetratingly analytic, but it is not fruitful." The tree of any form of religion should be judged by its fruits. Moved by a hunger for reality, for inspiration and guidance for daily living, one approaches the theological tree of either conservatism or liberalism in the mood of eager expectation but only to receive nothing but leaves of academic debate with a frequency that is tragic. Once the critical spirit has gained dangerous momentum, it fails to include within its purview factors of great positive and practical significance. Why not suggest as a cure for moral impotence that conservatives and liberals unite in a practical campaign for social betterment such as a crusade to make the world warless?

In the third place, the fundamentalist mentality is ecclesiastically presumptuous. It suffers from an institutional complex. Such a state of mind is discoverable and identifiable in each of the opposing camps. One pastor is said to have declared: "When I refer to religion, I mean the Christian religion; when I refer to Christian religion, I mean Protestantism; when I refer to Protestantism, I mean the Episcopal Church." Methodist conservative and Congregational liberal alike have been known to cherish and share this type of institutional exclusiveness. They remind one of John's complaint to Jesus: "Teacher, we saw one casting out demons in thy name, and we forbade him because he followed not us." John did not report, "followed not thee," but "followed not us." "And we forbade him." Suppression of others because they do not follow us is of the essence of intolerant fundamentalism.

Having surveyed psychological fundamentalism as a method and spirit in these three modes, how refreshing it is to hark back to the catholic approach of Jesus and to his attitude of cordial appreciation of values validated by experience! His outlook on life was subversive of the rigid and inflexible dis-

position. In his day and country the Pharisees were the fundamentalist conservatives and the Sadducees the fundamentalist
liberals. Jesus identified himself with neither party. He was
creative. He was in truth a religious eclectic and experimental-
ist of the first quality. He had a passion not for the preservation of opinion but for the furtherance of the abundant life.
He had convictions, but he held them without rancor. The
dynamic quality of Jesus' faith made room for change, growth,
experiment, and progress. It has been truly said that the
finality of Jesus lies in the vitality and creativity of his faith.
He possesses the endless power of growth and renewal.

The spaciousness of his spirit is a standing rebuke to all,
whether they be conservatives or liberals, who are blind to the
signs of an ever expanding manifestation of God's truth and
love, who sense no values in systems of thought other than their
own, and who refuse the right hand of fellowship to those of
alien faiths and races. In him there is no measure of institutional exclusiveness and no degree of intellectual captiousness.
Creative experience is the frame of reference in which his
teaching concerning God and man and society is set. Christ
was not absorbed in transmitting the past but in exploring the
unknown and shaping the future. "When the spirit of truth
is come he shall guide you into all the truth," is a prophecy
accredited to our Lord. Manifestly there is to be a progressive
revelation of the old Gospel, a revelation designed to scatter
the emotional fundamentalism of both conservative and liberal.
He who is informed by the genius of Jesus adopts St. Paul's
advice to prove all things and to hold fast that which is good.

Personality Types and the Form of Religious Experience

A number of years ago Professor George A. Coe made a
profitable study of the relation of temperament to religious
experience.[5] He learned that a great many people are trying
to be religious in ways utterly foreign to them. They are leading forced and unnatural lives. He made an intensive study
of seventy-seven persons, all of them college students of both
sexes, in order to discover why some people have dramatic

[5] *The Spiritual Life*, pp. 104 ff. (New York: The Methodist Book Concern, 1900).

religious experiences and others who desire them fail to induce them. The college students were under close observation and some of them were subjected to psychological tests and experimentation. In addition, a questionnaire elicited important data. "What would you do if you had to spend a day by yourself and were at liberty to do as you please?" is a question which proved especially fruitful.

Professor Coe learned that the combination most favorable to dramatic religious experience consists of the predominance of feeling in the individual, an expectation of striking occurrences, a vivid imagination, and a tendency to project or exteriorize the mental life in general. He concludes that those persons who have vivid dreams, hallucinations, and visions to which no religious importance is attached are predisposed to dramatic personal religious experiences.

One person reported to Professor Coe that he once dreamed of being cast into hell, having been expelled from heaven, and of seeing a heavenly procession which he was not permitted to join because he had failed to pass a qualifying examination. One is not surprised that this person saw streaks of light at the time of his religious transformation, witnessed joy in heaven, and had a vision of a narrow and a broad highway with the scriptural proportion of people on each.

Another student stated that one night he saw light springing up from a tomb in a cemetery. He believed that once he was touched by an absent friend. He was sure that on another occasion he heard his deceased grandfather's voice. He listened to angels singing. Twice in public speech he saw what he was describing. One is not surprised that he was subject to visions and voices in his religious experience, that he saw a luminous eye in the ceiling which he interpreted as the eye of God, and had a vision of Christ and the final judgment.

It is worthy to note that of the twenty-four persons who recorded striking religious transformations, thirteen reported that they were subject to analogous occurrences of no religious significance. Of the twelve who expected but failed to achieve a dramatic religious experience, only one could testify to other striking personal happenings. It should be plain that it is temperament which brings about the form of religious experience. The melancholic and the sanguine temperaments, which are characterized by a wealth of emotion and a lively imagination, are the temperaments which conceive of and express religion in dramatic forms. Expectation and one-sided mental activity coupled with the sentimental disposition induce visions and voices of religious import. The choleric temperament which is marked by reason and action does not, as a rule, express itself in a dramatic mode. Emotionally stable, intellectually alert, constitutionally active, this extroverted variety naturally seeks religious satisfaction in moral living and sacrificial service to mankind. The phlegmatic person, slow in thought and action, weak in emotion and imagination, is likewise temperamentally disqualified from inducing intense and startling religious effects. The form of religious experience depends not on the will but on the mental conformation of the individual.

St. Paul's conversion is illustrative. Before the walls of Damascus a light from heaven strikes him to the ground. A voice calls, "Saul, why persecutest thou me?" and when he answers, "Who art thou, Lord?" the reply is: "I am Jesus, whom thou persecutest." Following directions, humbled and blinded, he is led by the hand of another into the city. For three days he is without sight, and tastes neither food nor water. Under the prayers of the Christian brother Ananias his sight is restored and religious organization effected.

By way of contrast reference may be made to the conversion of Lydia of Philippi. One Sabbath Paul and his fellow-workers went to the banks of a river where a number of women had gathered for prayers. Among those who listened to Paul was Lydia. She is described as a seller of purple. Furthermore, she was a God-fearer, one who worshiped the God of Israel and practiced the Jewish code of morals. We read that God opened her heart to Paul's message and that she and her household were baptized. She insisted that if the apostles believed that her transformation was genuine they would abide in her home. This is the simple story of the experience of the first convert Paul made in Europe.

The conversion of the one was dramatic and that of the

other without abrupt transitions.   In the case of Paul we have
the light and the voice and the blindness and the fasting before
the disrupted personality achieves unity and self-consistency
In the other we have an open heart and a receptive mind and a
responsive will, all working together harmoniously.   The one is
like a volcano, the other like a sunrise.   Paul was a Jew with
the imaginative and emotional characteristics of his race.   He
had the glow, fervor, imagination, and energy of the missionary.   Lydia was a merchant, and as such presumably practical
and objective, a woman of poise and serenity.   Furthermore,
Paul's persecution of the Christians had induced in him points
of stress which were not easily overcome.   Lydia, on the other
hand, seems to have had no such inward conflicts to resolve.
They traveled different roads, but both arrived at the reintegration of personality with Christ as the point of reference.

It is well to bear in mind that the form in which the religious
impulse discharges itself, being temperamentally conditioned,
is of far less consequence than Christian character.   The voices,
visions, ecstasy, and rapture, however definite, arresting, and
decisive, which accompany the critical religious events of some
persons are after all not the final tests of Christian discipleship.

Failure to recognize this fact frequently results in unnecessary religious tension and even in the permanent impairment
of personality.   Mr. and Mrs. Frank Conrad were temperamentally and fundamentally different.   He was an introvert,
she an extrovert.   Under the pressure of an evangelistic campaign Mr. Conrad sought a religious transformation.   After
days of agony and depression, a power from without seemed
to fall upon him while he was walking home from church.
He was so affected that he quickened his pace into a run.   The
excitable and imaginative husband having achieved what he desired, regarded his experience as a standard to which others
should conform.   Mrs. Conrad made repeated and sincere efforts to induce a similar reaction but was uniformly disappointed in her expectations.   Her determination to accomplish
that for which she was incapable only brought about a conflict within her which imperiled her whole life.   Her husband
declared that she herself was responsible for the failure.   Fortunately a wise Christian brother who sensed the status of

affairs outlined to her the bearing of personality type on the form of religious experience. Once she understood herself, her poise was restored and she began to find satisfaction in living the Christian life in ways congenial and natural to her.

On the other hand, caution should be exercised lest the dramatic experience be undervalued. While the excitable and imaginative disposition is exposed to the danger of sentimentalism and of a divorce between emotion and morals, it gives rise to definite and glowing experiences which may profoundly influence personality for good. Feeling and imagination, trained and disciplined, play a significant part in the development and organization of personality. The prophet, the psalmist, the poet, and the singer are all endowed with emotional predispositions and gifted with creative imagination. So long as emotion is aroused by ideas and is controlled by ideas, so long as it discharges itself positively and constructively, the warm and imaginative dispositions are praiseworthy and useful. Zeal apart from knowledge makes the fanatic, knowledge apart from zeal makes the cold critic, harmoniously blended zeal and knowledge make the man of productive imagination and creative enterprise.

One temperament should not say to another, "I have no need of thee." Each should understand and respect the others. No person should be humiliated by an incapacity to experience what is natural only to another. All can and therefore should be centered in the simple fundamentals of Christian faith and practice and properly rate as temperamental the particular form in which a personal religious experience is cast.

CHAPTER VI

CAN ADULTS BE RECONSTRUCTED?

In his interview with Jesus, Nicodemus queried, "How can a man be born when he is old?" The form in which the question is stated implies the negative answer, "It can't be done." He received the declaration of Jesus that it was imperative that he, Nicodemus, a man of maturer years, undergo a radical transformation of ideas, ideals, and conduct with confused skepticism. William James, America's most popular psychologist and philosopher, seemed to take it for granted that a sort of congealing of the brain sets in during the late twenties and that consequently adults acquire new ideas especially outside their vocational spheres only with the utmost difficulty. We have inherited the traditional supposition that adult human nature is all but hopelessly static and inflexible.

Maxims which incorporate the assumed fixity and rigidity of the adult are numerous, popular, and frequently quoted as ultimate courts of appeal. For many years we have treasured the solemn if not inelegant assurance that it is impossible to teach an old dog new tricks. The Germans proverbially declare that what little Jack does not learn, old John will never learn. Repeated reference has been made to a Roman Catholic priest who is reported to have asserted that if he be permitted to supervise the religious training of a child from infancy to the seventh year any later efforts that may be made to divert him from the Catholic faith will be futile. Sometime ago a minister in an address before a student audience volunteered the statement that after a man is forty the only new thing he acquires is superfluous adipose tissue. Opinions of this kind have been so uncritically accepted and zealously transmitted that dissent from them has been rare.

Various inferences have been drawn from the supposition that adulthood is generally inflexible and unchangeable. For example, it has been concluded that since man is by nature a fighter all attempts to abolish war from civilization will in the end be fruitless.   Human nature in its mature state is static, we are told; hence man, impelled by an impulse stronger than himself, will always engage in warfare.   Again, years have been considered a sufficiently valid reason for arrested religious development.   Moved by the comfortable doctrine that adulthood releases from the obligation to alter and grow, many a man has remarked to his pastor: "I have had more than forty birthdays.   I am no longer young.   My habits are fixed, my opinions final, and my purposes established.   I am certain that you do not propose or expect any changes in the conduct of my life.   Any of your time or energy devoted to an attempted reconstruction of me would be wasted.   Permit me to urge you to apply yourself with all possible zeal and diligence to the training of our children and young people.   They are in the formative period and any program for their nurture in Christian principles which you may see fit to introduce will receive my financial and moral support."   Ingenious as well as ingenuous applications have been made of Jeremiah's question, "Can the Ethiopian change his skin, or the leopard his spots?"

Experiments in Adult Improvement

The ancient doctrine of the general unalterability of adult personality has been in recent times successfully challenged and contradicted.   Today the teachability of the adult is recognized not so much as a theory but as a demonstrable fact.   Experimental evidence, a deeper penetration into the resources of personality, and a more careful observation of the part which growing maturity plays in the progress of civilization have quite effectually disposed of the sayings and opinions quoted above and of the inferences which have been drawn from them. Everybody concedes that the educational process of the child is based on the plasticity and adaptability of growing personality.   The fact that the child's infancy is prolonged far beyond that of the young of any other creature on earth is educationally of the utmost importance.   His brain is incomplete at birth. Of all the inhabitants of this planet the responses of the child to his environment are the most various and modifiable.   These principles of the educational tradition are psychologically sound.   What we have not always appreciated is that human nature from the cradle to the grave is more or less elastic. Not only the youngster but also the oldster is endowed with a capacity for new experience and improvement. At no stage is personality completely static.

Professor Thorndike has published his conclusions derived from wide and intelligent observation and from scientifically conducted experiments concerning the teachableness of man at various periods of his life.[1] He is convinced that in general nobody under forty-five should refrain from trying to learn almost anything because of a fear that he is too old to master it. If one obeys the principles of learning and fails to subdue the subject matter, the inability, Professor Thorndike contends, should be attributed not to one's age but to the more prosaic factor of incompetence. Barring native lack of capacity, it is indolence, or sensitiveness to ridicule, or defective previous training, or improper use of time, or wrong method, or discouragement, or an attempt to master too much at a time, or a shifting of interest and the like, rather than aging, that accounts for failure to learn. According to Professor Thorndike's findings adult inmates of Sing Sing Prison learn such school subjects as writing, spelling, and arithmetic more rapidly than they would have learned them at the age of ten or twelve. He records the successful attempts of persons from twenty to forty years old to learn to dance, to skate, and to play the piano; to learn to relish foods for which there had been a dislike such as spinach, olives, and raw oysters; to conquer stage fright and to become effective public speakers; to overcome their dread of such fearsome natural phenomena as thunderstorms and snakes; and to revolutionize their social, religious, and political viewpoints.

The experiments and inferences of other investigators support and verify the conclusions of Professor Thorndike. Five male adults under the direction of Swift attempted sensori-motor improvement in keeping two balls tossed in the air with one hand. Ten trials were made each day. At first only from one to ten tosses could be made without failure. After five hours of practice four of the five men achieved more than one

---

[1] Thorndike, E. L., *Adult Learning* (New York: The Macmillan Company, 1928).

hundred tosses each before a failure occurred.[2] Wells supervised an experiment in which ten adults registered improvement in the observation of detail. The performances consisted in canceling as many O's on a page as possible in one minute. One hundred and ten trials in all were made. At first the average number of O's canceled in one minute was forty-five, at the last it was one hundred.[3] Blair conducted experiments in adult habit formation. Four adults served as subjects. Their project was to operate accurately in proper sequence six colored keys of a typewriter. Twenty-eight trials were made. At the eighth trial an errorless test was made in sixty-one seconds, at the twenty-eighth trial the same result was accomplished in thirty-seven and one-half seconds.[4]

Generally speaking and excepting pathological cases, so long as life endures, human personality may be enriched and enlarged. It appears to be experimentally established that adults are capable of making rapid, marked, and permanent improvement not only in the simpler sensori-motor activities and in the observation of detail but also in the more complicated and elaborate systems and functions of the intelligence. Adults can improve the more complex abilities of selection, analysis, and judgment.

But the finger of warning should be lifted. Failure to continue to progress decreases the ability to learn. Professor Thorndike declares that if a person stops learning at thirty he will in the course of time lose such gains in learning ability as he has previously acquired at school or by other means. Growth is the only known means whereby personality maintains itself, and growth is the result of revitalized thinking and adventurous activity. Only those adults who become as little children in open-minded teachable humility and in trustful abedience to the laws of growth are privileged to enter and possess the kingdom of personal development and power.

One may add to the experimental evidence for the ability of

[2] Swift, Edgar James, "Studies in Psychology and Physiology of Learning," *American Journal of Psychology*, Volume XIV, pp. 201 ff.

[3] Cited by Thorndike in *Adult Learning*, p. 7.

[4] Blair, J. H., "The Practice Curve," *Psychological Review*, Monograph Supplement, Volume V, Number 19.

the adult to learn the impressive fact that under favorable conditions the intellectual life of man grows for many years after the body has reached its fullest vigor and maturity. The finer abilities of personality achieve their consummation only during the adult years. There is an intellectual realm which only maturity inherits. There are ideas and ideals which only an active-minded adult is capable of understanding and receiving. The intellectual abilities are at their best from forty to sixty. The powers of judgment which develop through exercise generally reach their most advanced stage of balance and precision in middle life. The majority of the strategic positions in the business and professional world and in church and state are occupied by middle-aged persons. The elasticity and efficacy of the properly disciplined mind are not the illusions of a persistent and sustaining spirit of youth. Pretended attitudes and assertions, wish-thinking and imaginary accomplishments as protections against reality, have no place in the discriminating and creative life of personality on what is fallaciously called the wrong side of forty.

The Expansion of Adult Education

Confidence in the power of adulthood to transcend its limitations expresses itself in the present movement for adult education which is widespread, increasingly intelligent, and correspondingly productive. Millions of adults are exploring and exploiting opportunities for self-advancement. The annual enrolment of the correspondence schools in our country is estimated at two million adults. The governing objective of ninety-five per cent of these correspondence students is the improvement of vocational prospect and status. They are moved by a wistfulness and longing for a fuller expression of life. Our women's clubs boast a membership of three million. The women of this vast army are seeking the more abundant life both for themselves and for their children through better homes and better communities and through a more varied and a richer aesthetic and intellectual life. In our southern states there has been for some time a movement under way for the removal of the existing humiliating adult illiteracy. Adults in large numbers are attending the provided night or "moonlight"

CAN ADULTS BE RECONSTRUCTED? 87

schools. These adult pupils are not foreigners or immigrants, but the lineal descendants of old French and English American stock. They are as Nordic and as nearly without admixture as any people within our national boundaries. Again, the number of mature persons registered in our colleges and universities, especially during the summer sessions, is growing with amazing rapidity.

Participation in adult education has assumed international and world-wide proportions. It is impressive that in August of 1929 a conference of the World Association for Adult Education was held in Cambridge, England. Representatives from more than forty nations assembled to consider the motives, aims, materials, methods, and organization of adult education. Typical aims as disclosed by the conference merit mention. In Russia, India, and China adult education is primarily a war against illiteracy; in radical circles in England its main purpose is emancipation from the ideas and control of the governing class; in Denmark it centers in preparation for effective participation in the social order; in the United States its aim is the improvement of the vocational outlook. A prominent American delegate stressed the wise use of leisure time as a worthy objective of adult education. Participants in the conference freely voiced their needs and desires. Some wanted training in the science of boxing. Welsh miners demanded instruction in New Testament Greek! (Let American theological seminaries in which the study of the Greek New Testament has been made optional take note and ponder!)

Adult education is, then, no sporadic and fugitive interest, but a growing movement which, despite divergences of aim, method, and organization, unites in a vast fellowship of striving for the more abundant life millions of persons of mature years. "Why stop learning?" seems to be the slogan adopted by multitudes of individuals. To the institutions and agencies already mentioned should be added such available facilities for information, inspiration, and culture as art galleries, museums of natural history, libraries, musical concerts, public lectureships, the better radio programs, the more dignified magazines, and newspapers offering not only accounts of important current events but, in addition, stimulating editorials and reliable feature articles.   In their study of the reading habits and interests of adults, Gray and Munroe discovered that 7,500 copies of Robinson's *Mind in the Making,* as against 6,000 copies of one of Zane Gray's popular novels had been read.[5]   Dr. Will Durant's *The Story of Philosophy* was a "best seller." A placard conspicuously displayed in a bank presents the challenge: "If there is anything stopping you, get it out of the way. President Andrew Johnson was a grown man before he could read or write."

Professor Thorndike's dictum that the best time to learn anything is when we want to use it implies that the learning ability is coextensive with the emergence of needs which can be met by personality growth.   Educators are in many instances speaking of continuation education rather than of adult education and of continuation schools rather than of night schools.   The substitution of the term "continuation" is suggestive of an ideal of education which contemplates the uninterrupted expansion and enlargement of personality from the cradle to the grave.

One of the most impressive illustrations of the ability of persons of adult years to overcome limitations is the rehabilitation of the adult blind.   In our country each year some two hundred thousand industrial accidents which injure the eyes occur.   Many of these cases result in total blindness.   When a piece of steel, or stone, or glass destroys the sight of a man, he is permanently relegated to the company of the occupationally unfit unless he is reconstructed and readjusted.   Dropping a coin into the hat of a blind beggar does not give him the fundamental help which he so desperately needs.   Only when he has been so rehabilitated that he can read with his fingers and earn his bread by doing useful work does he triumph over his deprivation.   It has been abundantly demonstrated that persons blinded in the adult period are capable of mastering their depressing disability and of leading happy, wholesome, honorable, and productive lives.

[5] Gray, W. M., and Munroe, Ruth, *Reading Interests and Habits of Adults* (New York: The Macmillan Company, 1927).

The Religious Transformation of Adults

Is it psychologically possible to rehabilitate the adult individual who is afflicted by moral and religious blindness? The history of the Christian religion, to confine ourselves to the type of religion to which we are committed, supplies an affirmative answer. The New Testament as a whole may be interpreted as an account of a successful experiment in adult religious reconstruction.

Jesus, the central figure in the New Testament, as a child, grew in body, in intelligence, in religious outlook, in social responsibility. As an adult he continued the enrichment of his personality through temptation, meditation, disappointment, suffering, and obedience to the Father's will. The confidence of Jesus in the capacity of man for personal religious progress is challengingly courageous. He did not accept the philosophy that human nature is entirely fixed and unalterable at any stage. His entire ministry assumed that if men only would they could, under God, transcend their limitations. Men are not to be blind to the evil in themselves or to ignore it, but to face it and to overcome it.

Under the inspiration of Jesus, Nicodemus finally answered his question, "How can a man be born when he is old?" in his own transformation. In the first recorded interview with Nicodemus, Jesus gave his case the heroic treatment which it required, but he did not urge the doubting man to an immediate decision to break with the past. Two years later Pharisees resolve to have Jesus arrested and haled before them for summary disposition. The high-handed proceedings outrage Nicodemus' sense of justice. He is bold enough to make a plea for simple justice for Jesus before the court and for the elemental right of self-defense. Nicodemus has not yet accepted the leadership of Jesus in religion and morals, he has not yet abandoned his narrow and oppressive conception of the good life, but he has arrived at the promising stage of open-mindedness and fair play. A few months later Jesus was crucified like a felon. At the foot of the cross stands Nicodemus, who has come with spices with which to anoint the mangled body of Jesus. The presence of Nicodemus symbolized his definite break with the leadership that had killed

Jesus. It was his public declaration of his adoption of the program of Jesus, his open confession of faith in the redemptive work of Christ. A subtle and elusive but clarifying and creative work of grace had prospered in Nicodemus. Who can trace the intricate and delicate network of influences and connections which led him from skepticism through open-mindedness to ultimate self-committal to Christ?

In time Jesus realized that in all probability his ministry would be terminated, and perhaps abruptly, after a relatively short period of further activity. He faced the problem of devising means for the continuance of his mission after his death. He resolved to give a small number of his companions intensive training that would empower them to carry forward his cause.

There may be those who believe that ideally Jesus should have selected a dozen infants, all eugenically tested and hygienically certified, given them specialized instruction and supervision for a quarter of a century and then sent them forth to spread the Kingdom of God. But he did not have time enough for such a noble experiment. Perhaps he would have had no great inclination for such a project even if the circumstances had been favorable. As it was, he chose twelve adults, all mature men, and through fellowship and training remade them to such an extent that they furthered his cause after his death with tremendous effect. For example, Peter, who had been steeped in political notions of the nature of the Kingdom, under the tutelage of Jesus in the course of time comprehended such a measure of the purpose of his Master that he established the Jerusalem church, gave it its first doctrines and early form of organization. It is difficult to understand how the Christian religion could have been established and disseminated apart from its adoption by adults.

The Book of Acts, which outlines the history of the apostolic church, is a treasure store of cases of adult reconstruction. All the techniques for Christian service disclosed in this document are applicable to work with adults. The religious training of children is not mentioned in this book, although the baptism of entire families would naturally imply it. The primary task of the early missionaries and teachers was the conversion of the adult to Christianity, his growth in the Christian virtues, and his self-investment in service. In all teaching situations specifically revealed in the Book of Acts the subjects are adults.

Peter grappled with the religious problems of adults. He took the initiative in the determining of a successor to Judas and in so doing imparted instruction to one hundred and twenty persons, mostly adults, assembled for prayer. On the day of Pentecost he addressed the multitude with the result that three thousand souls, the majority of whom were adults, affiliated with the church. It is reasonable to suppose that most of these converts continued in the Christian faith and cultivated creative personalities. Peter, together with John, changed the outlook of the lame beggar at the temple gate and had to defend this deed and his message before the graybeards of the Jewish Sanhedrin. After he yielded the leadership of the mother church in Jerusalem to James the brother of Jesus, Peter carried the gospel with its transforming power to adults of other lands.

Stephen and Philip, both of whom were gripped and remade by the power of Christianity in the mature years, labored with adults with astonishing effects. Stephen taught in the synagogues in Jerusalem and converted a goodly number of Jews who had been born and brought up in foreign lands; he, too, delivered an apology for his life before the Council but sealed his ministry with martyrdom. Philip's work in the city of Samaria was rewarded with great numerical success. His winning of the distinguished proselyte riding in his chariot from Jerusalem to Ethiopia is a classic instance of religious work with an individual adult, and is replete with fundamentals of personal work which modern pastors might with profit take to heart.

Paul himself instructed in Christian principles and remade by the power of Christianity as a grown man, pressed the re-creating claims of Christ upon adults from Arabia to Rome, if not to Spain, with a cogency and persuasiveness which have made him the outstanding leader, pastor, teacher, and theologian of the Christian Church. He founded and supervised a chain of churches on the firing line of Christianity, composed for the most part of adults recruited from almost every degree of culture, ignorance, and iniquity.

The great leaders of the subsequent periods of the history of the Christian Church devoted themselves to the reclamation of undone, defeated, and despairing adults with a sublime audacity which abundantly vindicated and justified itself. Such contrasting personalities and representatives of opposing theologies as Luther and Zwingli, Wesley and Whitefield, Edwards and Bushnell, Beecher and Moody, all alike in their ministries, demonstrated the validity and practicability of the gospel of Christ to rehabilitate adults broken on the wheel of moral depravity or social injustice. Not that these outstanding Christian leaders neglected the training of the child in the principles of morals and religion. Luther, for example, in a day when only the nobility and the clergy had the benefits of a formal education organized schools in which the young of the common people were taught the rudiments. He wrote catechisms in which children and young people were instructed. Wesley was perhaps the first prominent clergyman to explore and exploit for the Christian nurture of the child the Sunday school founded in his day by Robert Raikes. And Bushnell is the morning star of modern religious education in America.

Persons who glibly declare that the children of the present are the hope for a better future seldom realize that those who are charged with the responsibility for the molding of childhood are adults. Adult control is absolutely essential to child education. The child cannot outline and supervise his own education. A child-centered program of education must be formulated and applied by competent adults. Civilization is determined and ruled by adults. They write our books, practice our professions, conduct our business, govern our communities, enact our legislation, and teach our schools. Progress must begin with those with whom responsibility is lodged. One of the most urgent tasks of the Church is to train and discipline adults so that they may efficiently and worthily discharge their responsibility for the religious culture of the child. The quality of the present adult leadership largely conditions the quality of the rising generation. If the human race is to be improved through the better training of childhood, parents, teachers, and others who touch the child at critical points must themselves first be improved if not actually remade.

Let the pastor who works with adult individuals thank God and take courage. Experience shows and controlled statistical studies demonstrate that it is not only psychologically possible but actually imperative to enlarge or remake adult personality. The history of the Church vividly sets forth the part which Christianity plays as a moral revelation and dynamic in the progressive development or rehabilitation of adult personality. The pastor's work with adult individuals is not easy; it is admittedly far more difficult than his delicate ministry to the children, for he has the inertia of entrenched modes of thought, feeling, and conduct to combat. When we give due consideration to the unfavorable conditions which depress many, in fact most persons, such as inadequate housing, malnutrition, monotonous toil, ignorance, and lack of recreation, a marked degree of personality improvement in a brief period of time is not to be anticipated. The experienced pastor will not despair if the ravages of long standing and of grim circumstance refuse to yield instantly to his treatment. He will not expect immediate transformations in the lives of those persons whose environmental circumstances are debasing and whose native endowments are meager. Sustained by the assurance that human nature, so far from being inflexible, is actually modifiable and adaptable, he will approach the individuals to whom he ministers in the mood of patient expectation.

CHAPTER VII

MOTIVES FOR PERSONALITY CHANGES

A COLLEGE professor one day while on his way home came upon a distingushed educator and colleague standing, apparently lost in thought, beside a mud puddle left in the street after a recent rain, in which his young son was splashing about and gleefully covering himself with slime. The astonished professor proceeded to interrupt the meditations of the father and to direct his attention to the activities of his child. "Stop daydreaming and compel him to leave the puddle," he exhorted. "That's just what I don't want to do," the father retorted. "I don't want to force him out of the mud. I am trying to devise a procedure whereby the boy of his own accord will stop playing in the puddle and go home with me."

The father's self-appointed task was a delicate and intricate one of motivation. How could he implant in his little son a desire to abandon an activity from which he was evidently deriving much pleasure but which was destructive of clothing and detrimental to health? Was there anything in the personality of the child to which the father could make an effective appeal? The resort to commands, threats, coercion, and violence would have been a confession of parental failure, however one might be inclined to justify such drastic methods in the existing circumstances.

The Importance of Motivation

A motive is an incitement to activity, an instigator of personality changes and social adjustments. What can the pastor do to induce individuals to make needed personality adjustments? To create in the immature or maladjusted personality the will and the ability to reorganize itself is the perennial responsibility of the pastor. It is an axiom in case work that it is impossible to aid so long as there is no desire for improvement. It goes almost without saying that the exercise of force or authority is quite out of the question in pastoral work, no matter how refractory or recalcitrant individuals may be. In order to accomplish his purpose the pastor must arouse dormant desires to action and reinforce already existing interests. It is of the utmost importance to know the hidden or conscious motives of actuation.

The pastoral problem is complicated by the fact that an intellectual comprehension of and assent to the validity and practicability of proposals for personality advancement are not in themselves sufficiently motivating to incite to the appropriate adjustment. Only applied knowledge is power. To know is not always to act. For example, physicians who have an adequate knowledge of what constitutes a balanced diet and who are fully aware of the deleterious consequences of overeating do not always themselves at home and at the banquet table practice what they know and prescribe for others. Good Dr. Blunt in his old age refused to take to his bed when his own clinical thermometer indicated that he had a temperature of 103 degrees, although he would have poured maledictions upon the head of any patient of his who would have ventured to do likewise. To give the reasons for doing a commendable thing is not enough. Appeals to reason apart from appeals to fundamental urges and interests are seldom if ever effective.

The theory that habit is independent of a dominating desire or interest is fallacious. Motivation is the root of habitual performances. Incited and sustained by an interest or urge, one persists in a series of operations the performance of which, through sheer repetition, has become automatic. A spur of some sort stimulates the mechanism of habit to activity. When the motivating element or principle has been suspended or disrupted the habit which has served it naturally collapses. Let us suppose that a mother gives her young son ten cents a week for brushing his teeth daily. Repeated performance establishes the laudable habit of the daily brushing of the teeth. After a period of three months the mother, relying on the force of habit to maintain the hygienic practice, informs the child that the payment of the weekly stipend will be discontinued. The outcome may be anticipated. Having been actuated by the economic motive alone, the little boy promptly interrupts the daily habit. When he is mature enough to appreciate the principles of dental hygiene he will as part of the routine of daily life and without extraneous supports make regular and intelligent use of the tooth brush. Divorced from its driving power, no habit, however strong or old it may be, can indefinitely maintain itself. After all a habit as a process is the automatic means whereby an underlying motive regularly expresses itself.

Knight and Remmers conducted an experiment which illuminates and enforces the point.[1] Ten college freshmen, after being subjected for five days to hard work, loss of sleep, hazing, and other torments and indignities, were given a series of tests in computation late at night. The freshmen believed that the results of the test would be an important factor in deciding their fitness for admission to a college fraternity. The motivating element was their strong desire to qualify for membership in this organization. The results of the tests were compared with those obtained from fifty college juniors whose work was not motivated by any special wish or want. It may be supposed that the juniors were at least as intelligent as the freshmen and had at least equal ability to solve problems in arithmetic. The freshmen averaged twice as many computations in the given units of time. The achievement of the freshmen is plainly not the product of a difference in biological equipment or in previous training but of a difference in motivation. Attention, interest, and desire lay at the base of the superior work of the freshmen. The prestige, the social life, the fellowship, and the post-college benefits of membership in the fraternity interested the freshmen, intrigued their attention, and created an intense desire to be pledged. These processes and conditions interlocking and interpenetrating formed a driving power which depressing and discouraging circumstances failed to disrupt.

Push and Pull

It has been customary to distinguish two kinds of motives— namely, the blind impulse and the conceived impulse. The

[1] See Knight, E. B., and Remmers, H. H., "Fluctuation in Mental Production When Motivation Is the Main Variable," *Journal of Applied Psychology,* Volume VII, pp. 209 ff.

propulsion without deliberation or clear definition is described as a push; the propulsion the ends of which are understood and treasured is described as a pull. The distinction has, however, within recent years become somewhat dim and confusing.

Instincts have been supposed to be the chief pushes from within man. But what is an instinct, and how many are included in our native equipment? The present tendency among psychologists is to describe an instinct as an inherited reaction pattern. It is an inbred readiness to act in a specific manner without previous training or experience when the appropriate stimulus is applied. Psychologists and sociologists who have in recent years resurveyed original human nature are persuaded that in this sense of the term we are endowed with but few instincts. The vast majority of responses once attributed to instinct have on closer inspection been discovered to be products of social interaction. The general and popular usage of the word instinct includes far too many acquired directive activities. To go so far as to claim that one has an instinct for doing everything one can do is to rob the word instinct of its restricted and specific meaning. The astonishing degree to which personality is shaped by tradition, custom, social institutions, and conventions should receive due consideration in a classification of human responses. With the growth and increased complexity of the nervous system many of the human instincts have deteriorated or become extinct. With the expansion and enrichment of our social heritage our instinctive heritage seems to have diminished.

According to some careful students of human nature only such processes as the digestive, the excretory, and the reproductive are determined by intact complex mechanisms in man. The tendency is to describe and interpret instincts in terms of reflexes variously organized and integrated. Watson, the crusader of an extreme form of behaviorism, teaches that there are only three human instincts—namely, fear, love, and rage.[2] These, one is led to believe, are after all inherited emotional responses. Watson holds that not all the fear reactions of the infant are instinctive but only his fear responses to the loss of

---

[2] See Watson, John B., *Psychology from the Standpoint of Behaviorism* (Philadelphia: J. B. Lippincott Co., 1924).

support of his body and to loud sounds. Others would add to
the three listed by Watson hunger, self-regard, self-expression, and gregariousness. The Freudians postulate only two
instincts—the instinct of self-preservation and the sexual instinct. Most psychologists are convinced that the number of
human instincts is a meager one, but pending further research
and experimentation hesitate to submit a list specifying them.

One thing seems to be established. The human instincts do
not long remain totally blind pushes. The instinctive reaction
may not be foreseen or understood by the animals, but in the
case of all normal human beings, with the exception of infants,
experience and reason throw light upon it. Intelligent lovers,
for example, have knowledge of the ends which the sexual instinct subserves. Even the digestive and excretory processes
are subject to at least partial control. The social culture in
which we are enmeshed modifies and directs to a greater
or lesser extent whatever of instinctive endowment we may
possess.

One should not conclude that the drive or desire which one
has acquired through social interaction is an inferior incitement
to action. In fact, once firmly entrenched and become an in-
tegral function of personality, it is just about as powerful and
important a determinant of conduct as if it were a biological
inheritance. Specific impulses, although for the most part
social products, become established and governing through
exercise and gratification. When, for example, the statement
is made that sympathy is not an instinct but a creation of social
interaction, the inference should not be drawn that sympathy
is not a mainspring of conduct. Acquired as well as inbred
urges instigate action.

An individual is as a rule incited to action by a combination
of circumstances or considerations. The course of a human
life is rarely, if ever, outlined by a single motivating cause
Motivation is complex. Impulsions tend to intertwine, to
support one another, and to join forces as if engaged in a con
spiracy friendly or otherwise. With one and the same stone
a person aims at several birds. The surgeon may be moved
to perform a delicate operation with all the skill he can muster
in order to save a precious human life and also in order to

enhance his professional status and to make an addition to his income. A person may be aware of only one actuating force in a given situation, but others, although he is not conscious of them, are significantly influential.

Professor H. A. Overstreet relates that one season at his summer camp in the mountains his family, being without the services of a maid, attempted to do their own housework.[3] The three boys of the professor and his wife were by no means inclined to engage and to co-operate in the daily routine of housekeeping. After breakfast with the exuberance and heedlessness of youth the boys would rush out of the house to the lake or woods, without having helped father and mother wash dishes, make beds, and sweep floors. Indeed, the boys would leave with unbrushed teeth and unwashed ears. It occurred to the parents that the unpleasant tasks might be joined to something which would grip the youngsters. Accordingly a schedule of daily morning chores was made for each lad. On the schedule card of each, spaces were provided in which the performances for every day were recorded. The boys were offered some financial reward for the work done and a bonus for each week's perfect record. The device accomplished miracles. The lads worked with a will. Professor Overstreet's analysis discloses a number of interlocking motives which wrought the change. Every child wants to earn money; hence the economic motive played its part. Every child wants to register progress and to compete with others; the desire to achieve and overcome was aroused. Every child wants the approval of his group; the wish for recognition and status made its contribution. Furthermore, the schedule of tasks gave to each boy specific assignments; everybody likes to know just what is expected of him; a clear conception of duty is necessary to its intelligent performance. The cumulative effect of these instigators to action can hardly be overestimated.

All of us are not equally responsive to the same set of motives; in fact, no two persons are so much alike that any particular incitement has for both of them an identity of meaning and value. The law of individual variation is operative

[3] Overstreet, H. A., *Influencing Human Behavior*, pp. 44-46 (New York: W. W. Norton & Co., Inc., 1925).

in the field of motivation as elsewhere. Nevertheless, while the same motive forces are not all present or equally potent in all of us, we do have many fundamental wants and desires in common. The elemental desires of the workingman and the capitalist are alike, although there is a difference in the motor expression of these longings. The workingman wants a job which because of the big pay or daring or skill it entails gives him standing in the eyes of others, comfortable shelter and enough food in the cupboard, security against old age and sickness, the love of another in whom he seeks completion, some means of self-expression, educational opportunities for his children, and some of the luxuries of life like the motor car and the radio set. The capitalist wants the same fundamentals but accommodated to his place in the social order; he desires standing in "society," to be a power to be reckoned in financial circles, to be the creator of something which expresses his personality, to love and to be loved, to give his children an opportunity to occupy positions of dignity and importance, and to lead a life of variety and luxury. The factors common to the workingman and the capitalist impel the rest of us. All of us who are normal are incited to action by such primary forces as the desire for security, for excitement, for intimacy, for distinction, and for the avoidance of the dangerous or disgusting. The constructive gratification of these wishes constitutes a universal basis of appeal which the alert pastor is quick to sense and utilize.

Mrs. Farmer's husband deserted her and their dependent children and made no provision for their support or care. She took in washing to earn bread for herself and her brood of children. One day her pastor, who was calling on her, referred to the hard work she had to do in order to hold the partially dismembered family together and expressed his sympathy. To his surprise Mrs. Farmer replied: "I have to admit that I love to attack a huge basket full of soiled clothing and linen and make everything clean and sweet and serviceable." His sympathy had been misplaced. The luscious sense of power and achievement and the exhilarating spirit of adventure sustained and supported the desires for security, social intimacy, and the avoidance of the disagreeable. It is easily conceivable

MOTIVES FOR PERSONALITY CHANGES   101

that under other circumstances Mrs. Farmer's urge for power and recognition would have taken a different form of motor expression. In general we may say that experience gives the primary wishes and impulses their specific form and content.

The Originating Power of Emotion

Emotions possess amazing propulsive force. It is suggestive that the word "emotion" is derived from Latin terminology meaning move. Woodworth describes emotion as a stirred-up condition of the personality.[4] Emotions are high explosives which should be handled with extreme care. Few religious leaders are aware of the perils of tense emotional states. Dean Willard L. Sperry refers to a director of music who in his talks to theological students used to remark that if the professor of chemistry were as careless in dealing with his chemical elements as the average pastor is in dealing with the emotions of people he would blow his laboratory and himself to atoms. To use emotion to make broken lives whole, and hampered and thwarted people victorious, is a delicate pastoral responsibility.

The intense emotional experiences which we call the passions are instigators of action which is at once unreasonable and destructive. Anger, hate, envy, jealousy, malice, greed, and lust are passions which, tolerating no interference, would crush all opposition as by irresistible forces. He who succumbs to any of them loses his balance, is disorganized by inward tension, is rendered miserable and morose, and acts on impulse and without due regard for consequences. A violent emotion narrows the field of consciousness to such an extent that wider considerations and corrective elements are ignored. Passion is a cancerous growth which spreads throughout the personality and affects every aspect of life. Passion is not only a menace to the peace and security of others; it turns on itself and corrupts and corrodes the personality that harbors it. It is significant that the passion-ridden person is often referred to as one possessed by a species of madness. One who has been the victim of his own passions may remark, "I was beside myself," or "I was not myself," and thereby confess that his

[4] Woodworth, Robert S., *Psychology,* p. 118 (New York: Henry Holt & Co., 1921).

conduct was like that of a man under the control of an extraneous and evil spirit. It goes without saying that the wise pastor in his efforts to motivate personality adjustments invariably shuns the arousal or the use of passions.

On the other hand, there are emotional possibilities which the discriminating pastor exploits. The appeal to pride or to its opposite, shame, often prompts creative motor expression. Pride is a feeling of self-esteem which may become a rallying center for conflicting or wayward impulses. Inordinate pride, or haughtiness, is of course of doubtful moral value. Self-discipline proceeds from due self-regard. A college dean reports that when students fail to make satisfactory progress in their courses of study his appeals to their self-respect and pride often prove most efficacious. Sometimes, the dean testifies, it is possible to shame the student into more heroic efforts and accomplishments. Shame, as a feeling of self-reproach and personal guilt, constitutes a form of motivation which should be utilized with caution lest the individual become too depressed to react positively to suggestion.

It is quite generally recognized that love and affection as incitements to self-improvement and advancement have no superiors or equals. Love of a worthy woman has been the point of reference in the attainment of a higher personality integration in the experiences of a multitude of men. Love releases the creative forces of mankind.

Affection for children motivates much of the conduct of parents. Parental affection is a powerful incentive to right living, to the practice of the homely but respectable virtues of industry, frugality, and honesty, and to the making of a delicate adjustment to a difficult mate. Affection for the child is restricted to neither sex; in the divorce courts fathers will battle as hard and persistently as mothers for the possession of the children. When husband and wife merely endure one another under the same roof for the sake of the child, parental affection is possessive and smothers the child, and therefore fails to develop its deeper possibilities. Only when their love of the child motivates a clearer understanding of each other, mutual sympathy, helpfulness, and co-operation, does it become a solvent of conjugal infelicity.

The central illuminating and organizing element of the Christian religion is ethical love. Christian idealism possesses tremendous emotional power. It must be confessed that religious leaders have not always exploited the dynamic quality of ethical love. Time was when large and influential areas of the Protestant Church in America considered fear and pity the proper emotional persuasive to piety. The terrors of a lurid hell were detailed with melodramatic vividness and startling consequences. The emotionally unstable and highly imaginative, frightened by the imminent prospect of being doomed to an awful fate, hastened to comply with the demands of the accepted religious leadership. To be sure, when anxious fears subsided there was likely to be chagrin and resentment. The fear state itself did not always bring forth fruits meet for repentance, for "the demons also believe and shudder."

Not content with the arousal and intensification of fear, our fathers attempted to induce the emotion of pity. A portrayal of the dying Savior was often relied on to produce the desired effect. The indignities Christ endured and the agonies he suffered on the cross were particularized, his innocence and holiness were contrasted with the iniquity and guilt of his murderers and of the sinful of the present day. Profoundly shaken by pity, men accepted the proffered salvation. It must be conceded that in too many instances the tears of pity symbolized an impractical sentimentalism. The religious appeal oscillated between fear and pity, and these emotions tended to bring to pass religious inoculation. The sturdy characters of the period were, one is inclined to infer, the products of the more substantial and morally creative principles of the Christian faith.

The emotional emphasis has been shifted to the ethical love which Christ himself both commended and exemplified. It is psychologically significant that ethical love has a rich emotional content. It brings all things under subjection to itself. We love Christ because he first loved an undeserving albeit needy world. On the cross so far from offering a sacrifice of blood and life to a vengeful deity, Christ lays bare the ethical love of the universe and demonstrates a passion for men which is stronger than death. Small wonder that Paul exclaims, "The love of Christ constraineth us." Loyalty to Christ moves in the direction of ethical power. Ethical love for Christ motivates not only sanity and sobriety but also active good will and intelligent social sympathy. Cynicism, skepticism, mockery, and cold-hearted criticism do not originate action which enlarges the individual or benefits society. "Perfect love casteth out fear" and begets that confidence and assurance which makes personality reconstruction psychologically possible.

CHAPTER VIII

RELIGION AS A RALLYING CENTER

OF what use can religion be to the person who is passing through a personal crisis? A few years ago a group of students under the direction of Professor Norman E. Richardson gathered original data from fifty-three books, all published within the previous period of seven years and representing the best current Protestant thinking, concerning the value and function of the Christian religion in individual experience. The functions selected for tabulation were for the most part considered desirable and constructive. More than one thousand items were thus summarized. The array of functions, despite duplications included for the sake of variation of emphasis, shows that religion may dominate the important areas of human experience. That the pastor has in personal religion a powerful ally in his work with individuals should become increasingly clear.

There are, as intelligent observers know, various ways in which different individuals interpret crises and react to them. For example, a man may assume the infantile attitude of blaming others for the misfortune that has overtaken him. If his employer discharges him on the ground of incompetence, he may complain that he is the victim of caprice, capitalistic jealousy, or lack of appreciation. If he is experiencing domestic infelicity, he may attribute the trouble to the malicious attitude and acts of his mother-in-law. Whatever the nature of his difficulty may be, he is positive that he is being discriminated against by others of evil intent. Those who have his welfare at heart and know him better than he knows himself may disagree with his diagnosis, but any efforts to convince him of the true state of affairs will serve only to confirm him in his notion that he is the innocent subject of an iniquitous conspiracy. So long as the delusion of martyrdom continues it is impossible for him to make the proper personality adjustment. In fact it is likely to induce a chronic state of cynicism, captiousness, and discontent, if not of active hostility and rebellion against others or what is denominated as fate.

Another may heap reproaches upon himself in the day of adversity. He may be inclined to blame himself for a misfortune in the precipitation of which he has had no part. Sensitive souls, burdened as they often are by a sense of guilt, have suffered extreme mental tortures. Mrs. Morgan's little daughter Jane made the lawn of a church near her home a playground. Almost every day when the weather permitted the child romped among the trees and the huge flowerpot stands of her favorite spot. One day while at play in this place she overturned a heavy iron stand and was crushed beneath its weight. Within a few hours life departed from the mangled body. For days Mrs. Morgan reproached herself for having allowed Jane to play for so long a time on the church lawn. "I was about to call Jane home when I noticed that she was unusually happy and made up my mind to let her enjoy herself awhile longer. If I had only summoned her as I had originally intended, the dreadful thing would not have happened," the anguished mother repeatedly lamented. It requires rare tact and wisdom to convince such a person that she is not responsible for the tragedy.

Still another resorts to philosophizing, to an attempt to understand why he has been afflicted. Instead of attacking troubles, eliminating what can be eliminated and bravely bearing what cannot be banished, he consumes his time and energy in accounting for the existence of adversity and suffering. The fact that no one has offered a comprehensive explanation of human tragedy which has won the assent of the majority of thinkers does not seem to undermine his confidence in his own ability. In some instances the explanation may be an assumption that one is suffering the just penalty for sin, although an objective examination of the situation fails to disclose any wrongdoing from which the specific crisis could naturally emerge. The inference is drawn that trouble is not to be mastered but meekly endured. A wise man stands in awe and reverence before the impenetrable mysteries of life, but a presumptuous person professes to have a theological plummet long enough to touch the bottom of the central secrets of the universe.   There are, to be sure, others whose insistent demand for a convincing explanation of the existence of pain, sorrow, and loss is never satisfied.   Their consequent philosophical bewilderment hinders a practical adjustment to stern reality.

The Religious Response to Crises

One may adopt the religious approach to perplexity or adversity.   A dynamic and motivating experience of God facilitates personality adjustment.   Religion in his case is a rallying center, the source of comfort and inspiration in the day of trouble.   Religion is not a triumph of hope over dismal experience but the dominance of experience by insight, courage, and power.   The negations of life are canceled by the affirmations of religious values.

Religion, if this experience is to retain its specific content and meaning, is not any form of idealism which takes a man out of himself and shapes his daily conduct.   Religion is essentially God-consciousness.   In the unforgettable phrase of Donald Hankey the religious man bets his life that there is a God.   In the comprehensive experience of religious people, God is the point of reference in the integration of personality.   God is the larger environment with which man may make creative correspondences.   The function of religion in the time of trouble is to construct a more courageous, a more competent, and a more victorious self through an active faith in God.   In the face of a desperate situation the consciousness of God is intensified and imparts to human personality a special impetus and momentum toward reorganization and unification.   Power moves in the direction of an attitude of confidence in God as a mighty helper.   Religion is, then, the endeavor of an incompetent and divided self to achieve consistency and completion by an appeal to an ideal agent of extra-human structure.

The supreme advantage of the Christian religion lies in its possession of an historical basis in the person of Christ.   One of the most amazing statements of Jesus is his declaration, "I have overcome the world."   He did not say, "I have escaped the world"; he did not say, "I completely understand the world"; but he did say for the encouragement of his friends, "Be of good cheer, I have overcome the world."   The comprehensive purpose within which he recognized and fostered every creative impulse is expressed in his announcement, "My meat is to do the will of him that sent me." The rallying center in the life of Jesus was the Father God. The Christian religion is a dynamic experience of that type of ultimate reality which Jesus uniquely disclosed and interpreted, an experience which gathers up into itself all the scattered energies of man and unites them in a creative synthesis.

Christ kindles in those who come under his spell a glowing love for others, loyalty to his moral principles, a readiness to make sacrifices, and a desire to transcend personal limitations. In the matrix of the leadership of Christ gates of significance are opened and fountains of personal power are unsealed. His personality supplies to the individual who stands face to face with grief, loss, misunderstanding, or persecution the incentive to make the appropriate adjustments, together with the requisite stabilizing principle and spirit of tranquillity. An appreciation of Christ may result in a new union of life forces and the recentering of personality. The example of Christ is a perpetual inspiration. By an unwavering purpose to discover the will of the Father and to do it, by prayer, by meditation, by facing grim facts, by clear thinking, by courageous action Christ overcame or rose above peril, pain, turmoil, loneliness, misunderstanding, and a sense of desolation. As an object of devotion the radiant personality of Christ can accomplish what no set of abstract rules and regulations for the reconstruction of imperiled or broken human lives can bring to pass.

Not that the follower of Christ leads a charmed life. He is not immune from the distress, loss, and affliction which are the common lot of mankind. He is so limited in knowledge that at times his ignorance will seem to be abysmal. He possesses the eternal values in earthen vessels. The Christian may be cast down but he is not destroyed, persecuted of men but not forsaken of God, perplexed but not in despair, subject to the perils of a complicated world but not defeated by them. Some one has said that the Christian cultivates the heroic possibilities which he possesses. There is in every one of us, either potentially or actually, a hero and a coward. The coward shrinks from life or lets it overwhelm him. The hero attacks life boldly and tries to exercise dominion over it. The hero carries his burden without bitterness or rebellion, without demanding comfort and security, asking only the privilege of living and loving. The hero that a man can be is his best possible self. After all, men do not differ so much in the nature and intensity of their troubles as in their attitudes toward them. The Christian life is not a refuge from affliction but as another has suggested a field for adventure in which the potential hero develops at the expense of the possible coward.

Religion in Typical Adjustments

Adjustment to bodily handicap may be encouraged and furthered by the religious attitude. People who are deformed, or blind, or deaf, or lame, or bereft of an arm or a leg, or unusually homely of face have to cope with peculiar problems and make special adaptations in order to achieve the fulness of life. One source of their embarrassment is the fact that normal people fail to take them for granted but persist in showing them sympathetic consideration. Well-intentioned but misguided persons are inclinded to pamper the handicapped, to shield them from the ordinary incidents of living, not realizing that such preferential treatment makes the recipient self-conscious. Physical defect makes one hypersensitive. When such a one walks down the street he feels that people whom he passes stop, turn their heads, nudge one another, and speculate as to who or what is responsible for the defect. Those who must shoulder a physical handicap have to make a special effort in order to function adequately in the economic and social order. The self-respecting who prefer to earn their daily bread have, as a rule, a difficult occupational adjustment to make. When marriage becomes a possibility, its appropriateness and wisdom are not always easy to determine. Surely these people have a right to claim the assistance of whatever will enable them to make that personality adjustment which will banish their sense of inferiority and give them a chance to lead wholesome, happy, and economically independent lives.

When four years old Mary Fulton fell from the partially built porch of a house in process of construction, lighting on her left side on the crushed rock in cement forms. Her left

arm was badly fractured; three bones in the wrist and the cap
of the elbow were broken. Normal recovery was made, and at
the end of three weeks the splints were removed. Little Mary
demonstrated that she could move her fingers. Two days later
she was stricken with what the physician in charge diagnosed
as spinal meningitis. At first she was unable to walk. The
malady yielded partially to medical treatment, and in the course
of time the patient could walk. But the paralysis of the left
arm was permanent, the result, it seems, of the weakened condition induced by the fracture.

Mary had to deal with the stern fact that in all likelihood she
would have to go through life with the use of only one arm.
To be sure, now and then her parents clutched at a faint hope of
her complete restoration. One practitioner assured them that
under his treatment the use of the paralyzed arm would be recovered in three weeks. When he failed to redeem his pledge,
the indomitable spirit of Mary expressed itself in statement:
"Let's not go to that doctor any more, I don't need my arm. I
can be an art teacher and won't need it."

Gradually Mary adjusted herself to the handicap. The process was not always easy to further. One day when she was at
the railway station a locomotive engineer sitting in his cab
saw her while the train halted and with a crass attempt at
humor called to her, "Did you lose the arm in the war?" She
took refuge from the offensive question in more strenuous
work in the newspaper office in which she at the time was employed. Like others in similar situations, the most difficult
thing to overcome was the fact that so many people, most of
whom were kindly disposed, called attention to her defect by
failing to treat her as though she were normal.

When she was in college a young man of ability and character fell in love with her. She returned his love. When she
began to take the thought of marriage seriously, a number of
questions arose to perplex her. For example, could she take
care of children without any aid from others? She set about
to answer this question in a practical test. One afternoon she
took charge of a baby during the absence of the mother from
home. Alone with the six-months-old infant Mary proceeded
to attack her problem. She dressed and undressed the baby,

carefully supporting the little back, prepared a bottle of food
and fed her.   Mary did everything that she felt was necessary
in the care of a baby.   She discovered that the task was not
so difficult for her as she had anticipated.   Her efforts were
successful.   The experiment demonstrated that she could undertake the personal and independent care of children.   Mary was
relieved and thrilled.

Mary Fulton is now happily married and takes her part as
the wife of a professional man with graceful distinction.   She
does her own housework, sews and embroiders, drives an automobile, dances, swims, plays tennis, and does almost everything
that physically normal people do and in almost the same length
of time.   Bodily handicap, so far from embittering her, has
been the occasion of an adjustment which has developed sympathy, courage, and resourcefulness.

It is significant that the quality of her background is religious.   She was reared in a Christian home, was carefully instructed in the principles of religion; her early associations and
social contacts were colored by religious considerations, she
united with the church, and she married a minister of the gospel whom she assists in his parish work.   To be sure, her
courage in facing her defect, her determination to triumph over
it, the means which she adopted to further adjustment might
have been cultivated apart from religious idealism, but the fact
is established that the subsoil of her personality was fertilized
and enriched by religion.   She lived and moved and had her
being in an atmosphere charged with creative religious attitudes.

In our country money is all too generally the measure of
one's success. A non-lucrative career, like that of a teacher,
although it benefits society, is tolerated rather than recognized.
It is, therefore, not strange that when a person in our commonwealth suffers a serious loss of income a change in outlook
on life as well as an accommodation to a restricted mode of
living is necessary.   Stimulated by an adequate working philosophy, the loser may learn the validity of Jesus' statement
that after all a man's life does not consist in the abundance of
things which he possesses.   The striving for social prestige
and power over others, often intimately associated with the

acquisition of wealth, may in a revaluation of life prompted by financial reverses seem petty and sordid, if not actually illusory and ridiculous. Adversity may restore to their proper places the various items in the scale of values.

So long as the individual is able to provide the necessities of life, as these are determined by a modest if not minimal mode of living, health, self-respect, friendship, and a chance to lend a hand to those who are less fortunate may take on a significance which was ignored in the day of prosperity. The homely virtues of industry, thrift, frugality, and self-control, formerly supposed to be antiquated, may be restored to respectability and activity. There may be leisure enough to cultivate some things which money cannot buy, such as good taste, and the appreciation of literature, music, and the other arts. The religion of Jesus commends the simple life, warns men of the subtle dangers of wealth, and exhorts them to lay up treasure in heaven. The one who has sustained an embarrassing reduction of income may discover in plain living, in the simplicities of life, enrichment, and satisfaction which more than compensate him for his loss.

Adjustment to the loss of a beloved companion by the hand of death is a complicated process. As a rule the extent of the loss sustained by the survivor is only gradually appreciated. The aching void which a growing consciousness of deprivation creates is difficult to fill. Death is relieved of its ugliness and acquires dignity when faith in personal immortality is intensified. The belief that the dear departed live and that we shall meet them is a religious consolation of no meager significance.

Often death removes not only a companion but the breadwinner as well. Consider, for example, the case of the financially dependent mother of young children who has been recently widowed. She faces the prospect of loneliness and the necessity of supporting herself and her children. She may repine and withdraw into herself. She may let life be too much for her, continually bemoan her lot, and cultivate a martyr attitude. On the other hand, she may adapt herself to her altered circumstances with fortitude and intelligence.

Widowed, say at thirty-five, and with dependent children, she may never attract another mate and build a bridge across which she may walk from loneliness and poverty to companionship and economic security. Nevertheless, her outlook for matrimony, such as it is, will be more favorable if she accepts the responsibilities of widowhood with courage. The battle for bread for herself and her brood of children may develop latent capacities and prove exhilarating. In her occupation she may find companionship with her fellow-toilers; their points of view, ambitions, and accomplishments may stimulate her. Active participation in the educational programs of her children may revive and expand her own intellectual and cultural interests. The church of which she is a member will supply her with the fellowship of kindred minds, of congenial people of taste. Religion may afford her background, encouragement, and hope so that her widowhood is not merely tolerable but dignified and serenely satisfying.

Persons who are ill may constantly draw upon religious reserves for courage and strength. Religion is often the master sentiment which develops a fighting spirit, a firm determination to recover from physical ailment which is of more therapeutic value than drugs. James Andrews, a lad of fifteen years, was suddenly smitten with appendicitis and summarily prepared for a hospital and surgical ordeal. The pastor, Mr. Mark, arrived at the home just before the removal of the patient to the hospital. James was bearing up bravely and displayed an attitude of calm fortitude. This was no time, Mr. Mark felt, for any word suggestive of the "dark valley" or of an uncertain outcome. In the few moments at his disposal the pastor spoke an encouraging word and fortified the already splendid spirit of the lad. Mr. Mark considered it best under the circumstances to offer no prayer. In parting, he added, "James, take this with you," and gave him a small card taken at random from a supply of about sixty cards, each of which bore a different Bible verse and hymn stanza. The card which James carried with him to the hospital gave him this message: "Fear not, for I am with thee; be not dismayed, for I am thy God; I will strengthen thee; yea, I will help thee; yea, I will uphold thee with the right hand of my righteousness."

The surgical operation was critical, for infection had already

set in and developed. For days James lingered on the border-
land but finally rallied and ultimately fully recovered. His
father, who sat at his beside during the long days when no one
else was permitted to visit the patient, later told the pastor that
throughout the crisis the lad held in his hand the card, and that
it inspired in him the fighting mood. In his struggle with the
grim prospect of death it was religious faith, faith in the goodness of God, faith in the power of God to support him, that
psychologically speaking summoned his vital forces and organized them for victory.

The sharpness of death itself is overcome by religious faith
Accommodation to the process of personal physical dissolution is often made by focusing the attention on the prospect of a blissful immortality. Something bigger and stronger
than death occupies the field of attention. The dying Catholic
gazes intently upon the crucifix which the parish priest holds
before his eyes, and the symbol of the world's supreme sacrifice imparts courage, gives assurance that his sins have been
atoned for and forgiven, and promises him endless life under
more desirable circumstances. In an appreciation of the in-
carnation of love, the pangs of death are banished. In man's
final adjustment religion, so far from reserting him, offers him
the support nothing else in the world can supply.

In cases of particularly difficult or delicate personality reorganization religion sometimes functions for a season as a haven
of rest and security. Despite heroic endeavors, the individual
has failed to make a necessary adjustment. He is perplexed
and weary. He does not know what to do next. He does not
admit defeat but is moved to retire from the conflict in order
to recuperate. He exercises a passive religious faith. His confidence in God as his keeper is calm and serene. His respite
from effort gives him time to reorient himself to his problem
and to summon his energies for a fresh attack. If the attempted process of adaptation is accompanied by painful
elements temporary cessation of effort serves as a palliative or
anodyne. Refreshed, composed, and collected after a period
of relaxation, the individual is prepared to resume his fight for
freedom from obstacles.

Religion and Mental Pathologies

Frequently men are saved from insanity by ordering their lives around religious values which they consider real, potent, and abiding. Conventional and facile consolations are ineffectual in the presence of one who is persuaded that the foundations of his mental integrity have been undermined. When one feels that one is about to become the victim of a disordered mind, the only thing that can serve as a rallying center is something that has for one an authentic note. In such a desperate extremity religious values are often the stabilizing forces.

Sometimes melancholy takes the distressing forms of a panic of fear. William James includes in his discussion of the sick soul an account of such a case written by the sufferer himself.[1] The victim states that one night when he was in a state of extreme mental depression suddenly a horrible fear of his own existence fell upon him. Simultaneously the image of an epileptic patient whom he had seen in an asylum arose in his mind, the image of an idiot with greenish skin and black hair, with his knees pressed against his chin and his body covered by his undershirt. The idiot sat there looking absolutely nonhuman, moving only his dark eyes. The image of this creature and his own fear of life merged and produced a dreadful combination. The sufferer was certain that he would become like that idiot and that nothing could save him from such an awful fate. He was reduced to a quivering mass of fear.

After this experience the entire universe was altered for him. Every morning he woke up with a horrible dread at the pit of his stomach and with a devasting sense of the insecurity of life. For months he was afraid to go from the house into the dark alone. It seemed incomprehensible that anyone could live unconscious of the abyss of insecurity beneath the surface of life. He maintains that his fear of life was so powerful that if he had not clung to texts like "The Eternal God is my refuge," etc., "Come unto me, all ye that labor and are heavy-laden," etc., "I am the resurrection and the life," etc., he would have gone mad.

[1] *Varieties of Religious Experience,* pp. 160, 161 (New York: Longmans, Green & Co., 1911).

The part which religion plays in the strange behavior of the insane is frequently misunderstood. Taking religion too seriously is supposed by some to result in pathological obsessions and delusions. Psychiatry teaches that delusions of grandeur, which the mentally disordered often entertain, are not, as a rule, the root but rather the fruit of insanity. Patients whose religious interests were negligible before their minds disintegrated, sometimes harbor phantastic religious notions. The world of the insane man has collapsed. Obeying some obscure urge, he may identify himself with some mighty personality. In his own blind way the patient is trying to reorganize his shattered personality around some agent of dignity and power. However pathetically absurd such a delusion of grandeur may seem to others, it helps the insane to achieve a sense of important selfhood denied by reality. The fusion of his identity with that of God or Christ is, then, the attempt of an insane man to integrate his personality in terms of a larger and more victorious self. When those in charge of the patient succeed in temporarily disillusioning him, he is immediately reduced to a state of bitter despair. His support has been removed and the self is torn and divided and impotent. Only when the delusion has been reinstated is the self again restored to a degree of order and coherence. The grotesque projections of the sick mind so far from being the origin of the pathology constitute a rallying center.

How Religion Becomes Effective

What determines the efficacy of religion in the reorganization of personality? The answer to this question is of importance to the pastor who would make the fullest possible use of religion in his personal service. The answer is that in general religion functions in individual experience when it is understood and sincerely accepted. The pastor who will take the pains to investigate will discover, perhaps to his own chagrin, that the majority of laymen have a pitifully inadequate conception of the structure and function of religion. Most of them have never attempted to clarify their notions of religious values. Although they have received instruction in religion in the church school as children and have listened to sermons as adults for a quarter of a century, their ideas of the nature and significance of religion are confused and nebulous. They may be able to recite a few shibboleths, or to repeat catch-words to which they attach religious value, but their comprehension of the content of religion is tragically feeble. Religious leaders should take seriously the conclusion of psychology that man is not endowed with a religious instinct which functions without guidance once the appropriate stimulus has been supplied, with an inborn mechanism for a religious pattern reaction, but with a capacity for religion, a capacity which can be properly developed only through example, instruction, practice, and worship. While religion embraces verities which transcend our powers of comprehension, it is equally true that religion depends for its vitality and usefulness in part on the degree to which its cardinal principles are understood by the individual.

Furthermore, in order to be effective religion must be a passion. It can become the dynamic center of personality only when it is emotionally experienced as well as understood. Religion remains impotent so long as one's attitude toward it is objectively impersonal. To an adequate understanding of the nature of religion must be added a hearty acceptance of its implications for conduct. The will is influenced and directed by the emotions generated through the internalizing of religion. Man is swayed by his admirations and enthusiasms rather than by the processes of logic. Conduct has an emotional incentive which an intellectual pursuit of truth as such fails to supply. Ideas which are emotionally sterile are morally dead. The religious consciousness involves a high potentiality of emotion that possesses propulsive power. The faith, hope, love, and loyalty which religion includes entail dynamic emotional experiences. Once embraced with ardor and candid devotion, religion establishes itself as a drive which regulates and harmonizes the facts of personal experience. Emotion attaches to its object a sense of personal security, confidence, and personal identification which the belief in the mere existence of verities never achieves.

Of all workers with individuals the pastor is to make intelligent and effective use of religion in removing obstacles to personality development, in inculcating germinal truth, in encouraging constructive action. He is to employ religion in challenging and bringing to fruition the latent powers of personality. Religion is to provide motivation for the adoption and application of the laws of continued renewal and growth. It is to meet man's fundamental need for reassurance, comfort, and consolation in a world that is full of trouble and too big for him. It is to supply a set of authoritative sanctions for a way of life that will ennoble the individual. Religion, wisely directed by the pastor, is a catalyzer energizing the emotions, arousing constructive desires, and conditioning conduct and character.

CHAPTER IX

THE COMPLEX

A MULTITUDE of personality problems of which representative specimens have been indicated in previous chapters originate in clearly recognizable experiences or situations. The sources of strain are more often obvious than concealed and active primarily above rather than below the level of awareness. Personality clashes arising from known causes are not only of frequent occurrence but are also as menacing and disorganizing as the conflicts which are born of submerged memories or desires. Many persons are distracted and unhappy because unrepressed impulses have destroyed the unity of their lives. The wilful exercise of urges which are at variance with the cravings of the self for integration in terms of standards admittedly proper or right is altogether too common to be ignored.

We do not need the help of the clinical psychologist in tracing the majority of our perplexities or misdeeds to their respective origins. Ordinary intelligence and power of observation will bring to consciousness a variety of motives from which we act. Candid self-analysis will disclose patent factors underlying many of our mental processes. For example, reluctance to accept demonstrated contributions of modern science may be recognized as a consequence of inherited beliefs to which religious importance is attached. I may know that I am afraid of fire because I have touched a hot stove and not because an obnoxious but subconsciously smoldering love affair is expressing itself symbolically. Incendiarism is not invariably expressive of inhibited sexual stimulation, but sometimes of a deliberate plot to collect fire insurance. Caution should be exercised lest we interpret the attitudes and acts of others as well as of ourselves in terms which are far-fetched or utterly irrelevant.

In the conduct of his daily life the individual is, nevertheless, actuated by a multitude of motives of the existence and potency of which he is entirely unconscious. Urged to explain why he did a certain thing he may give good reasons but not the real reasons. Although he is positive that he was incited to action by the plausible motives he advances, a more penetrating analysis may reveal determinants of which he has been in total ignorance. The revelation of the hidden springs of conduct would take him by surprise.

The strata of personality which have their being below the level of awareness condition many of the variations from the usual and wholesome. A psychologist refers to a young man who was abnormally afraid of being bitten by horses. The victim of this exaggerated fear felt more secure at a horse's heels than at his head. The young man invariably moved to a position behind a horse. The origin of his fear was a mystery to him until an uncle of his, whom he had not seen for many years, explained that when he, the nephew, was a little child and too young to remember, a vicious horse actually bit him and of course terribly frightened him. Although the painful episode was forgotten, it prompted feeling and action for many years. We may forget occurrences like that, but they will hold us in active remembrance.

One form of subsconscious motivation is technically known as the complex. Unfortunately the term "complex" has been appropriated by the popular imagination and has been assigned meanings and applications which do not commend themselves to the reputable psychologist. Almost any deviation from what may be considered the conventional, or any anomaly is called a complex by the uninformed. Recently a lad told his rather garrulous younger brother that he had a "talking complex." The term "complex" should be stripped of the foreign connotations with which it has been invested and be given a consistently scientific significance.

A complex in the more scientific sense of the term includes at least three fundamental items: it is a system of ideas with their emotional involvements; it is in conflict with the accepted standards of the individual; it is subconsciously dynamic. These three aspects of the complex are conceded by most theories of psychoanalysis. In some other respects there is a wide difference of opinion. The strict Freudians maintain that all complexes proceed from experiences of early childhood and are related to the sexual impulse. Others refer the genesis of all complexes to a consciousness of inferiority. Still others hesitate to assign the origin of every complex to any one specific urge or condition, but are disposed to consider the manifold impulses and wider experiences of the personality prolific sources of repressions and conflicts. We shall have occasion to revert to some of these controverted points; meanwhile the generally uncontested features of the complex should be surveyed.

The System of Emotionally Toned Ideas

A complex is, then, first of all a group of ideas with their emotional accompaniments. Human experiences tend to hang together in the form of clusters. Related mental processes or conditions, mutually attracted as it were, join forces and exist and move as a unit. Personality consists of a hierarchy of constellations of wishes, drives, impulses, and interests. A complex is an organization of ideas heavily charged with emotion. It is, of course, more than a system of emotional toned conceptions, for not all groups of ideas suffused with emotion are complexes.

There are two primary feelings: pleasantness and unpleasantness. Pleasantness is associated with the free and unobstructed neural discharge of impulses. It accompanies an adjustment to a behavior pattern to which there is no opposition. Unimpeded activity is pleasurable. Unpleasantness is attached to the neural blockage or interference of impulses. When the discharge of an impulse is impeded, no matter by what, tension results. When there is antagonism between two impulses, as when they seek the same channel of discharge, the consciousness of unpleasantness arises. When the appropriate adjustment is made, when adaptive reaction occurs, tension is relieved and the quality of the feeling tone changes and becomes agreeable. Pleasantness and unpleasantness are feeling states each of which embraces a variegated group of characteristic emotions. For example, the emotions of thankfulness and joy are specialized manifestations of pleasantness, and the emotions of grief and rage of unpleasantness.

The complex is marked by a feeling tone the quality of

which is disagreeable. The basis of unpleasantness is to be found in the internal clash of impulses which distinguishes the complex. Energy of the complex-driven individual is obstructed; there is confusion, frustration, or conflict. The unpleasantness associated with the complex assumes differentiated emotional states. The emotions which are related to the variety of complexes include those of hatred, jealousy, malice, fear, anxiety, anger, resentment, exasperation, irritability, and depression. Such emotions exhaust the stores of nervous energy and dislocate personality. Only when the appropriate adaptive response is made to the requirements of the self as a whole does human energy discharge itself freely and then the unpleasantness evaporates and the consciousness of agreeableness in terms of relaxation and satisfaction is aroused.

Conflicting Values

In the second place, a complex is a form of motivation which is contrary to the tastes and ideals of the individual. A norm of conduct once accepted as valid assumes the form and force of a personal obligation. In the progressive integration of personality the regulative evaluations are the centers of appeal. But not every system of emotionally charged ideas is in full accord with the central governing aims, purposes, and ideals of the personality. Man's primitive self-assertion and the organized social pressures to which he is subjected often clash. When the forces in human life and in its surroundings destroy the harmony and unity of personality a state of civil war ensues. The complex is an organization which is diametrically opposed to accepted principles and obligations.

There are a number of ways in which the individual may react to impulses or memories at variance with his ideals or social standards. For example, a struggle or conflict may be avoided by keeping the unacceptable attitude and the sense of fitness apart. Vital contact between the two may not be allowed to occur. The two contradictory systems may, as it were, be confined in separate areas of personality. Each may follow its own course without interference from the other. So long as the condition of double-mindedness persists no opposition arises.

Persons who lead inconsistent lives without suffering qualms of conscience and without attempts to unify them in terms of the higher values which they profess to accept give the faithful pastor many an anxious hour. Unfortunately cases of this kind are discoverable in almost every parish. Albert James is a Kentuckian living in the "Blue Grass" region, well educated, the husband of a wife of the same class, and the father of five children. He and his family are all church members. He boasts that he has drunk whiskey to excess all his life, but he says his prayers every night, intoxicated or sober. For years he took no responsibility for the support of his family. His wife earned bread for herself and their children teaching school. Finally she and the children went to other parts to live where he cannot molest them. He is now living alone in the attic of a garage, apparently contented and without registering complaints against anyone. He is devoid of all personal pride; he, a Kentuckian, will labor in a ditch with Negroes. He is not conscious of any inconsistency between drunkenness, profanity, and the neglect of his family on the one hand and church membership, prayers, and orthodox religious beliefs on the other. His faithful pastor proposes to give the errant parishioner a more adequate conception of the meaning of the Christian life. Alas, none are so blind as those who will not see that faith without works is dead.

Sometimes a conflict is evaded by making a change in the principles that govern conduct. Reacting against the exacting requirements which one has hitherto accepted, one, so to speak, goes shopping for a standard or authority whose demands permit indulgence in what one craves. Such a readjustment is most easily and readily made by those who are dependent on others for the guidance of the currents of life. The religious dependent, dissatisfied with present affiliations, is inclined to adopt the expedient of appealing to an authority willing to countenance if not positively sanction the allurement. Mr. H. C. Miller refers to a young woman whose religion was of the mother type and who was disappointed and depressed because her confessor had forbidden her to participate in dances during Lent.[1] A few days later she made her appearance at a ball.

---

[1] *The New Psychology and the Preacher,* p. 127 (New York: Albert and Charles Boni, 1924).

When asked to explain how she proposed to make her peace
with her confessor she naïvely responded: "Oh, it's all right;
I've changed my confessor." True to the type of personality
she represents, such an individual senses no ethical defect in
her normative alterations and is conscious of no self-deception.

Subconscious Motivation

The complex is subconsciously active. When the conflicting
impulse or impression is banished from the field of attention
it may become a subconscious possession. At this point a
number of questions demand answers. What is the subconscious? What is its relation to the waking consciousness? For
what phenomena does it account? In the nature of the case the
subconscious eludes direct introspection, and the meager information of it which we do possess has been gleaned by indirect
means. One should add that our knowledge of the nature and
the effects of the subsconscious while admittedly sparse is
actually increasing.

The subconscious may be described as that vast area of one's
mental life which is not the material of present reflective
scrutiny. There is no sharp division between the conscious and
the subconscious activities of the self. The two fields are
loosely separated by what is called the threshold of consciousness. There is no gulf fixed between them; each affects the
other; the one merges into the other.

The subconscious is not a subterranean storehouse in which
every experience is deposited as a permanent possession and
from which the accumulated items may be withdrawn one by
one. Nor is the subconscious a factory in which in isolation
from the rest of the personality marvels are manufactured
from tenuous stuff and delivered to the conscious self. Mental
states and processes, conscious or subconscious, are not substantial and material.

Furthermore, the subconscious is not an independent and
individual existence and as such the source and basis of a
self of its own, a self wiser and more efficient than the self
of clear consciousness. The terms "subconscious mind" and
"subliminal self" are misnomers and as such have false philosophical implications. "The subconscious" as a name is less

objectionable if it is understood that the definite article "the" does not indicate a distinct and exclusive entity. The relation between the subconscious and the conscious is one of identity and continuity, although the subconscious may include fragments or growths which are disconnected from healthful interchange with the personality as a whole. Personality which is wholesome is at once unitary and composite.

Again, esoteric and mystical qualities and effects should not be postulated of the subconscious. Subconscious processes are not independent of the nervous system; there is a correlation between the physical and the mental throughout the total range of subconscious states and activities. It is not a gate through which occult entities or forces with which awareness may have no intercourse invade human life. It is not an inexhaustible reservoir of supernatural or superhuman energy. Although the field of the subconscious is difficult of access, the phenomena of it which science has surveyed and analyzed are all included within the general and universal system of natural and orderly sequences. The subconscious does not possess magical properties and powers, however weird, bizarre, or miraculous some of its manifestations may seem to one who is unfamiliar with the techniques and classifications of psychology.

Chance or magic has no part in the mental life, however difficult it may be to account for apparently discontinuous phenomena. For example, let the reader pause long enough for any letter of the alphabet to become the object of momentary attention. Be assured that the letter thought of, whether it be a, g, m, or z, is conditioned by the mental state of the time. One particular letter and no other emerges into awareness. The brilliant inspiration of the poet, however unheralded and unrelated it may seem, is in all probability a subliminal uprush. The orator has moments when stimulated by a social situation he rises to unanticipated heights of thought, feeling, eloquence, and power which bend the audience to his will. Now and then repartee darts into a usually sluggish mind with all the force of an external revelation. In all such occurrences there are determining psychological antecedents and sequences, however subtle and elusive they may be.

Any form of mental experience which is not clearly recognized and definitely identified by the personality is subconscious. It is the function of the clear consciousness to cope with the novel or unusual conditions. If problems are solved often enough, awareness refers the repeated operation to the automatic apparatus. Shaving is a delicate and complicated task, but most men accomplish it without much conscious effort and direction while they are planning the work of another day or devoting their attention to other affairs foreign to toilet making. The mechanical operations which are so largely subconscious conserve time and permit the individual, if he is so disposed, to engage in activities requiring conscious supervision.

Subconscious activities are frequently creative. Memory and habit are subconsciously reproductive, but many subliminal processes are productive. Given an initial expenditure of conscious effort, a period of incubation occurs, a subconscious maturing through the formation of new nerve connections. After the individual has entangled himself in an intellectual project, the fruition of it is often accomplished by the life-forces which are resident in the personality. The subconscious activity in such undertakings as the solution of mathematical problems during sleep, the construction of a complicated plot for a novel after conscious striving has been abandoned, and the production of an invention after cessation of effort is generally recognized and admitted. The experienced sermonizer knows that a theme with which the mind is charged develops and gathers to itself suitable material without conscious labor or intent. While engaged in some foreign activity there will flash into the mind a principle or illustration which unfolds or enforces the theme. Good sermons are not mechanically made like an article of furniture, but subconsciously nurtured, elaborated, and matured.

The realization of suggested ideas is an excellent example of creative subconscious response. In our ordinary waking condition the subconscious expression of suggested ideas is a natural and common occurrence. It is certain that any idea held steadily before the mind to the exclusion of contrary considerations generates belief in its worth, exerts a pressure upon the nervous system, and, if it is a concept of action, tends to realize itself with a minimum of conscious effort or guidance. The subconscious accepts the challenge of expectation. Of course the length of the period of subliminal development varies. In response to the declaration that I am blushing, the blood may rush to the surface of my face in copious quantity at once. On the other hand, considerable time and repeated stimulation may be necessary in inducing a headache through suggestion. The amount of time consumed by subconscious incubation is a variable quantity and is determined by the mental state of the individual, the vitality and responsiveness of the organism, and the complexity of the suggested idea. The state of hypnosis is, as we shall have occasion to specify, marked by an unusual degree of suggestibility.

The field of abnormal psychology embraces many subconscious processes and determinants of attitude and action. Dissociated or multiple personality, automatic writing, manias, neurotic symptoms, delusions, phobias, amnesia, hypnotic manifestations, dreams, faith cures, speaking with tongues, and kindred phenomena are all largely reducible to subconscious affiliations and involvements. The dream is an excellent and representative example of subconscious experience. The dreamer is generally not aware of himself as dreaming, does not control his dreams, is deprived of objective reference and self-criticism, and is dependent on his own subjective resources. Hallucinations constitute another significant type of subconscious products. A tract states that in Sweden a company of three hundred people returning home after an all-night prayer meeting saw a hand pointing to these words written in large letters in the heavens, "See, I come quickly." Where there is concentration on a group of exciting ideas, an abundance of emotion, imagination, and expectation, false perceptions are likely to be the result. It may be said in passing that the evaluation of the religious factor in instances such as the one just mentioned is not the task of the psychologist as such but of the theologian and philosopher.

Purposive minor mistakes like slips of tongue and pen, and such aberrations as losing articles or forgetting unpleasant data partake of the nature of disguises for real intentions. One hesitates to affirm that all errors are symptomatic of inhibited impulses.   Doubtless many of the little accidents of speech and deportment so far from being acts of repressed tendencies are simply the results of lowered organic vitality or ordinary incompetence.   Fatigue, a slight illness, preoccupation, and sheer inability account for many of the lesser mistakes of daily life.   Nevertheless, it cannot be denied that underground proclivities do obtain expression in trivial singularities against the individual's will.

Dr. Brill records that an acquaintance requested an introduction to a friend who was on the point of sailing for Europe.[2] The Doctor did not want to comply with the request but felt that he could not refuse with good grace.   He said to the petitioner, "If you will come to me next Saturday, I will take you to his office."   Mrs. Brill, who was present, interrupted, reminding her husband that his friend would sail Saturday. The Doctor corrected himself saying, "I meant Friday."   The mistake was the obvious response to the query, "How can I avoid introducing this man to my friend?"

A woman wishing to say that her brother had recently lost flesh and that he weighed only one hundred and seventy-five pounds, remarked instead, "Now he weighs only a dollar and seventy-five cents."   The slip becomes intelligible when we are informed that the brother was at the time bankrupt.

A gentleman who up to the age of forty had never done any productive work decided to mend his ways.   In a letter to a friend he wrote, "I am really making a strong effort to find some suitable vacation."   We anticipate "vocation."   His real inner life, however, was revealed in the mistake.   Vacation was of more importance to him than vocation.

In *The Merchant of Venice,* Portia, hampered by an oath from the open avowal of her love, says:

> "One half of me is yours, the other half yours—
> Mine, I should say."

Furthermore, we have a tendency of which we may be unaware to forget or lose or break what we dislike.   The woman who does not like a certain dish or vase is likely to let it fall

---

[2] This and the following two cases are presented in Brill, Abraham A., *Psychoanalysis,* pp. 224 ff. (Philadelphia: W. B. Saunders, 1922).

to the floor in order that it may crash into fragments and be thrown away. The man who dislikes a necktie is likely to mislay it where it cannot easily be recovered. It is a matter of common knowledge that we are inclined to forget our failures but to remember our successes. It is said that Darwin made a written record of any discovered observations or ideas which contradicted his own general findings, for experience had taught him that such data escape the memory much more easily than those which are compatible.

Dr. John B. Watson records a case of forgetting which illustrates this type of repression. He went with a woman of his acquaintance to the railroad station to meet three of her girl friends who were on their way from Boston to Washington. She proposed to buy flowers for each of them. She went directly to the florists but purchased only two bouquets, one of violets for Miss A and one of orchids for Miss B. She did not at the same time buy flowers for Miss C. Dr. Watson called her attention to the omission and inquired why she disliked Miss C. She thanked him for having saved her from a social blunder and later admitted that Miss C was a thorn in the flesh.

A physical disability is frequently the symptom of an unrecognized aversion of some sort. A child may induce a headache when distasteful food is set before him or when he is commanded to perform an odious task. Pfister records the case of a boy who repeatedly almost committed self-destruction by falling or by sustaining injuries in other ways because in his home he was denied the attention and affection which he needed and craved.

When the conflicting memory or urge is not destroyed root and branch but merely inhibited it may express itself in symptoms which seem to have no direct connection with it. The complex leads a furtive and eccentric existence and takes the form of disturbing and disrupting motivation. Doubtless the vast majority of potential complexes never develop but mercifully evaporate. It is only the occasional conflicting experience which, denied conscious existence and repressed, creates pathological conditions. Only now and then does an inhibition imperil the unity and sanity of the self. The com-

plex possesses a dual quality: it is at once attractive and re-
pellent. It arouses the double attitude of repulsion and fascination. One disapproves of the complex but is at the same time
unable to cast off the spell which it exercises. A memory or
desire is repressed because it is unpleasant, but its peculiar
attractiveness preserves it from complete destruction.

The individual is conscious of the symptoms of the complex
but not of their underlying cause. He may engage in some
feverish activity or embrace some strange belief against his own
inclinations; he may be in the clutches of ideas and impulses
that are so foreign to his character and tastes that he seeks to
deliver himself from their power. Dr. Bernard Hart cites a
case which illustrates the point.[3] A Sunday school teacher, to
the surprise of his friends, became an avowed atheist. He
maintained that after a prolonged and diligent study of the
subject he had abandoned all faith in the existence of God. He
did actually have a wide knowledge of controversial theological
literature. He marshaled his arguments for atheism with great
skill and submitted a coherent and well reasoned case. Personality analysis disclosed the complex which was the source of
his atheism. The girl to whom he had been engaged to be
married had eloped with the most pious of his fellow Sunday
school teachers. His standard of conduct did not permit him
to express his resentment against a successful rival in an open
and direct attack or alienation. He repressed his antagonism
Below the level of recognition it motivated atheism. The rejection of the cardinal belief which had been the chief bond of
union between himself and his fellow-teacher was symptomatic
of his submerged enmity. The arguments for atheism were
at bottom a defense of his hidden but dynamic attitude toward
his rival.

[3] *Psychology of Insanity,* pp. 71-73 (New York: The Macmillan Company, 1912).

CHAPTER X

THE INFERIORITY DISPOSITION

A VARIETY of real and imaginary disabilities is subsumed under the head of the inferiority complex. Fortunately the majority of such cases are not extreme enough to disrupt the personality. The inferiority complex, strictly speaking, is a pathological mental disorder. A sense of deficiency is, however, present with many people, a condition which assumes the form of a depressing anomaly. This disposition is not so intensely dynamic as to disorganize the self, although it is morbid and vexatious.

The inferiority attitude is entirely different from the ordinary consciousness of inadequacy which actually nerves one to face a situation and to attack and subdue it. The sense of inferiority which is an anomaly or singularity obstructs and diverts the energies which should be expended in achievement. It keeps one from girding one's self with confidence for the responsibilities of daily life. In normal cases the sense of deficiency is a spur to action. Edward Payson Weston was a weak, sickly child and as such displayed no athletic ability. When eighteen years old he began to overcome his physical inadequacy by walking. At the age of seventy-two he walked from New York City to San Francisco, a distance of four thousand miles, in one hundred and four days. Such behavior differs from the attitude and acts of a person in the power of the disability which is properly called the inferiority disposition.

One encounters persons who are handicapped by a sense of inconquerable deficiency in every area of human activity. The number of individuals who are persuaded that they are incapable of rising to the occasions which emerge in the trend of their lives is amazingly large. While not technically pathological the assumption of incompetency is in most instances a patent obstacle to the fulness of life. Educators, for example, are constantly working with students of real ability who are firmly convinced that they are unable to master the academic

131

requirements for a college degree. To guide the student in the
delicate process of delivering himself from servile subjection
to an inferiority fixation is one of the major tasks of the student counselor. It often occurs that the depressed student, to
his utter amazement, sustains an academic examination to the
satisfaction of the instructor. Expecting to fail, he is surprised
at and puzzled by his success. Although such a person often
really does more than he imagines himself equal to, the level of
actual accomplishment is lowered by his lack of self-confidence.

People who are rendered morbid and unreasonable by the inferiority disposition are embarrassingly present in every parish
It is impossible for the pastor to escape them. They are cold
grouchy, and subject to despondency, care too much about what
others think of them, feel that they are unappreciated if not
actually unjustly treated or persecuted, attach too much significance to praise or censure, are preoccupied with their own
emotions, ideas, and plans. Mrs. Green is disgruntled because
she does not occupy the position of leadership among the
women of the church to which she feels herself entitled; Miss
Wood is peevish and fretful because she lacks social and edu
cational advantages; Mrs. Aroni is unhappy believing that
others look down upon her because she is a foreigner; the
frustration of Miss Bell's natural desire for marriage mani
fests itself in a Uriah Heep type of humility. They are
markedly different from others and are often referred to by the
troubled pastor as "difficult." Hitherto the distraught pasto
has been exhorted to exercise patience, tact, and diplomacy in
his relations with such uncomfortable and uncongenial souls
Such an approach rarely reconditions the singular individual
and at best only reconciles the pastor to their peculiarities. A
knowledge of representative sources of inferiority states and of
their scientific treatment should outline a more productive
pastoral procedure.

Sources of the Inferiority Disposition

In general it may be said that the inferiority persuasion is
fear of inability to meet situations, which has its foundations i
debilitating experiences, possessions, or circumstances. The
idea of inferiority arises most frequently from sensitivenes

to bodily defects or malformations, from disparaging forces in the early training both in the home and the school, from real or imaginary disadvantages of ability or race, and from an actual failure or frustration long forgotten but subconsciously dynamic. The pastor does well to bear in mind that in many cases the individual is not chagrined by the past that renders him incompetent but is preoccupied with the mood or conviction of inability to comply with the requirements life is now making. Of course in many instances the depressed person has a correct understanding of what originates his inferiority but does not assume the right attitude toward it.

Disadvantageous comparisons of the individual with others lie at the root of his self-disparagement. The apparent superior advantages of others are erected into a standard by which a person measures himself to his own humiliation. He realizes or fancies that he is not on a parity with others whom he regards as at least normal if not superior in gifts and achievements. The young child is surrounded by forces and persons that make him feel relatively insignificant. Nevertheless the child strives for power and recognition. He wants to be an adult. The aim to be a strong man is suggested to the child by the powerful presence of such persons as mother, father, the policeman, and the locomotive engineer. If he is normal, the will to power develops in him and by the conquest of circumstances he constructs an aggressive ego. If the environing social pressures or the personal conditions are too formidable to be overcome or to be gracefully accepted as invincible, he is likely to lose self-esteem and to engage in an intense protective struggle. When he is defeated in the battle for recognition, or status, or new experience, or security, or the avoidance of the offensive, or the gratification of organic desires, he may devise a guiding fiction which leads him to behave as if he were superior.

It is not hard to understand how deviations from the physically normal engender a sense of self-depreciation. The tangible and the visible are naturally the points of comparison most frequently taken into account. The organism is of the utmost importance in the adjustment of the personality to the conditions of life. Such bodily malformations as crippled limbs, hunchback, harelip, cleft palate, facial birthmarks, and dental irregularities are all so conspicuously disfiguring that there is no adequate protection against invidious comparisons and uncomplimentary remarks. Blindness, deafness, and dumbness are other disabilities too formidable to be ignored either by the handicapped or by others. The person with a visible physical defect is discouraged and humiliated by the realization that he is in some conspicuous particular inferior and as such the object of unfavorable comment or of ridicule. Comparison with the normal is invidious. His ego suffers degradation.

A bodily defect may be none the less mentally depressing because it is invisible. A disorder of the digestive apparatus, Adler contends, may express itself in psychic nutritional activities.[1] He sees a correlation between gourmandism and acquisitiveness. A disturbance of the balance of the glandular system may induce a loss of proper self-esteem and aggressiveness. The fact that one is unaware that one's anxious timidity is rooted in an irregularity in the glands of internal secretion such as the thyroids or gonads only complicates the case. Whatever the nature of the specific defect of the organism may be, the victim feels uncertain, incompetent, incomplete and insecure.

One who signs himself H. I. W. writes Dr. Joseph Jastrow that he has become fearful and deficient because he is the issue of a marriage of first cousins and has small feminine hands.[2] When a student in a law school H. I. W. read a book stating that the majority of the offspring of first cousins are either mentally or physically defective. The suggestion which the author's contention conveyed found a tenacious lodgment in the impressionable mind of the student. A short time later he attended a lecture given by a psychiatrist which increased his anxiety and further reduced his self-regard. The lecturer in his discussion of types of mental disability maintained that there is a correlation between the size and shape of the hand and the quality of the mind. The suggestible listener examined

[1] Adler, Alfred, *The Neurotic Constitution,* p. 6 (New York: Moffat Yard & Co., 1917).
[2] *Keeping Mentally Fit,* p. 284 (New York: Greenberg, Inc., 1928).

his hands and found them small. Although he is five feet
seven inches tall and weighs one hundred eighty pounds, he
has the hands of a little girl. He states that his hands are
constantly brought to his attention by the comments of others.
He writes that when he is proceeding brilliantly in the daily
routine for some time he is reminded of his small hands, loses
interest in life, and in his work drops to the level of mediocrity.
Dr. Jastrow hastens to assure him that very frequently the children of first cousins are mentally well endowed and that big
things can be done by men with little hands. He infers that his
correspondent is too sensitive to unimportant things and ad-
vises him to forget his parentage and his hands.

Other cases of the inferiority fixation originate in the social
forces in which the person is enmeshed. The child is frequently discouraged and repressed by elements in the social
setting which because of his immaturity he is unable to rise
above or to remove. The child who is persistently scolded or
nagged by his elders is likely to develop a feeling of inferiority.
On the other hand, when parents lavish excessive care and attention upon the child he will in all probability lack the initiative and independence which are indispensable to wholesome living. When there is dissension between them one of the parents may seek compensation for the painful conjugal relationship by petting and pampering the child. The result is that
when circumstances deprive the child of the overindulgences to
which he has become accustomed he is overwhelmed by the realization of his helplessness and incompetency. Furthermore,
children are exceedingly sensitive to and humiliated by any
moral taint or social disapprobation which attaches to a parent.
That many cases of inferiority are directly attributable to detrimental family influences will not be denied by any who have
access to the home life of American childhood and youth.

A mother brought her young son to Dr. Morgan's clinic
for examination.[3] She was convinced that the boy was mentally deficient and that she herself was in some mysterious way
to blame. She desired advice as to the best course to pursue

[3] Morgan, John J. B., *The Psychology of Abnormal People*, p. 539 (New
York: Longmans, Green & Co., 1928).

in his education and vocational training. The boy prefaced all answers to the test questions given with the remark, "I'm not very good in that." Asked to indicate the grade he was in at school he replied: "I am in the fifth, but I should be in the sixth. I am not very good in school work." His intelligence quotient was 105, but he and his mother were positive that he was mentally retarded. Dr. Morgan learned that the boy had a sister, brilliant and several years his senior, who spared no pains to impress her superiority upon him. What with the captiousness of the sister and the unreasonable expectations of the mother the fact that he felt woefully inferior should occasion no surprise. Surely the distance which separates the child from the potency and distinction of adulthood should not be increased by arbitrary standards of attainment.

Our American system of public education must be held to accountability for the failure of a multitude to live creatively. Someone has remarked that the most serious defect of our public school system in its decided tendency to accustom children to failure in their studies. To become habituated to failure is a major tragedy. The program of our schools is not adapted to the natural capacities and requirements of all children. Many are not receiving the schooling which they need, but they are allowed if not compelled to compete with children whose native competencies are being developed. The misfits are at first discouraged and then permitted to sink into indifference and lethargy. Failures are numerous and a settled feeling of incompetency is engendered. Failure is taken for granted. It is assumed that nothing but a dismal series of unsuccessful experiences is to be expected. Until we organize and apply a variety of school programs coextensive with the variety of distinguishable personality types and vocational capacities, our system of public education will continue to produce personalities at a disadvantage in a competitive social order.

Poverty in an age like ours which considers wealth the symbol and reward of successful living arouses in many sensitive persons morbid introspection and extreme self-condemnation. They infer that their lives are failures and that they are social outcasts. Even when economic reverses are the consequence of uncontrollable conditions they are reduced to a mental state compounded of fear, timidity, dejection, and servile submission to their lot. The collapse of self-esteem and self-respect renders the rehabilitation of their financial status difficult. This type of inferiority is not restricted to the vocationally unfit and socially inept but often disorganizes persons of character, ability, and charm. There is perhaps no more pathetic and tragic product of the present economic system than the man who is competent and willing but is denied the opportunity to earn his bread.

The Macdonald family had been active in the life of the local church for several years. Mrs. Macdonald, a talented musician, was a capable and devoted member of the choir. Mr. Macdonald attended the worship services regularly and responded willingly whenever his co-operation and assistance were requested. About Christmas time Mr. Macdonald became increasingly irregular in his church attendance and by March discontinued it altogether. Mrs. Macdonald, while continuing her choir service, was often absent from rehearsals. Pastoral calls at the home failed to uncover the real reason for the change. Several attempts of the pastor to win the confidence of these parishioners were met with evasions and inconsistent explanations. He was apprised of the source of their altered attitude by others.

One day the pastor happened to meet Mr. Macdonald in the lobby of a hotel. The pastor pulled the embarrassed parishioner down into a seat next to his and, summoning his courage, told him that he was going to have a conference with him then and there. He told Mr. Macdonald that for some time he had known that he was unemployed and volunteered whatever help he might be able to give. Mr. Macdonald burst into tears and poured out his story. He admitted that he had not been gainfully employed for months, that his credit was exhausted, and that his family was almost without food. He maintained that no one wanted to hire anybody like himself, that he was a failure and knew it, that no one, not even the members of his own family, were fond of him, and that he could not endure the situation much longer.

The origin of Mr. Macdonald's inferiority disposition with the attendant withdrawal from the life of the church was the loss of position and needed income. The pastor introduced Mr. Macdonald to a member of his congregation who was at the time employing competent salesmen. Mr. Macdonald was added to the sales force and became one of the most successful men in the employ of the company. The outstanding bills are all paid, the members of the family are happy again, and both Mr. and Mrs. Macdonald are more active and zealous than ever in church affairs.

Escape Mechanisms

The person who feels inferior is disposed to resort to the use of protective measures in an attempt to conceal or disguise his attitude. He is likely to select from his available resources striking expedients for the enhancement of his status. He behaves as if he were competent, as if he surpassed others. He becomes a bundle of contradictions. Caution and impatience, discontent and complacency, loquaciousness and brooding silence by turns characterize the one who is incompetent and degraded in his own sight. He is sensitive to ridicule, adverse criticism, and disapproval, susceptible to flattery, and craves attention and popularity. If he is belligerent and storms and blusters, it is not because he is confidently aggressive but because at heart he is insecure and shaken. When taken at his surface value and challenged he promptly collapses and capitulates. He may be so destitute of inward supports despite his professed superiority that he is the victim of insomnia.

Moved by his sense of deficiency, the individual is likely to construct extreme forms of defense mechanisms. In order to create a favorable impression he may set himself a goal which is unattainable. The goal is imaginary and his professed ambitions a pretense. He advances plausible reasons why his objectives have not been attained. Decisions which might reveal his inadequacy are postponed; fatigue, the opposition of the envious, and uncontrollable circumstances are alleged as factors which conspire to delay but not to frustrate the accomplishment of his published purpose. He boasts that when conditions are ripe he will act and succeed. He endeavors to escape responsibility the assumption of which would affect or injure his pride. He lives in a world of wish-phantasy, a world which would crash if he were subjected to the test of actual competition with other persons. Daydreaming accompanied by neglect of duty brings about degeneracy of the will.

Sometimes an effort is made to elevate the depressed ego by ridiculing or belittling the competent. In order to augment his value the neurotic assumes a captious and superior attitude toward those whose actual accomplishments transcend his own. He attempts to convey the impression that the mastery of areas of achievements in which he is really incompetent is beneath his dignity and entirely unnecessary. If he is a business man, he pours contempt upon the artist, the painter, the musician, the poet, and regards them as specimens of an inferior type of humanity. He implies that the world he lives in is the only world that is real and of value, and that the world of the artist is intangible and illusory. He himself is a red-blooded man, the artist is effeminate and unable to compete with such as he. As a business man he may assert that it would be a waste of time and effort to acquire the technical knowledge and skill which play such a significant part in our modern industrial age. He boasts that for a modest stipend it is possible to hire all the technical brains which his business or industry requires. He could, of course, excel in the technicalities, but why should a superior man like himself specialize in such things when men unequal to the struggles of the business world are willing to serve him at a nominal wage? It does not occur to him that his own lack of confidence, his own disability real or imaginary, his envy and malice, his incompetency in the arts or applied sciences, are dramatized in his contemptuous superiority. Unable to rise to the level of the accomplishments of the more gifted and trained, and far from respecting them as men and appreciating their contributions, he disguises his inferiority with an attitude of disapproval and caustic depreciation.

Not infrequently others or what is called bad luck or fate are blamed for disadvantages. The responsibility for inadequacy is disowned and transferred. One is the innocent and helpless victim of a diabolical conspiracy or power or condition. The number of persons who doubt that they are the children of those who profess to be their parents is impressively large. Many of these attribute their weakness to imaginary irresponsible parents who deserted them or deposited them as infants on the doorsteps of those who are their foster-parents but pretend to be their real parents. They may claim that they are the offspring of inferior parents, hence they are incompetent themselves. Parents are often held to accountability for inadequacies which are patently acquired and remediable. Others maintain that they are too small physically, too weak, too homely, or that they are cross-eyed or crippled, and therefore hampered by defects imposed by fate, which cannot be removed and the limitations of which should be passively accepted. One may believe that one is bad by nature or constitutionally dull or irreparably deficient and supinely submit to the inimicable decrees of fate. The individual blames others or some imaginary malicious agency for his inferiority in his effort to preserve his ego from complete collapse.

A sense of inferiority frequently leads to drunkenness. Contrary to popular opinion, alcohol is not a stimulant but a narcotic. So far from sharpening wits and increasing bodily strength, alcohol actually retards mental processes and weakens muscular responses. The radical element in grain alcohol, which is consumed in spirituous liquors, is not a tonic like the drug in tea or coffee but a depressant. Alcohol first attacks the higher brain centers, the seat of intelligence, then robs one of motor co-ordination and finally induces stupor. That alcohol is habit-forming seems established. The power of alcohol over the victim may be lodged in the chemical changes which it effects in the organism. But this is only one reason why men drink. To the physiological basis of drunkenness should be added the psychological condition of inferiority.

Intoxicating beverages afford an escape from the consciousness of undoneness, from emotional depression, from failure and hardship, from monotony and boredom, and admit the drinker to the dream world of fancy and freedom. The drunkard tries to "drown his sorrow" in the jug. But the

solace is temporary.   One cannot indefinitely walk in the Ely-
sian fields of alcoholic bliss and freedom from care.   The capacity for self-criticism may be dulled for a night, and the restraints of civilization may be cast off for a season, but when
stupor has evaporated there is a fearful awaking with a throbbing head and a vengeful conscience.   The ego, inflated for the
time being, falls to earth and collapses.   The habitual or periodic drunkard may again and again seek the consolation and
flight from reality that lurks in the bottle but only at the cost
of all we hold dear.   His taskmaster exacts all for an illusory reward.   Alcohol solves no problem, does not deliver a man
from his defects, and does not construct a more victorious ego.

Remedial Measures

The cure of inferiority, like that of other mental singularities
and pathologies, depends in part on the skill of the worker with
the individual.   Self-help alone is difficult if not precarious in
most cases of inferiority.   The condition of the personality is
generally such that one is either too discouraged to help one's
self or is so deluded by an escape mechanism that one feels no
need of reconditioning.   Futhermore, the memory of the originating experience of the inferiority consciousness is often
submerged beneath the level of awareness.   In such instances
the person does not realize what is the root of his depression.
Assistance usually comes from one who has had technical training and who has done considerable clinical work.   In the majority of cases it is useless if not definitely complicating to
give the sufferer the cheery advice to collect his energies and
to extricate himself from his predicament.   He needs help in the
process of the reconstruction of his ego.

In the second place, the cure is in part dependent on conditions which inhere in the individual himself.   The subjective
aspects are of the utmost importance.   Does he sincerely desire to overcome his weakness?   It is patent that where there is
no consistent and deep longing to conquer disability no deliverance can be expected.   How firmly established is the circumstance or condition which gives rise to the inferiority?   An
intense originating experience is more difficult to combat and
subdue than a superficial one which the individual does not

take very seriously. How chronic is the disorder? Has it assumed the character of an habitual fixation? Evidently the more firmly entrenched an abnormality has become, the more difficult it is to dislodge it. It is not easy to reverse the habits, decisions, and delusions which have become increasingly dominant with the lapse of the years. The success of the remedial measures applied is intimately associated with the source and nature of the mental disturbance, with the attitude of the victim, and with the quality of the helping hand extended in relief.

In general it may be said that the cure centers in the reconstruction of the ego. Such states of mind as insecurity and delusion must be uprooted. The producing causes must be exposed and either dispersed or relieved of their power to depress the ego. A new self must be created, a self that is honest, fearless, and brave, a self that is competent to challenge the issues of life, a self that is victorious in defeat, a self that recognizes limitations of ability without envy or captiousness and makes the most of its own resources. To help the undone person to reconstitute his ego is, then, the primary task of the pastor or other worker.

The anomaly or complex is grounded in and supported by emotional tension and instability. The central fact of inferiority is a controlling emotional disturbance. The person is in the grip of a complication of such devasting emotions as fear, timidity, uncertainty, jealousy, false pride, superiority. It is these qualities which enfeeble the will and lead to rationalization, projection, wish-thinking, and other deceptive intellectual processes. The reconstruction of the ego consists largely in an emotional reconstitution. Fear must yield to confidence, envy to good will and appreciation, inordinate self-esteem to self-respect. Such reconstructive emotional attributes, born of a changed attitude, invigorate the will, induce intellectual honesty, and eventuate in the attitude of serenity.

The attainment and preservation of equanimity is a major objective of mental hygiene. The doctrine of tranquillity is not in the tempo of our times and when it is advocated protest voices itself in the query, "Who wants to live like that?" It is tragically assumed that by crowding more late hours, action, sound, and shifting scenes into each day's existence, the joy and value of living are augmented. The truth is that the delicate nervous mechanism of the human body can be driven at such a rate and under such a burden that the returns of daily living, so far from being increased, are actually diminished. Similarly, emotions which are both intense and prolonged consume an exorbitant amount of energy and in time bring about nervous collapse. Anger, hatred, malice, vindictiveness, anxiety, and other emotional constituents of inferiority are archdestroyers of the unity, poise, and sanity of personality. On the other hand, emotional stability is marked by the temperate and creative attitudes. Sentiments are entertained but not sentimentally, gratitude for benefits received but not effusiveness; one is sympathetic but not maudlin, self-controlled but not indifferent, aggressive but not destructive. Serenity of disposition imparts vitality to thought and seeks outlets in considered activity and is the end which the worker with the inferiority-ridden person keeps to the fore.

A specific case must be approached in accordance with its own demands. Some of the remedies for cases attributable to definite sources have been implied in the above discussion. For example, if loss of income is the root of the inferiority, the remedy is self-evident, although not always easily supplied. In our competitive social order an adequate income is one of the most effective builders of self-esteem. That life in this world has an economic basis is a fact which we cannot ignore in our ministration to financially broken men.

When inferiority originates in a defect of the organism that fact must be reckoned with in the reintegration of the personality. Plastic surgery, dentistry, and other scientific resources are competent to remove or diminish many visible bodily impairments and disfigurements. Teeth may be supplied or straightened, crooked or crushed noses restored, unsightly blemishes eliminated. If the malformation does not lend itself to surgical treatment, its presence may be surmounted. Lord Byron, for example, afflicted with a clubfoot, became a great swimmer. The recognition that people with conspicuous organ defects have led happy and fruitful lives should be an inspiration to those who have to contend with similar handicaps.

Social pressure rather than organic malformations originate many cases of inferiority. Not that all who have been repressed and retarded by social forces are beyond reconstruction. Many of them can be reconstituted. The deflated ego can be expanded and fortified. Joseph French was a shy, retiring lad in the final year in high school. Although a boy of parts, the school curriculum bored him and a succession of grades below the level of college entrance requirements was recorded against him. He did not take his failures to heart, his defense being that he applied himself only to what was of special interest. During the summer vacation he was taken in hand by a person of insight. The lad was given a membership in a golf club and encouraged to play golf. His progress in the acquisition of skill as a golfer was amazing. His timidity fled, his confidence in himself grew, his outlook was transformed. In addition he was taught to drive an automobile. His growing mastery of the machine increased his sense of power and fortified the will to overcome obstacles. By fall he was a new creation. In a special examination he met the conditions of admission to college. His record as a freshman in college is excellent.

The moral effects of a victorious ego are often so pronounced that they assume the nature of a transformation of personality. Mrs. Basil Moore had a sharp tongue, a cantankerous disposition, and an attitude of superiority. She considered her husband beneath her in almost every respect and was therefore determined to divorce him. She was so ashamed of him that she refused to accompany him to church. One day an acquaintance handed the pastor a copy of a poem which Mrs. Moore had written. The pastor sensed in her literary effort an opportunity to serve her. He told her that the poem contained some noble sentiments and suggested that she enrol for a course of study in literary composition offered by a correspondence school. She adopted the suggestion and made a careful study of the technique of poetry. It was a momentous day in her life when two of her poems appeared in the local newspaper. The moral change which followed was remarkable.

Her self-pity vanished, her shrewish disposition gradually dispersed; she became cheerful, sympathetic, tolerant, and lovable. Her attitude toward her husband changed. She was no longer ashamed of him but went with him to church and other public places. She was a poet! She was a person of consequence! Springs of creative vitality were released within her, and the incentives for wholesome living were fortified.

Fear is a form of inferiority. Fear paralyzes the ego. When the origin of the fear is obscure the sense of inferiority may express itself in irrational behavior. One is unequal to situations that others meet easily and almost automatically. The behavior is motivated by no identifiable circumstance although explanations may be attempted. Professor Bagby refers to a man who was afraid of being grasped from behind.[4] The strange fear began in childhood and persisted to his fifty-fifth year. He was under compulsion to look back over his shoulder at intervals when walking on the streets. In a group he always insisted on placing the back of his chair against the wall. He avoided crowds and did not go to the theater. In his fifty-fifth year he returned to the village in which he had grown to manhood. The same merchant was behind the counter in the corner grocery. In the course of a conversation the merchant recalled the incident that motivated the fear compulsion. When the visitor was a small boy he often took a handful of peanuts from the stand in front of the store. One day the merchant, determined to end the petty larceny, hid behind a barrel and, just as the boy was in the act of stealing peanuts, grabbed the culprit from behind. The boy screamed and then fell to the sidewalk in a faint. The visitor remembered the painful episode and after a period of adjustment was relieved of his phobia. In all such cases the cure involves the discovery of the determining experience.

[4] Bagby, English, *The Journal of Social Psychology,* Vol. XVII, p. 271.

CHAPTER XI

FEAR

FEAR is a painful attitude aroused by the apprehension of an evil or danger. It is anticipatory pain. It is a form of the inferiority consciousness. Not every fear reaction is instinctive. Watson affirms that only two fear emotional responses are biologically inherited—the young child's fear of sudden, loud sounds, whether they be musical or discordant, and the inf it's alarm when the supports which sustain his weight are released and he is dropped. The vast majority of our fears are acquired, are actually learned, are transmitted to the child by parents and others.

The physiological accompaniments are numerous, and many of them are distressing enough to emerge into consciousness. Consider the individual stricken with stage fright. The heart beats more rapidly, the blood vessels contract with resulting cooling of the skin and pallor, cold sweat covers the brow, breathing is labored, the salivary glands refuse to perform their function, and consequently the throat is dry and the voice feeble, the eyes protrude, the pupils are dilated, there is trembling of torso and limb, the arms swing upward in a protective motion, and the processes of digestion are arrested. The person in the grip of terror is a shriveling creature at once ludicrous and pathetic.

Flight from the painful stimulus is the ordinary fear adjustment attempted. If escape from the fearsome is impossible either the courage of desperation enables one to combat the danger or the paralysis of fright renders one an easy prey to the object of terror. Fear that one is unequal to a crisis is likely to induce the failure one is so anxious to avoid. On the other hand, a measure of fear is often a stimulus to heroic effort. The orator face to face with an indifferent or a hostile audience, apprehensive of the outcome of his address, may give himself to the task of espousing his cause with such abandon that fear is dissolved and a sense of exhilaration controls.

Types of Fear

No intelligent man is wholly without fear. No person of imagination is absolutely fearless. Only the moron and the idiot may be altogether unafraid. Whether it would be best for humanity to be delivered from all its fears is a subject for debate. Only human beings brood over the dangers and alarms of the past and fret about the hazards, imaginary as well as real, of the future. Once an animal has escaped from danger it no longer devotes attention to the object of fear. Only man clings to the fearsome memory and looks forward with dread to worse evils which may befall him.

Worry has properly been recognized as a major disease of civilization. Worry may be described as extended fear, as a continual state of undue anxiety. It harasses, plagues, and torments many of its victims literally to death. It may develop into fatal chronic fear. Suicide, pernicious anemia, and acute indigestion claim many of its victims. Anxious expectations and horrible imaginings become habitual, often dethrone reason, and reduce personality to a state of chaos. Persons governed by chronic anxiety always foresee the worst as imminent. Many of them are unable to identify the roots of their fears, for often their emotional excesses are secondarily attached to definite situations or objects.

It is impossible to make a complete list of the fears which terrorize mankind. A catalogue would include fear of the dark, the wind, thunder, lightning, inclosed spaces, future punishment, poverty, disease, solitude, old age, water, high places, doing or saying improper things, snakes, mice, insomnia, loss of property or income, and vocational failure. These fears are so common that they may well be called everyday fears.

When we search for an underlying connection which binds all fears together and gives the agglomeration general significance, we may find it in man's insuperable aversion to the partial or total disintegration of the self. Fears attach to obstacles, to the preservation or enlargement of the individual. Only when the conditions in which the individual is caught and held fast are exceedingly painful and hopeless does he cry out for relief in death. That fear itself is in most cases an ineffec-

tual weapon against the enemies of man does not invalidate
the thesis.   However irrational a fear may be, such as the fear
of thunder, it is a painful emotional reaction against the fancied
threat of the impairment of personality or death.

Perhaps no exception to the rule will be made of the suicide,
once we understand his state of mind.   It is not so much death
itself which the person contemplating suicide seeks as escape
from the pressure of the moment or hour.   It is the agony of
the present which shatters his intelligence.   He does not want
to be delivered from life itself but to overleap the intense distress of his situation in order that he may find peace and balm
for his spirit.

Phobias are ordinary fears exaggerated, fears out of proportion to their uses, morbid reactions not commensurate with
their stimuli.   Vocational phobias are perhaps the most insidious and baneful.   The barber who dreads that he will cut
each patron whom he is shaving lives in perdition.   The housewife who is afraid that another woman will detect a fleck of
dust in her home is driven by a pitiless taskmaster.   The
minister who constantly fears that he will offend his constituency lives in perpetual nerve-shattering agony.   Anxiety to be
successful in one's calling or station in life arouses morbid and
crippling fear attitudes.

Sometimes a phobia is transmitted from one generation to
another by a process of suggestion.   A boy twelve years old
had from his childhood a horror of toads.   Investigation disclosed that he had derived the phobia from his mother, who
had in turn acquired it imitatively from her mother.   In fact
the phobia originated with the lad's great-grandmother who on
her deathbed was terrorized by the hallucination that toads were
crawling over her body.   The daughter, who witnessed the
delirium, became similarly affected—in fact, on one occasion at
the sight of a toad she fell to the ground in a nervous paroxysm.
Many adults who are apparently well have had phobias which
in the course of time have disappeared.

Superstitious fears are closely related to phobias.   Perhaps
fully one half of all college educated persons entertain super-
stitions.   The persistence of superstitious fears, in spite of the
development of reason and the growth of science, points to a

predisposition to belief in non-rational interpretations of coincidental or trifling events. Superstitious fears are legion—one spontaneously recalls the conception that thirteen is an unlucky number, that Friday is crowded with hazards, that harm will come to one who walks under a ladder, or passes through a funeral procession, or breaks a mirror, or spills salt at the table, or looks at the moon over the left shoulder, or whose path is crossed by a black cat before breakfast. Although reason is applied to such superstitious fears, they are difficult to uproot. To be sure, a splinter of glass from a broken mirror may lacerate one's hand, and some paint may fall upon him who walks under a ladder, but what is the connection between such events and the sinister evils they are supposed to portend?

Fear in Religion

We do not know exactly how or to what extent fear functioned in primeval religion. That fear has been exploited by more or less undeveloped religions seems established. No doubt when primitive man was sick, or defeated by his enemy, or had no food supply he concluded that the gods were punishing him or taking vengeance on him or were capriciously malicious and that therefore it behooved him to placate them. Fear was indubitably one of the earliest motives of worship, sacrifice, ritual, and ceremony. But religious behavior probably originated in several more or less related attitudes and experiences of which fear was but one.

Fear no doubt has had much to do with the rise and development of the system of intermediaries in religion. Since God is so far removed from man in holiness and power, man is impelled to call and rely on a priest to plead and pray for him. We may be afraid of the majesty of God to such a degree that we refrain from offering extemporaneous prayer and, lest a mistake be made for which we may suffer painful consequences, we may read or recite prayers which have been composed by experts in religious form and procedure. Some religious bodies still teach the doctrine of the total depravity of human nature. Since God is so morally exalted and man so degraded, a priesthood with a system of sacrifice must be interposed between them. God is not a Father but a monarch whose subjects live in a state of fear and trembling.

The pastor is especially interested in the specific moral and religious fears which torture individuals. Fears originating in conscience generally play a governing part in the lives of the ethically sensitive. Children being both immature in judgment and impressionable, are often tormented by fears inculcated by parents and teachers. Little children often imagine that the world is so ordered that their evil deeds are punished on the spot.[1] They believe that they will be hurt, or arrested by a policeman, or overtaken by some other misfortune if they are guilty of misdeeds. There is here and there a disposition to put the theory to the test. A boy of ten ventured to test his teacher's statement that if he played on Sunday he would sustain a bodily injury, and in doing so he hurt his knee. He was so impressed by the apparent fulfilment of the prediction that he kept the Sabbath rigidly for ten years thereafter. A girl of eight was so moved by the statement of a minister that all persons were like a woman clinging for protection to a rock in the form of a cross amid the violent waves, as represented in a familiar picture, that she developed a horror of water and the obsession that she was predestined to die of drowning. Such fear is pathological.

Fear of the end of the world is still prevalent in large sections of the Christian Church. It is frequently elaborated to such an extent that it invades and disorganizes almost every normal human relation. A young woman writes that as a child she learned to interpret current events as signs of the approaching end of the world foretold in the Bible prophecies. She believed that the world was desperately wicked, that God's indignation and wrath were aroused, that the longer the final catastrophe was deferred the more awful it would be and the more surely every sin, however trivial, would be punished. The fact that what she liked best outraged God most cast a gloom upon her life for years.

Probably most children pass through a stage when ghosts are feared. This fear often originates in the tales told children

[1] See Hall, G. Stanley, "A Study of Fears," *American Journal of Psychology,* Vol. VIII, pp. 147 ff.

by thoughtless servants and nursemaids. It sometimes arises in
an intense wish to associate with a beloved one who is dead.
The child gifted with an abundance of emotion and a daring
imagination is especially subject to a belief in the existence and
malignant activity of ghosts, evil spirits, demons, goblins,
phantoms, and similar mystic agencies. Many apparitions are
born of dreams, illusions, and hallucinations. A girl believed
that her home was haunted, that ghosts were always walking
in the halls and up and down the stairs. The fear which the
belief instilled made her sickly. The dread and its injurious
bodily effects persisted even after the servant who had misled
her was discharged. In order to disabuse her mind of the fearsome error her father took her to a meeting of spiritualists
where he was allowed to speak to his dead daughter Bertha
through a tube. Since he had never had a daughter Bertha the
experiment permanently cured the girl.

Closely linked with conscience and religious fears, the fearful
expectation of the speedy end of the world, and the belief in
the power of ghosts to harm or help us is the dread of eternal
torments. The fear of hell as a persuasive to piety is fortunately not as prevalent in religious circles today as it was a
generation or two ago. Nevertheless, many neurotic persons
owe their mental disorders to their horror of hell and Satan and
his cohorts. There are still many of slender intellectual attainments who are being alarmed by well-meaning but misguided
religious leaders. That the consequences of evil are too ter-
rible to be disregarded need not be confused with the doctrine
of an angry God who abandons the wrongdoer to the ever-
lasting torture of perdition. One should, to be sure, be prepared
to meet one's God and be ready for the end of the world—
one's little personal world.

Moral and religious fears are most frequent from thirteen
to eighteen, during early and middle adolescence, when personality is fermenting and emotionally unstable. The fear consciousness in religion is decreasing. An increased knowledge
of the nature of the physical universe, the recognition that fear
is an inadequate or defective method of meeting danger, and
the dissemination of a less harsh conception of God have
brought about a decline of fear in religion.

The Cure of Fear

What are the remedies for fears? Obviously there is no single prescription which will cure every type of fear or phobia. Some fears yield to one kind of treatment while others require an entirely different procedure. That the average man can conquer every sort of fear to which he is subject is hardly to be expected, but he ought to be relieved of the terrors that maim personality.

No doubt a clear definition of the object of fear will in many cases relieve one of torment. Thunder, for example, is entirely harmless, and most snakes are non-poisonous. There are, to be sure, many dangers the nature of which one should appreciate in order that proper adjustment may be made to them. An adequate knowledge of destructive agencies should result not in dread, but in caution. Earthquakes, cyclones, wires heavily charged with electricity, motor trucks, enraged bulls, darkened unfamiliar spaces are all dangerous, but the recognition of them as such, so far from striking the heart with terror, should lead to wariness. Careful attention should be given to the probable effects of dangers in order that harm may be avoided or averted. An understanding of one's environment is essential. Although exercising due caution, one should realize that no man can escape all the perils of living. Unnecessary dangers should be avoided, but in order to live and achieve some risks must be taken. It is far better to die young in a brave attempt to accomplish something worthy than it is to become a centenarian through an excess of conservatism.

Economic independence should relieve one of many torments. Financial embarrassment and abject poverty breed fears which fill the heart with anxiety and tortuous forebodings. The fear of poverty, of a penniless old age, of dependence on charity, of loss of position is eliminated by the acquisition of even a modicum of worldly goods. The man who lays by against the proverbial rainy day a portion of the surplus of the present earnings is dealing some of the most harassing worries a deathblow. Many a man would hold his head high, look the world squarely in the eye, and laugh at the minor misfortunes of life if by self-denial and extra effort he deposited a thousand dollars in a savings bank. The homely virtues of industry, frugality, and thrift might be cultivated by some who profess to despise them, for their normal rewards are freedom from financial worry.

The strengthening of bodily energies for daily living reduces fear. Bodily illness breeds fears by the score. The healthy man, for one thing, is not the prey of anxieties rooted in physical disabilities. The individual who is suffering from a bodily disorder is in a condition which makes him susceptible to nervous anxieties. Only when the bodily ailments have been banished or, if incurable, have been accepted with fortitude do the fears they have originated subside. When overwork has depleted the energy of the organism one becomes the victim of vague, undefined, and dreadful expectations. Rest and mild recreation afford the overworked organism a chance to recuperate and build up its reserves. The person whose vitality has been restored may no longer be haunted by the specters of his troubled imagination.

Play and recreation are destroyers of fears and phobias. Games, especially those played in the open, direct the attention from the self to objective concerns, send the blood coursing through relatively unused areas of the brain, increase the circulation, tone the muscles, improve the digestion, and generally exhilarate the mind. Dancing is one of the most natural expressions of the play impulse. Right dancing gives nervous control and poise, harmonizes the workings of the finer and heavier muscles, restores the balance between feeling and intellect, makes the heart glad, and inspires one to attack life with confidence and vigor. Persons whose occupations are sedentary do well to acquire proficiency in some sport or game which entails at least a moderate amount of physical exercise. The construction of an ego which is aggressive and victorious lays the ax at the root of debilitating fear. With each visit to the bowling alley, or ballroom, or tennis court, or golf course the scale of values is readjusted. The problems and worries that seemed so formidable dwindle. The true perspective is recovered. One leaves the scene of recreation with an inward glow and filled with zeal or fortitude for whatever may come.

Some fears can be dispelled only by the excavation of their hidden origin. Other means employed for their eradication are only palliative, for eventually they return with all their power to disorganize the personality. Knowledge of their source which may be inconsequential is the only permanent cure. Professor English Bagby records the pertinent case of a young woman who in her childhood developed a phobia of running water.[2] She was unable to account for the disorder which had persisted from her seventh year. Her fear reaction to splashing water was intense. It often required the combined efforts of three members of the family to give her a bath. At school when she saw children drinking from the fountain standing outside the classroom she would be terribly frightened. In her twentieth year an aunt, Mrs. G, visited her family. Mrs. G had not seen her niece for thirteen years. When informed of the phobia, she recalled the originating occurrence. One day the aunt and her niece, then only seven years old, took a walk in the woods. The little girl, disobeying her aunt, ran off alone. Her aunt after a search found the child in a small stream, held fast by rocks, with a waterfall pouring down upon her head. The child was screaming with fright. Mrs. G rescued her from her perilous position and went with her to a farmhouse where the wet clothes were dried. The child was deeply concerned lest her mother learn of her disobedience, but her aunt reassured her with the promise that she would never tell. The aunt left the home of her niece the next morning. The little girl was thus deprived of a confidant and endured a period of painful anxiety. Shortly the phobia manifested itself. The young woman was able to recall the episode. It was as if a flash had thrown light upon the hidden recesses of her mind. The phobia disappeared. There are no doubt persons in almost every parish whose fears are forms of conditioned reflexes which can be obliterated only by an exposure of the subconsciously dynamic causal factor.

Self-understanding and adjustment to circumstances is the only cure for a variety of paralyzing fears. The Reverend Arthur H. Line is a faithful and conscientious minister of the Gospel. He describes a professional fear neurosis and his management of it. Journeying to a distant place where he was to

[2] *The Psychology of Personality*, pp. 44 ff. (New York: Henry Holt & Co.).

deliver an address on matters with which he was not intimately familiar, a panic of fear seized him and aroused in him the desire that the train might be wrecked, or that bandits might hold it up, or that a sudden illness might disable him. The same sort of fear would overcome him now and then on Saturday night when the sermon for the morrow had not been adequately prepared. Sometimes the desire to be rendered helpless would weave itself into a dream of an accidental injury or an acute bodily ailment, a dream from which he would awake with a thud. Mr. Line adds that such experiences were of more frequent occurrence throughout the earlier days of his ministry than they are now. He diagnoses the case as a fear neurosis in which he seeks to be delivered from tasks to which he feels himself unequal. Sometimes the summoning of the will to deliver the address or sermon dissolves the conflict, although in such instances a residuum of fear reduces his powers of oral expression. Rest gives partial relief. More thorough preparation for public appearance as a rule conquers the seizure or forestalls it.

Fear and Reverence

That religion has instilled fears that have depressed and distracted mankind must be admitted. On the other hand, the tender-minded religions of which Christianity is an outstanding example have quelled the anxieties of their adherents. The fear propensities have been transmuted into such progressively refined attitudes as awe and reverence. Awe may be defined as fear mingled with respect. We stand in awe before God when our fear of him has been modified and tempered by wholesome esteem and deference. The Old Testament contains many admonitions to fear God. To fear God in the Old Testament sense is not to stand in His presence filled with a superstitious and brutalizing dread but to render Him loyal and intelligent obedience and respect. When Jonah says, "I fear Jehovah," he does not mean I am afraid of, but I am a worshiper of, God.

Awe as an emotion of solemn wonder is inspired not only by a morally elevated person to whom we owe allegiance, but also by such natural phenomena as the grandeur of a mountain range or the vast solitude of a desert. On the other hand, reverence as an attitude of profound veneration and affection is invariably aroused by the appreciation of the moral superiority of a personality. One does not, strictly speaking, reverence a storm or a lion. Reverence is inspired by and directed toward an ideal or idealized personality. Now the center of a leading type of worship is reverence for God, a reverence that is a fusion of respect, admiration, honor, and humility which leaves no room for the cringing apprehensiveness of alarm which is the essence of fear.

In many quarters of the Christian Church the divine fatherhood in the teaching of Jesus is the point of reference in religious living. We are told that the God of Jesus is a Father, a God of love, a God whose property it is always to have mercy, a God who makes provision for our needs even before we can formulate them, a God who shares our sorrows. We are exhorted to love God with our whole selves. What we have often failed to recognize is the double quality of our love of God. Authentic love leads us to approach God with alternating trust and holy awe. The relationship which exists between God and man is not a relationship between equals. Man is not on a parity with God, for between the two there is a difference which can never be removed. The true love of God induces in us successive moods of confidence and reverence. Our attitude toward God cannot be completed in a single mood or in one conception. At the root of religion lies a mystery which alternately exalts and humbles us, which both attracts and overwhelms us. Jesus is conscious of the holiness as well as of the mercy of the Father. He bows before the Lord of all being in reverent submission, and he stands in the presence of the Father filled with joy and trust. The mercy of God is never tepid. When Jesus taught his disciples to pray, "Our Father who art in heaven, hallowed be Thy name," he united the tender and the awesome. God is our father, but the Father is in heaven—that is to say, the Father is shrouded in mystery, girded with righteousness, and pavilioned in splendor. His name is to be hallowed, is to be held in profound respect, and not be profaned by irreverent use or flippant sentimentalism.

The Master brings together in a synthesis the two fundamental attributes of the character of God.

Reverence is the heart of the form of worship which Protestantism is now cultivating afresh. Crass fear is banished by the consciousness of the good-will and glory of God. Veneration of the sacred mystery which is the center of the universe possesses a general tonic quality which makes the experience of worship stand in its own right. Love that is at once a reliance on the resources of God and a sense of his sublimity casts out fear. Many a man who has for years been tormented and divided by phobias has shed his fears through confidence in the divine goodness that passes all understanding.

"Yea, though I walk through the valley of the shadow of death, I will fear no evil."

"Jehovah is my light and my salvation; whom shall I fear? The Lord is the strength of my life; of whom shall I be afraid?"

CHAPTER XII

SEXUAL CONFLICTS

THAT many emotional disturbances originate in sexual relationships no one who has worked with individuals for any length of time will be disposed to deny, although one may not be inclined to subscribe to the contention that all forms of inward conflict have a sexual source and significance. The pastor of matured experience knows that sexual difficulties are so intimate, complicated, and deep-rooted that rare insight, patience, and skill are the preconditions of their relief or eradication. In fact, he realizes that many of them are so delicate and baffling that they require the services of one who has made a special study of their ramifications. Nothing more than an approach to a few typical sexual conflicts which often claim the pastor's attention can be attempted here.[1]

Primitive man mated early and therefore had fewer sexual upheavals than present civilized man who marries at a comparatively late age. Sexual restraint is part of the price which we pay for civilization. The sexual urge ripens spontaneously in the teens and threatens to break all barriers. Nature, which recognizes no conventions or injunctions, clamors for expression of this biological impulse. Thwarted sexual desires induce many nervous ailments. In addition, as we shall presently specify, there are forces within the domestic circle itself which tend to aggravate and to complicate the sexual proclivities of the growing personality. A normal sexual life, that is to say one that is free from shame and undue repression on the one hand and satisfying and exhilarating on the other, while by no means rare among religious people in America, is altogether too infrequent. What should be the rule is relatively sporadic.

[1] Forms of sexual perversion, such as sadism (the derivation of sexual pleasure from the infliction of pain upon others), masochism (the finding of sexual satisfaction in cruelty and abuse from one's associate), or nymphomania (uncontrollable and morbid sexual desire in women), or homosexuality (a sexual passion for an individual of the same sex), since they should be referred to the psychiatrist, are not included in the following survey.

It is generally supposed that the present generation is as a whole preoccupied with sex. Whether increased frank discussion of sexual topics reflects less hypocrisy in modern society or more actual promiscuity is not easy to determine. It is moreover still too early to measure the effects of the gradual diffusion of the knowledge and use of contraceptives. It is certain that prostitution has become less popular and seduction more difficult. The triple terrors of promiscuity—pregnancy, venereal disease, and social censure—have been materially reduced. Compromises between marriages difficult to dissolve and unsanctioned clandestine sexual unions, such as trial and companionate marriages, are being proposed and tested. Many contend that the pleasure of sexual intimacy should be dissociated from social disapproval and from the responsibilities of parenthood. Although sexual activities cannot pre-empt more than twenty-four minutes of each twenty-four hours, as a psychiatrist recently declared, they do arouse almost endless discussion, argumentation, research, and experimentation from all of which some hope that a body of substantial principles will issue for the guidance and welfare of mankind.

The attitude toward sex both in its physiological and psychological aspects is still in some social groups tragically unnatural, unwholesome, and conflict-inducing. Many children are told that they were dug up in a garden or brought to their parents by the stork. They are admonished not to inquire into the functions of their sexual organs. All questions concerning sexual matters are still frequently met by embarrassment, evasions, fictions, and reproofs. Parents and other adults pretend that there are no such things in existence as sexual desires and satisfactions. Children are deceived and misled by the very persons to whom they have a right to appeal for information and counsel.

Not that most children who are systematically duped remain in total ignorance of the elementary facts of sex. Other children partially instruct them and at the same time teach them that sexual relationships are intrinsically vile but momentarily pleasurable. Sex knowledge gleaned from the streets is demoralizing, but it contains an element of truth which is sufficient to make it plausible. Children so misled acquire the confirmed belief that the sexual life, while necessary to the propagation of the species, is thrillingly indecent and as such to be studiously concealed. A prurient curiosity which may become lasciviousness is engendered and fostered. On the other hand, a girl may react to the vile account with disgust. She may become a useful and refined woman, but the emotion of disgust which is revived in her at the recollection of her early information may so poison her outlook that sex will never be regarded in a normal light. The attitude of deception and shameful secrecy should retreat before the advance of an open and forthright consideration of the right of the child to know the facts.

There should be frank recognition of the fact that sexual problems are no worse ethically than other conflicts. As it is, sexual involvements are taken most seriously by morally sensitive persons, especially by those who have accepted as valid and obligatory a stern code. The approach to disorders arising from sexual complications should be candid and objective. The assumption that sexual desires as such are unholy, to be tolerated rather than to be pressed into the service of human welfare, renders one incapable of offering the distracted individual the practical help he so desperately needs. The pastor's conception of the quality and function of sexual promptings and gratifications is of primary importance. He can minister to personalities disorganized by sexual conflicts only when he presupposes that sexual intimacy between a man and a woman who are living together, loving not only each other but many things in common, rearing children and making a home for them, and in the course of their partnership contributing to the betterment of the community, is natural, wholesome, and elevating.

Sexual Self-Stimulation

Adolescence is a period of rapid sexual development. It is in the course of adolescent ferment and stress that many individuals resort to masturbation. Researches reveal that this form of self-stimulation is not restricted to either sex, although it is more prevalent among adolescent boys than among girls. According to reliable statistics, more than ninety per cent of adult males and about sixty per cent of the females masturbated during adolescence. Nearly all young people who masturbate will abandon the practice after marriage.

The sexual impulse is strong in boys who have attained puberty and clamors for release. Although he wants to be a man and to be accepted by others as such, the adolescent is too immature and emotionally unbalanced to cope successfully with all the forces and emergencies which fairly overwhelm him. Marriage is inexpedient if not practically impossible. In the circumstances the habit of masturbating is easily acquired.

The actual situation is seldom understood either by the youthful victim or his harsh critics. Multitudes of young people are still being taught that masturbation is of all sins the vilest and most unpardonable, and that it induces insanity, to say nothing of sexual impotence. Believing what he has heard but seemingly unable to break the pernicious habit, the victim stands condemned in his own eyes, isolated and lonely, the prey of his fears, and helplessly remorseful. The furtive practice fills him with such a deep sense of shame and guilt that he cannot summon the courage to confide in and seek the help of his most trusted adult friend. Nervousness, restlessness, and lack of application to duty are among the ordinary accompaniments of such a wretched existence.

The pastor who is sensitive to the symptoms of this type of sexual distress and can win the confidence of the boy may render him a service almost beyond compare. To be sure, in order that he may give the lad the guidance he so sorely needs, the pastor's own attitude toward youthful masturbation must be both objective and sane. He must realize that the majority of adolescent boys masturbate and that he is therefore not dealing with a rare case.

When assurance is given the misinformed boy that only excessive masturbation undermines the health and that the practice while by no means to be commended, is perhaps as common as and no worse than prevarication, he is relieved of the burden of terror and disproportionate guilt under which he has been staggering. The lad should be warned that persistent masturbation may make the normal intimacies of marriage difficult. The wise pastor tries to discover the roots of the

indiscretion. Analysis may disclose that masturbation is the
extension of a form of the narcissistic interest in and enjoyment of the youth's body, an attitude which should have been
outgrown together with childhood. It may be that the indulgence is an attempted solace for loneliness or failure. It may
originate in a lack of proper adjustment to the other sex.

Self-knowledge may lead to adjustment. A redistribution
of the vital energies and the enrichment of personality through
the cultivation of the fascinations of social contact may prove
effective correctives. The multiplication of the outlets for
vitality, especially in the form of hobbies and outdoor athletic
and recreational activities, will make the preoccupation with
sexual inclinations more difficult. If masturbation is motivated by loneliness and a sense of inadequacy, active participation in organizations and societies of various kinds may be
efficacious. Furthermore, the companionship of a modest and
refined girl sublimates the sexual urge by arousing the chivalric
and knightly in the boy and by giving him a steadying ideal o
womanhood. Fellowship with a man of maturity and judgment is a source of inspiration and moral strength to the boy
who is endeavoring to overcome the depressing habit. On
lad remarked to me that what he needed even more than a Go
in heaven was a friend on earth.

The same treatment with obviously necessary adaptation
may be applied to masturbating girls. The pastor will invariably refer such girls of whom he has knowledge to an under
standing and competent woman for counsel and adjustmen
She may discover that the causal factor is physiological. A
local irritation in the vagina is often the root of masturbation
and when the physiological discomfort has been removed b
mild douches the basis of the objectionable practice has als
been eliminated. A deeper appreciation of the dignity of th
function of the reproductive impulse is sometimes emotionall
stabilizing. The erring girl should be instructed in the hono
able part which the wife and mother plays in the progress c
civilization. Once she realizes her partnership with God in th
creative process and the importance of the sexual life in ma
riage, she will not lightly misuse her functions.

Youthful Delinquency

Sexual delinquency among young people is the originating factor in some of the most distressing cases of personality disorder which perplex the faithful pastor. In the life of many a high school student sexual tension creates an area of major difficulty. Kissing and fondling are in some instances compensations for sexual intimacy and in others incitements to amorous desire and its natural consummation. In reply to the question, "Why do you permit or indulge in more or less indiscriminate kissing and caressing?" the following responses given by high school girls living in various parts of our country are typical: "I want it," "Boys expect it," "To pay a boy for a good time," "Because it is forbidden by the home or the school," "I crave a new experience," "I desire response," "I don't know what else to do." Many girls who participate are impelled by a spirit of playful disreputability. Fear, shame, thrills, nervousness, and shock are numbered among the results of fondling which have been tabulated by young girls.

A diligent and sympathetic student of the critical problems of adolescents, Mr. Ernest E. Piper, is convinced by his findings and observations that the majority of high school girls are technically incompetent to cope with boys of dishonorable intentions. Many girls have so habitually complied with the demands and expectations of their mothers that before they realize to what they are about to commit themselves they say "yes" to a tempter. The parent who has so dominated and subordinated the daughter that she has developed no power of discriminating resistance has much to answer for.

Many a girl who wants to have a boy friend is in a quandary. How can she get one? How can she really know him once she has attracted him? How can she make him behave without losing him? In justice it should be said that many girls report that the boys with whom they associate exert an elevating influence. And the boy is by no means invariably the aggressor in sexual delinquency.

Academic failure in high school or college is frequently attributed to lack of interest in and application to study. The wise educator seeks an explanation of the negative attitude which the deficient student displays. When a student of demonstrated ability fails in his school work for no other apparent reason than lack of concentration and effort, teachers do well to probe beneath the surface for concealed reasons. An emotional conflict, sexual in origin, may be the distracting element.

Annie Bacon, whose case Dr. Menninger reports, entered college with a brilliant high school record.[2] She began well but at the end of the first twelve weeks was failing in two of her studies. She explained that although she worked hard she was unable to retain the subject matter studied. Investigation showed that she was not dissipating her energies in social affairs. An intelligence test indicated more than average intellectual aptitude and ability. Her dean, faculty adviser, and teachers failed to find the root of her apathy and negligence. When Dr. Menninger first conferred with Miss Bacon she was only mildly depressed by her deficiency and did not seem to appreciate that her case was critical. He asked her point-blank where her lover was. She burst into tears and gave him an account of a romance which involved pregnancy, abortion, separation from her lover, mental anguish, and disillusionment. She had been doing her best to forget the harrowing past, to cast out of her life the memory of an experience by affirming to herself that it had never existed in fact. Fortunately in the emotional outpouring she reproduced the causal circumstances and experienced a release from inner tension. She followed the corrective directions given her so faithfully that she was awarded a place on the roll of honor in her sophomore year.

It may be remarked in passing that psychiatrists employed by industrial and business corporations have learned that many vocational failures for which there are no other and obvious explanations are rooted in obscure sexual conflicts. A harrowing love affair, the rankling memory of which is repressed, lowers the efficiency of the individual, be he student, salesman, or cook.

Sexual appetite is such an insistent craving that it is likely to confuse and disrupt the adolescent personality. It tends to warp and overrule judgment, especially if it is dissociated from other

[2] Menninger, Karl A., *The Human Mind*, pp. 408, 409 (New York: Alfred A. Knopf, 1930).

interests and capabilities. Sexual propulsions should be related to the sum total of the interests and obligations which mark a wholesome personality. In order that the sexual impulse may function to the enrichment and liberation of personality, training and guidance must be made available in youth. The church should offer education for marriage and parenthood, unless the facilities for such a project have already been provided by another community agency. Growing boys and girls should learn that sexual desires are not the only important urges. The distinction between the reproductive impulse as such and the desires of love, and the implications of each for personality organization, should be clarified. Good taste should be cultivated and the habit of discrimination against prurient fiction and lascivious plays established. Youth should be taught that love as an emotion is not self-renewing, that as an isolated experience it evaporates, but grows and yields its choicest fruits of satisfaction only in a partnership of two congenial persons who propose to live together through joy and sorrow, maintain a home, rear children, respect one another, and be affective in community enterprises. So long as responsible adults withhold preparation for happy and unselfish family life the reproaches which they cast upon the rising generation will be boomerangs.

Excessive Attachments Between Parents and Children

In the normal course of maturing the lad falls in love with a young woman whom he desires to make his wife. The self-reliant mother gracefully relinquishes her son to another and rejoices in the acquisition of a daughter. Tender filial regard for his mother persists—in fact, it acquires depth, dignity, and beauty with the passing years. Similarly, the current of the love-life of the normal budding woman converges on the young man she ardently wishes to marry. The normal son and the normal daughter leave their respective homes and parents and cleave to one another in a wholesome abandon of love.

Sexual abnormality and frustration often originate in an abnormal attachment of the child to the parent of the other sex. A morbid preference of a son for his mother or a daughter for her father makes love for a member of the opposite sex impossible. The excessive love of the son for the mother is called an

Oedipus complex, and the father fixation of the daughter is
called an Electra complex. Such abnormalities are often er-
roneously commended as singularly beautiful and distinterested
examples of filial devotion.

It is common knowledge that the love that a son cherishes
for his mother differs in kind and often in degree from the
love he has for his father. If the mother has nursed him in
infancy, lavished affection upon him as a little child, protected
him from the harsher exigencies of life, and taken his part
against the sterner attitudes and expectations of his father, an
intense love of her is the natural consequence. In addition
mother and son may be mutually attracted by sex characteristics.
The father's attitude toward his own mother and toward the
son's mother may intensify the boy's attachment. The mother's
ardent attachment to her son may in part arise from her disappointment in her husband and to that extent be a form of compensation. If the attachment becomes abnormal, the element
of morbidity is more often the creation of the mother than that
of the son.

The mother as a rule wants her daughters to marry and therefore promotes their love affairs, but is unalterably opposed to
the marriage of her son if she has nourished a morbid affection
for him. In such a situation father and son may be rivals for
the attentions and love of the same woman. Possessive love
is a pernicious influence. Many a man is a bachelor because
he cannot free himself from his mother who from his infancy
has dominated him and made herself necessary to him and
demands his undivided loyalty. Such a son has never been
psychologically weaned. In many instances the adult son has
outgrown the morbidity of the attachment and at heart desires
marriage, but rather than wound his mother he continues to
submit to her will.

The origin and development of the daughter's attachment to
her father are analogous to the origin and development of the
son's attachment to his mother. When the father gratifies the
whims of his daughter, takes her part against her mother,
shields her from the rough edges of life, and fondles her excessively a fixation for him sometimes arises. The mother's
attitude toward her own father and toward her husband may

stimulate the tendency of the daughter to lavish her love upon her father. The father's partiality for his daughter may be compensatory. Mother and daughter may be competitors for the favors and tender devotion of the same man. The ingredient of jealousy is present in such a crosswork of the affections, although the parents and the daughter may be unaware of their participation in the triangular clashes of love.

Although the father rather than the daughter is responsible for the cultivation of such a fixation, she will reap a harvest of abnormality or frustration. An occasional young woman deliberately rejects all proposals of marriage and prefers to remain single in order that she may, as she supposes, be true to her father. The morbid attachment between father and daughter now and then leads to incest. If she does marry, the marital relations will be a series of irritations. She will be restrained by compunctions; a sense of possible disloyalty to her father will hang over her like a sword ready to descend upon her head. Sexual liberty will not exist. Her husband will be checked and cheated.

Such fixations, once they have gained momentum, are admittedly difficult to correct. About all that a pastor can do is to help the victims to discover and face the underlying causes and their unfortunate results. Insight of rare quality is required to discern in the exclusive devotion existing between father and daughter or mother and son a reprehensible rather than a praiseworthy situation. A complete change in point of view is essential to proper adjustment. The pastor may exploit the possibility of separating the parent and the young man or woman. In the circumstances it may be advisable to encourage the son or daughter to leave home. The parent as well as the young individual should be given to understand that emancipation from a morbid attachment is essential to a wholesome outlook on life and the reconditioning of the affected personality. Parents should be brought to a realization that the possible future mates of their children have a right to expect all that love between the sexes implies. Preventive means in terms of the instruction of parents in the mental hygiene of childhood and adolescence are of course more effica-

cious than the application of corrective measures to their complex-driven sons and daughters.

Conjugal Infelicity

It is common knowledge that sexual embarrassment, irritation, and frustration render many marriages almost intolerable.
It is estimated that fully one-half of all American wives who
are well educated, have a good family background, live in the
cities, are married to business men or professional men of
moderate income and are each the mother of one or two children, are definitely dissatisfied with married life. The primary
cause most frequently cited for marital infelicity is sexual in-
compatibility. Complaints about interfering relatives-in-law
and disagreements about the management of the home, the
rearing of the children, and the distribution of income, while
often mentioned as points of conjugal friction, are after all in
many instances derived and secondary. Every woman of ordinary physical and mental development has the capacity for
satisfactory marriage relationships. Whether this capacity
eventuates in serenity or frustration depends on a conspiracy of
favorable educational and environmental increments.

Women are by nature and social conditioning more sex-con-
scious than men. For a prolonged series of years the woman
menstruates periodically, she develops the impregnated ovum
within her body, she gives birth to the child and nurses him.
She plays the stellar rôle in the biological process of race renewal. As a woman she is surrounded by special social restrictions and expectations. If she is sexually delinquent, the greater biological and social penalties are meted out to her. The
part of the man in the procreation of the human species, as
compared with hers, is brief and casual. However strong
the sexual urge may momentarily be, it is after all more or less
episodic in the life of the man. Nature and society never let
a woman forget that she is a woman. In the multiplicity of
his interests the man often forgets his sex and is just a human
being. It is not strange that when the emotional equilibrium
of the wife is disturbed her world collapses.

Of the specific causal factors of sexual conflict in marriage
not already mentioned, one of the most pronounced is defective

early religious training. Taboos and fears implanted during childhood and adolescence by religious teaching are likely to produce conjugal tension. Religious prejudice may be the obstacle to sexual satisfaction. Some religious sects teach that sexual union is justified only when the objective is reproduction, and that sexual intimacy for its own sake is the partaking of forbidden waters. The acceptance of the doctrine accounts for the prudish reluctance and the sense of wrongdoing which depress many wives and some husbands and irritate their partners. The use of contraceptives by persons who share such a restrictive conception of sexual intimacy is likely to result in an anxiety neurosis. Furthermore, the sexual relationships of husbands and wives of divergent religious convictions and of conflicting views of other fundamentals cannot afford a full measure of psychological stimulation and gratification.

A frequent cause of frigidity in women is the fear of pregnancy. For various reasons a woman may not want to bear a child. Conscientious scruples may restrain her from the use of the means of birth control. On the other hand, she may have no moral objections to the employment of contraceptives but lack confidence in their efficacy. Her phobia and consequent unapproachableness may attach themselves to symbolic objects and induce a neurotic disorder.

The husband's own selfishness or ignorance may be responsible for the fact that the sexual act is distasteful to the wife. She may be reluctant if not positively unapproachable because she derives no pleasure from sexual union. Only when she experiences one or several orgasms does her sexual participation complete itself. Many a wife has never had this emotional thrill and therefore, frustrated and dissatisfied, she plays a passive if not hostile sexual part. She is dependent on her husband for the normal culmination of sexual intimacy, and when he is too selfish or too ignorant to serve her, being preoccupied with his own desires, she is emotionally repressed. The husband should know and be guided by the fact that the sexual desire of the woman develops more slowly than his, that in her case its consummation is usually deferred longer than his, and that once aroused her state of emotional intensity subsides more gradually than his. He should take into account the biological fact that in most women desire is most intense immediately before and after the menstrual period. After all in order to be most satisfying to either partner sexual union must be satisfying to both. The considerate lover has his reward.[3]

Narcissism is frequently the root of frigidity. In such cases the current of the love-life turns on itself instead of outward to an individual of the other sex. Narcissism is a form of physical self-love characteristic of childhood but abnormal in adults. It is a form of emotional immaturity. Women who cultivate it flirt with men but do not love them. They are inclined to be absorbed in dress, personal appearance, and social standing. Lucy, as pictured in *John Brown's Body,* by Stephen Vincent Benet, looks at her reflection in the tall mirror in her dressing room, admires her body, kisses her shoulders, whispers words of love to herself, vows never to marry, but plans to be graciously charming to all men in order that she may always have beaus with whom to dance. If a narcissine woman for economic or other reasons does marry, she is likely to be unapproachable or reluctant.

The transition stage in the woman's life known as the menopause is frequently productive of marital stress and conflict. The duration of the child-bearing period is about thirty-five years. The climacteric of the woman usually makes its appearance in the middle forties of her life and the monthly functions cease at about forty-eight. Healthy women who have borne children generally experience the menopause later than those who have had no sexual life or no children. The symptoms of the physiological changes are pronounced and force themselves upon the attention of the woman, although they may be misinterpreted by her. The change of life is accompanied by mental disturbances, such as alarms, hysterical outbursts, extreme nervousness, irritability, jealousy, and contentiousness. Instances of sexual delinquency are by no means rare.[4]

[3] See Wright, Helena, *The Sex Factor in Marriage* (New York: Vanguard Press, 1931).

[4] The wise pastor exercises caution in his relations with women, married or single, especially with those who exhibit the characterictics of nymphomania or who are passing through the disorders of the climacteric. Dr. William J. Robinson (*The Menopause,* pp. 122, 123, Eugenics Publishing Company, New York, 1930) reports a case which should be a warning to all pastors. Under the pretense of desiring religious counsel a middle-aged

In some cases the woman's sexual desire diminishes during this trying period and finally perishes. In other cases, despite the involution and atrophy of the ovaries which, it is supposed, biologically condition the sexual impulses, desire is actually intensified. The excess of sexual ardor is often the fruit of the confidence that pregnancy, formerly feared, is now impossible; sometimes it appears to originate in a temporary increase of the ovarian hormones; frequently a spurious but none the less potent desire is created by the irritation and inflammation of the sex organs. It may be the outcome of a spinster's effort to capture romance before it is everlastingly too late. The theory has been suggested that the neural centers governing the sexual response may function after the ovaries have wasted away or been surgically removed.

At approximately the same age the man undergoes a change which while not so pronounced as the menopause is critical and sometimes morally hazardous. During the transition period he is emotionally unstable, irritable, and morose. Sexual desire is likely to be erratic. It may decrease in frequency and intensity, and his energies may be absorbed by such things as business, sports, and the education of his children. On the other hand, sexual desire may be exaggerated to such a degree that it is likely to ignore reason and social restrictions.

If there is in the husband and wife a synchronous increase or decrease of sexual appetite during the period of change through which both are passing, there is no occasion for sexual conflict and infelicity. If the sexual attitudes of husband and wife do not harmonize, as is frequently the case, jealousy and strife may ensue. If he is ardent and she is reluctant or frigid, he may

spinster, who was subject to the severe emotional distress of the menopause, induced her young minister to visit her frequently. Whenever he called she saw to it that they were alone in the house. One day, in an effort to obtain sexual satisfaction she locked him in the room with herself and removed her clothing. When the minister indignantly refused to gratify her desire she raised an outcry which brought the neighbors to her home, and then in their presence accused him of attempting to assault her. The bishop of the diocese investigated the case and acquitted the young minister of all blame, nevertheless the unsavory publicity and the resulting mental anguish moved him to resign his pastorate and to leave the district. A later act of indecency of which the woman was found guilty changed the attitude of those parishioners who had been skeptical of their former minister's innocence, but all expressions of regret and confidence and good wishes could not remedy the injury already done.

seek relief and satisfaction outside the marital relation.   On the other hand, if her desire is vigorous and insistent while he is unresponsive, she may accuse him of infidelity, adopt the rôle of a wronged wife, and engage in jealous persecution. She may take a lover.   In such cases the husband or the wife unwittingly or deliberately causes the partner not only physical suffering but also almost intolerable mental anguish.

The woman in the climacteric needs the advice and care of a competent physician.   A knowledge of what is actually transpiring within the organism and its relation to her outlook and behavior will relieve her of terror and encourage a measure of self-discipline.   The understanding husband, appreciating the source of his wife's temporary attitude and conduct, will reduce the conjugal strain by the exercise of discretion, consideration, and patience.   On the other hand, the man who is experiencing the corresponding change should have an adequate knowledge of his condition and of the origin and nature of a possible inclination to overstep the bounds of ethical propriety.   He may welcome intelligent pastoral service.   A sympathetic and wise wife can do much to tide her husband over the period when the sexual urge may clamor for a final fling before serene and dignified middle age arrives.

An abnormal clinging to a past disappointment in love may induce domestic tension.   Professor Mackenzie was consulted by a young married woman who was suffering from general boredom and loss of sleep.[5]   She was of the opinion that her husband neglected her.   Analysis of the case disclosed that she had married him on the rebound from a painful love affair. Although she was the mother of three children, she was unhappy in her personal relations with her husband.   She became acquainted with a man who was accustomed to stroll in the park to which she herself frequently went.   She confided her marital difficulties in him.   Although her conscience troubled her, she felt attracted.   A kiss which he stole seemed to make her conscious that her love life was centering in him.   The symptoms which sent her to him for advice developed.   This skilful counselor showed her that in all probability she was

[5] *Souls in the Making,* p. 126 (New York: The Macmillan Company 1929).

indifferent if not hostile to the advances of her husband because she still desired her early lover. She responded to analytic treatment so readily that when Professor Mackenzie last saw her she was so transformed in appearance and attitude that he hardly recognized her.

Now and then sexual irregularity occasions morbid states of mind which seek release in injudicious if not indiscriminate confession. The individual feels under obligation to go from one friend or relative to another disclosing the experience of which he feels guilty and ashamed. He imagines that if he fails to make confession to all with whom he is associated he is adding hypocrisy to immorality. He may not distinguish between a sordid memory of the distant past and present conditions and obligations. The recently married Mrs. Joseph Rockner was given to morbidity, preferred solitude, and, to the distress of her pastor, took no interest in the program of the local church. The case puzzled and perplexed the pastor, for he was unable to excavate the causal element. Finally an elderly woman of the congregation came to his study in order to enlighten and consult him. She informed him that when Mrs. Rockner was a girl of twelve she was seduced by an older boy. Before her marriage she confessed the tragedy to her intended husband who overlooked it. Now she believed that she was obliged to confess the delinquency to her husband's mother and sister. What should the elderly woman advise Mrs. Rockner to do? The pastor recommended that both she and the young married woman read Margaret Deland's story, "Good for the Soul," included in *Old Chester Tales*.

The young wife found in this story a situation which was similar to her own and a satisfactory solution of her problem. In the story Bessie Donald, an actress with an unsavory past, married Peter Day, a simple-hearted farmer. He was unaware of her previous conduct. She loved her good husband and was a good wife and a good mother, but the memory of indiscretions of former days oppressed her. Was she in honor bound to confess all to her unsuspecting husband? She consulted that expert soul-surgeon, Dr. Lavender. In the progress of the interview she realized that it was her duty to carry the burden of silence and thus to stand between her husband and unatoning pain. Mrs. Rockner sensed the wisdom of Dr. Lavender's philosophy and its application to herself. She was convinced that in her case there was nothing to be set right and no reparation to be made. Her resolution to confess the unfortunate girlhood episode to her relatives-in-law evaporated and her mental peace was restored.

Ghastly marriage relationships which the pastor discovers in every social class represented in his congregation could have been avoided by a natural and sane outlook on sexual desire. Ibsen in his *Ghosts* has dramatized the havoc and misery which a false idea of respectability can produce. Oswald, a youth, goes mad from syphillis. How did he contract the disease? He inherited it from his father. And how did his father acquire syphillis? He consorted with women of loose morals. What prompted him to do that? It was the priggery and prudery of Mrs. Alving, his wife, and the dullness of the community in which they lived. What reduced Mrs. Alving to the status of priggish respectability? It was the false ideal which she had been taught as a child and had unquestioningly accepted as right and mandatory, a standard of conduct which excluded natural passion and joy and filled life with gloom and irksome duty. *Ghosts* presents the tragedy which an unworkable ideal of life can bring about in the lives of all members of a family. Mrs. Alving's marriage is a failure, the foundations of her husband's life are blasted, her son is bereft of reason.

It is the duty of the pastor to drag such demons of folly, superstition, and intolerance from their caves and to let the light of knowledge begin its work. The sooner those who contemplate marriage and family responsibilities draw the moral from such tragedies and cultivate an ideal of life which welcomes and ennobles the fundamental desires of human nature the better for them and for the children they may be fortunate enough to rear. They should realize that, so far from being motivated by bestial impulses or lust, sexual union may be the outcome of a desire for the surrender of the one partner to the other in a common mood of tenderness, or for self-completion through the identification of one personality with another.

CHAPTER XIII

PROTECTIVE RESPONSES

WHEN life is too much for us, many of us devise means of escape from reality. We construct an imaginary world in which life is more secure and felicitous. Defeated in one area of experience, we may strive for success in another; what life withholds from us in actuality we may seek in reverie and make-believe; denied recognition and status by opposing circumstances, we may admire and applaud him who has won distinction; shrinking from self-condemnation for a transgression we may with withering indignation accuse another of the identical wrongdoing; we may proceed to justify and convert into a commendable deed what others call a reprehensible act. Of course the only method of adequately disposing of any conflict is to face it and to resolve it or, if it cannot be eliminated, bear it with dignified fortitude. It is, however, human to protect ourselves against the assaults of life by retreating behind barricades of our own invention.

If we did not construct tension-reducing procedures, many more of us would be victims of hypochondria or insanity. The frustrations, the inhibitions, the deprivations, the struggles, and the monotony with which we are compelled to contend generate intense emotional upheavals which threaten the integrity of the personality. Unreleased intense emotion creates havoc. The escape mechanisms which we contrive serve as safety valves which prevent explosions. As such they are psychologically indispensable.

To point out that protective reactions are emotional outlets which preserve the self from disruption is not to imply that they should invariably be given free rein. On the contrary, a knowledge of their existence and significance should lead to control, to discrimination against those types which are disabling, and to the proper employment of those which afford us that measure of relief and inspiration which sends us back into the battle of life with fresh courage.

175

One should hasten to add that there are many defense reactions of the originating forces of which we are in ignorance.
We are often unaware of the underground currents which
construct protective responses. For example, lacerating but
repressed urges and memories may be subconsciously active,
evoke severe emotional tension, and manifest themselves in
symptomatic defense structures. We may be positive that we
have trustworthy knowledge of the propulsions which underlie
our words and deeds, but be self-deceived. The inhibited incompatible dynamic element may express itself disguised in a
form of defense mechanism. Such a response frequently
wears a mask which conceals its real identity and origin. When
we understand the nature of subconscious promptings to protective behavior we are less inclined to berate the individual as
a dullard or a deceiver.

The characteristic masked expressions which the pastor most
frequently encounters are the following five: compensation,
identification, projection, transference, and rationalization.

Compensation

Repulsion from the unpleasant and irksome in the daily
routine of life is likely to induce various forms of what is
called compensation. A compensation is a substitute formation
for a lack of vexation. The blind, for example, in an effort to
counterbalance their lack of sight exploit to a greater extent
than do the seeing such senses as hearing, touch, and smell.
Sometimes a man of small stature will speak in a loud tone,
boast, and bluster. Compensation makes the social, physical,
and other deficiencies which burden us more tolerable. If
life is merely ordinary and monotonous, one tries to inject a
measure of variety and excitement into the humdrum of uniformity.

Total or partial vocational maladjustment or failure is often
compensated for by aggressive and successful participation in
other affairs. One seeks relief from the depressing sense of occupational inferiority in more congenial associations. The Reverend Amos Rand declares that for a season his ministry was
of doubtful value. A contagion of weariness, beginning with
himself, passed through the congregation like a plague. The

down-town church of which he is the pastor, moved by pride,
kept up external appearances.   Fellow-townsmen with only a
superficial knowledge of the state of affairs might have given
a flattering appraisal of the work of the church, but in reality
the church had no effective program and no fervency of spirit.
The discouraged pastor sought to counterbalance his unsatis-
factory ministry by active membership in several service clubs.
He became a service club addict.   In these clubs Mr. Rand
found what his own church lacked—enthusiasm, man-power,
and civic projects.   If this form of compensation had not di-
verted too much energy from the religious organization he was
called and pledged to serve, no valid objections could have been
raised.   Fortunately the story does not end at this point.   Mr.
Rand attended the summer sessions of a theological seminary
and, stimulated by teachers, fellow-students, and professional
study, clarified his ideals and changed his point of view and
thus recovered the lost zeal and radiance.

Often one creates a world of fancy, a world according to the
heart's desire, a world in which one escapes from the fetters
and obstacles of stern and relentless reality and in which one
for a time achieves freedom of action and self-realization.
What the individual is unable to do under the actual circumstances in which he is enmeshed may be imaginally and vicari-
ously accomplished.   So long as this form of compensation
sends us back into the world of reality better fitted to cope with
its difficulties it is beneficent.

The reading of certain types of fiction offers deliverance
from the thralldom of the commonplace and the hampering.
The romantic novel temporarily sets the bored housewife free
from bed-making, cooking, dish-washing, dusting, and sweeping and admits her to a realm inhabited by handsome gentlemen
of impeccable manners and beautiful ladies of charm and
distinction who are surrounded by the refinements, adornments,
and luxuries which wealth and culture command.   If the plight
of the lovelorn couple in the novel wrings the housewife's
heart and drains her tear glands, the experience affords her relief from her own nervous tension.   The man whose occupation is drab and so monotonous that there is but little deviation

from routine may in imagination gallop over the western plains, a heroic son of the open spaces, mounted on a spirited horse and emotionally share the thrill of bringing to earth a desperado in a quarterless hand-to-hand combat. Detective stories are the solace and refuge of many men whose lives are relatively uneventful. It is said that Kant, the great philosopher, wrote accounts of adventures in strange foreign lands, although nothing could induce him to leave even for a season the little university town where he lived and thought and taught. Variety, excitement, suspense, color, adventure, romance, and distinction, all of which daily life may withhold, are bestowed by the magic wand of fiction.

It is significant that we often call the theater a playhouse. The contagion of the audience assembled in the mood of festive expectancy, the stage presentation and interpretation of life's extreme points, the glamour and color with which drama is invested all conspire to make the theater a place where one seeks and finds relaxation and release from the emotional tensions of business or professional life. The state of mind of the person in the theater is akin to reverie. He lives an imaginary life as if it were real, although he is vaguely aware that he is daydreaming. Millions are flocking to the movies for the romance or adventure of which their dreary lives are devoid. Here the god of things as they are is for a time forgotten. Here emotional substitutes are discovered and cultivated. Thousands of women fall in love with a matinée idol or a popular moving picture star either because they have no real lover or the husbands they do have are such indifferent lovers. Many a wife's adoration of a stage lover is the direct product of her desire for the refinements of love-making of which her husband is either neglectful or incapable. Like much of daydreaming, this variety of compensation is a form of wish fulfilment.

Repressed domestic impulses often manifest themselves in compensatory activities. Miss Alden is a maiden lady of seventy who with the passing years has become queer, sensitive and lonely. Many years ago she withdrew from the social affairs of her friends and began to lead a secluded life. She ha

however, given herself to a project which has made her reasonably contented. She accepted the secretaryship of the local
chapter of the Society for the Prevention of Cruelty to Dumb
Animals. She expends the same thought and care on the animals which another woman would bestow on her little children
and needy or feeble relatives. Miss Alden's frustrated desire for a mate and family life has made her eccentric, but
her watchful regard for the dumb animals in the community
has kept her from becoming morose and mentally incompetent.
If she had participated to a larger extent in the fellowship of
the church at her door and co-operated heartily in the various
church school and missionary programs, she might have been
less lonely and odd.

Doctrinal orthodoxy is now and then an overcompensation
for moral integrity. An intense devotion to the religious beliefs of the fathers is not necessarily matched by the ethical
conduct which is above reproach. The more ethically lax some
people are the more they contend for the tenets of a reactionary
theological system. They seem to be prompted by a vague feeling that the intellectual acceptance of a doctrinal formula is
an adequate substitute for moral uprightness. Some of them
go so far as to inflict persecution upon others whose theological
opinions they consider irregular or heretical. Contrary doctrines are stoutly resisted as a Christian duty, while reprehensible practices are either openly or secretly countenanced. A
pastor of wide experience and discrimination declares that
when a member of his congregation is extremely and intolerant-
ly orthodox he is prepared to discover a skeleton in that individual's closet.

Identification

Identification may be considered a variety or extension of
compensation. We may seek compensation for omissions in
our lives by identifying ourselves with those who, at least
according to our opinions, have achieved the fulness of life.
In linking ourselves in an emotional relation to those who in
real life succeed in doing or being that in which we have failed
we experience satisfaction and a sense of completion. The
emotional values of success attach to the identification. The

object of identification becomes a kind of *alter ego*. Those whose sexual impulses are repressed often identify themselves with characters and their experiences in erotic novels.

William Thomas, minister of a large parish in a metropolis, attends all the major and many of the minor prize fights staged in the city. He is a diligent student of the technique of the leading boxers. He is intimately acquainted with the careers of the outstanding prize fighters. After witnessing a bout he goes home muscularly tired but contented. Mr. Thomas has disclosed the basis of his attachment to the boxer. As a boy he cherished a secret ambition to become a prize fighter, an ambition which was of course never realized, but which induces emotional identification with prize fighters and finds an outlet in his permanent enthusiasm for all things pertaining to prize fighting. One is not surprised to learn that the pugnacious proclivities of this minister are occasionally expressed in aggressive leadership in church and civic enterprises.

A form of compensation is closely allied to hero worship. Sometimes we admire and applaud a hero because at heart we ourselves wish that we were capable of his deeds and were the recipients of his honors. The boy identifies himself with Admiral Byrd and merging his personality with that of his hero takes command of an expedition to the frozen antarctic zone, makes the successful dash over the south pole in an airplane, and returns to his native land where he gracefully receives the plaudits of the admiring populace. Romantic girls sometimes in a daze act the part of the heroine who walks across the pages of a novel, in imagination wearing her jewelry and gowns, voicing her sentiments, enduring her trials and heartache, and at last sinking into the strong arms of her Prince Charming. In such cases one is more than a mere spectator of a colorful pageant; what one admires is internalized and personalized through a process of intimate association.

Parents who have had only meager educational opportunities often follow the college careers of their children with an emotional intensity which amounts to identification. Their children do for them what they themselves could not attain. Every college victory makes joy-bells ring in the hearts of the parents each campus defeat grieves them beyond measure. Often such parents derive more satisfaction from their vicarious participation in the college course than the children do from their actual experience.

Projection

Projection as a defense reaction consists in imputing to others faults of which we ourselves are guilty and ashamed. An attack directed against the character of another sometimes diverts just self-censure from ourselves. The originating repression may mask itself in what is felt to be commendable and brave zeal for the right. The one accused may be consciously guilty of the charge and therefore infers that he is being justly condemned by a righteous judge. He may not suspect that his judge, who also is guilty, is trying to escape the pangs of conscience.

Dr. Menninger cites a typical case of projection.[1] Helen and Walter, college students in love with one another, were widely separated during the summer vacation. In their correspondence throughout the period of separation protestations and vows of fidelity were frequently exchanged. When they returned to college in the autumn their attitude seemed at first unaltered, but in the progress of their first tête-à-tête a quarrel broke out which neither at the time could understand. Helen was apparently resolved to find fault with Walter, and when he branded her accusations as false she became all the more contentious. She maintained that during the summer he had had an affair with another girl and charged him with disloyalty to herself. What Helen masked from herself as well as from Walter was that it was not he but she who had been carrying on a flirtation. Helen had been flirting just enough to hurt her conscience and to induce the defense reaction of projection.

Projection is a treacherous process, for it tends to detach a person from the dictates and compunctions of conscience. It would relieve us of moral responsibility by imputing to others our reprehensible conduct. Projection is not a denial of the wrongfulness of an attitude or deed but an effort to evade ac-

[1] *The Human Mind*, pp. 271, 272 (New York: Alfred A. Knopf, 1930).

countability by making another a scapegoat. We go free and
often the innocent are made to carry our guilt.

Transference

Transference is another mode in which inhibitions find
indirect release. Sometimes we direct love or hatred from its
original object to another person. The two persons have something in common which accounts for the transfer of an attitude from the one to the other.

An elder asked Mrs. Pierce why she no longer attended the
services of the church. She replied that she could not endure
the looks of the preacher. The elder expressed surprise and
ventured to say that in the judgment of most members of the
congregation the preacher was a handsome man. "Well," she
insisted, "he looks like my brother-in-law. I can't stand him."
The elder in reporting the case to the pastor explained that Mrs.
Pierce had been embarrassed by a lawsuit which her brother-
in-law had brought against her husband for undue familiarity
with his wife. The pastor's similarity in appearance to her
brother-in-law at once recalled the humiliating lawsuit and
provoked the resentment which she directed to him. The transfer of her antagonistic attitude reduced the high emotional tension generated by repressed hatred. The case shows how transference, although it affords one relief, does a third person injustice, prejudices one against him, and blinds one to his worth.

Rationalization

We may be ignorant of being motivated by considerations
other than those which we publicly profess. The giving of
specious reasons for one's behavior is called rationalizing.
Words may be a camouflage for real but unrecognized intentions and impulses. Motive forces are at times quite unconsciously disguised with pretense and rhetoric. Sometimes
rationalizing as a form of defense thinking begins as downright
intellectual dishonesty, but through frequent repetition it assumes validity in the mind of the self-deceived individual.
Furthermore, as soon as we have done the questionable we proceed to defend and justify it. What we wish were true may be

supposed to be true.   The difference between reasoning and rationalizing should be grasped and borne in mind.

A pastor writes that there are in his parish several persons who are in desperate financial straits brought about by personality maladjustments.   Some of them are in economic distress because they have married shiftless and improvident mates, others because they are vocationally miscast.   When they consult the pastor they invariably ascribe their misfortunes to causes other than those which are actually operative.   Their interpretations and the facts as the pastor knows them are not in accord.   They sincerely believe that they have arrived at their conclusions by a logical process of reasoning.   Pride is no doubt a factor which confuses the issue and makes a dispassionate view of the actual situation difficult.   Only when such persons can be induced to face reality, however subversive of false self-esteem that process may be, can their maladjustments be corrected.

The reason we give is not always the cause.   Suppose that we think more evil of another than should be imputed to him.   We dislike him.   Why do we experience an excessive feeling of resentment?   It may be because the offensive person has wounded our vanity or caused a loss in our income or that we fear him as a business or professional rival.   The moment we comprehend that we are resentful not because there is a valid cause for our attitude but because our grievance is petty or imaginary the feeling of resentment loses its fascination and vanishes into thin air.

The probabilities are that most of us are all the time engaged in at least the milder forms of rationalizing.   We are generally swayed by a combination of motive powers, although we may be unaware of the admixture.   We may be persuaded that the single incentive to which we refer is the only one which influences our behavior, although it may be quite patent to others that several desires or impulses, varying in ethical quality, are actuating us.   For example, the minister of the gospel is solicitous for the salvation of my soul and also for the financial support of his church which I may give and for the statistical growth of his congregation.   The schoolmaster has a passion for the development of the personalities under his tutelage and also for his own standing and the reputation of his school. The statesman seeks the welfare of the citizens, the stability of his party, and the power and emoluments which his election to office entail. Self-regarding and other-regarding motives tend to mingle. Each one of these men may be fully aware of and make public only one of the propulsions which undergird his activities, his zeal and devotion. He may persuade himself that only other-regarding considerations enter into his plans and purposes, but his deeds betray other and perhaps less worthy purposes. There is, then, in many instances a breach between what we ourselves believe to be our motives and the underground promptings which actually determine our conduct.

Of all persons, the pastor should know the secret forces which actuate us. It is his task to detect their real identity. The pastor must penetrate the surface of our professions and explore the deeps out of which are the issues of life. If he is to improve human nature, he must first of all recognize our defense mechanisms. Psychological analysis is an instrument with which he may probe the interior conditions which incite to action. In the hands of religious leadership personality-assaying may not be an instrument of unerring precision, but the intelligent if not expert application of its principles will lay bare conditions which may well be the objects of further pastoral care.

The pastor should mistrust the individual's own interpretation of his anomalies. The physician does not accept the patient's diagnosis of his ailment. He proceeds to give the patient an examination in order that he may determine as objectively and scientifically as possible the nature of the disability. Similarly the pastor has a right to be suspicious of the self-diagnosis of the troubled consultant. The possibility of the presence and influence of a form of defense mechanism should be entertained.

CHAPTER XIV

SPECIALIZED DIAGNOSTIC METHODS

THE discovery of the springs of irrational conduct is in many cases a difficult and delicate procedure. Ordinary introspection or recollection, responses to direct questioning, or unguarded self-expression frequently afford no clue to the pernicious sources. The tracing of irrelevant remarks, of sensitiveness to certain topics of conversation, of mannerisms, of slips of the tongue or pen may not bring to light the irritating experience or possession. The defense reactions may be quite impenetrable. The lacerating increment may be too deeply and securely embedded in the depths of personality to be extracted by the usual method of informal confession and self-disclosure. In cases of this kind the clinical psychologist may apply one or more of the technical methods of diagnosis, such as dream analysis, word association, and hypnotism.

Dream Analysis

Mankind has attached an importance to dreams which neither the psychologist nor the historian can ignore. A collection of the treatises on the nature and interpretation of dreams which have been bequeathed to us by the past would be large, fanciful, and diversified. The mystical interpretation persists despite the invasion of the dreaming mind by science. Dream books are so numerous and popular that they can be purchased at the five-and-ten-cent stores. The literature of religion is replete with the accounts of influential dreamers and their dreams. Some students of the historical origin of religion have seen the genesis of the concept of spirits in the varied dream experiences of primitive man. However that may be, not one of us has an adequate comprehension of the contributions of his own dreams and those of others to his personal life. What I have dreamed of last night and forgotten may, to a large extent, determine the mood and decisions of today.

No theory of the significance of dreams is complete unless

185

it recognizes the contribution of Freud to dream-psychology. His conception is that all our dreams are expressions of repressed wishes. A wish unfulfilled in real life is gratified during sleep in our dreams. It must be conceded that many of our dreams are actually the direct outcome of our desires. Miss Josephine Carter wrote a letter of censure and exhortation to a friend guilty of serious moral lapses. The accused recipient resented the charges and displayed an unrepentant and rebellious attitude. The reprover thereupon dreamed that the accused acknowledged the error of her ways and promised immediate and permanent reformation. The desire for such a response was the obvious force which invented the dream-structure. That this dream was, in addition, an outlet for a submerged sexual desire or memory, as some would hold, may be challenged and rejected.

Not all dreams involve buried focuses of mental infection. Many of our dreams merely reinstate the experiences of the day which have impressed us. Such dream-states are relatively insignificant and their interpretation obvious. The incoherencies of a dream often reflect the multiplicity of employments and concerns which occupy our waking hours. As Koheleth remarked long ago, "A dream cometh through a multitude of business."

Other dreams originate directly in sensations aroused by external stimuli. Many and varied are our dream responses to such familiar nocturnal sounds and distractions as the rumbling of trains, the roaring of automobile traffic, the rolling of thunder, the rattling of shutters, the flapping of curtains, the moaning of the wind, the pattering of rain, the buzzing of the mosquito. Typical dream vagaries arise from the disturbance of the internal organs of the human body. Headache accompanied by the throbbing temples may excite a dream of driving nails. Toothache has been known to give rise to dreams of murder. Persons suffering from heart trouble are subject to dreams of effort, perspiration, and labored breathing. Indigestion throws the dreamer into a state of agony and terror. Sometimes in our dreams we experience intense emotional excitement not because we dream we have done a deed of violence, but we dream that we have committed a crime because we are in terror.   Cause and effect are often inverted.   Since the simplest interpretation that accounts for all the facts is probably correct, the Freudian exposition need not be invoked when dreams of this kind are being explored.

The anxiety dream is perhaps the commonest type of dream. It reflects the dreamer's dread lest he fail in the projects he has undertaken.   He dreams of frustrations and failures such as missing trains or traveling without being able to reach his destination, being defeated in competitive games, and losing his job or position.   The emotional tone of such dream states is one of irritation, futility, and painful suspension.   It is characteristic of human nature that our anxieties rather than our achievements and demonstrated abilities occupy our minds, especially when we are fatigued.

In a sense some dreams are more real than the activities of our hours of wakefulness.   During sleep the vigilance and resistance of awareness are relaxed and the suppressed material is woven into a symbolic dream.   An unbiased study discloses a surprising amount of dream experience which the psychoanalyst can adequately dissect and interpret.   A gentleman who was considering the dissolution of his marriage to an unloved wife whom he secretly wished out of the way dreamed that she was borne into his room dead.   The psychologist sees in such a dream a typical instance of wish-fulfilment.   The dreams of Joseph which are recorded in the Old Testament clearly indicate youthful ambition and have their roots in his father's preference for him.   The dream of the sheaves bowing down before his sheaf, and of the stars, sun, and moon making obeisance are the signs and symbols of the fundamental attitudes of Joseph.   His dreams remind one of a little boy's dream of possessing a bicycle or some other toy for which he has an ardent desire.

When we go to sleep there is relaxation of mental as well as muscular tension.   During sleep the vigilance of ordinary censorship is suspended, the criteria that controls conduct during the waking hours are ignored, the corrective and inhibiting influences and agencies of society are held in abeyance.   It frequently happens that during sleep impressions which have escaped attention during the day become prominent enough to construct dream scenes. Albert Peterson, a lad of fourteen, lost a pocketknife in the barn where he was playing with his companions. He sought it but was unable to find it. At night Albert dreamed that it was in a certain manger in the barn. The following morning he recovered the knife where the dream had located it. In all probability he had out of the corner of his eye seen the treasured article fall into the manger, but being occupied at the time by other matters the impression was too weak to attract and hold the attention. During sleep the delicate perception emerged from the fringe to the center of consciousness and the resulting dream came to the lad with the significance of a special revelation.

Sometimes impressions too faint to be clearly perceived are not only subconsciously registered but also elaborated in the mind before they become the texture of dreams. There is subconscious progress in reasoning and judgment. When Pilate was sitting in judgment upon Jesus he was warned by his wife who said, "Have nothing to do with this man, for I have suffered many things this day in a dream because of him." Doubtless her harvest of impressions both perceptible and imperceptible of the merits of the man on trial crystallized during sleep and induced a dream of warning. It is said that Professor Hilprecht, the Assyriologist, discovered in a dream that the two fragments which he had in vain been trying to decipher were parts of one and the same tablet. It is not uncommon for dreamers to be warned against persons in whom they are unwittingly misplacing confidence. During sleep automatic processes of the mind tend to bring to completion the unaccomplished efforts of the waking life. A somewhat masculine woman who had no lover but desired to attract one dreamed of a magic talisman, a powder puff. Evidently the dreaming mind was suggesting that more use of feminine arts might lead to the fulfilment of her desire for a mate.

Other dreams originate in self-criticism and fear of one's faults. The dread of self-censure may represent itself in a dream symbol. Recognition and criticism of feebleness and instability of character in a recent instance expressed itself in a dream of a donkey with weak legs. Such dream structures often afford the analyst a clue to the state of mind which undergirds a debilitating peculiarity or anomaly. Shakespeare in *Macbeth* describes the Lady walking in her sleep after the murder of the king and gives her physician's reaction:

Doctor: What is it she does now? Look how she rubs her hands.

Waiting Woman: It is an accustomed action with her, to seem thus washing her hands; I have known her continue in this a quarter of an hour.

Lady Macbeth: Yet here's a spot . . . . Out, damned spot! Out, I say! . . . . What! will these hands ne'er be clean?

Doctor:

> Foul whisperings are abroad; unnatural deeds
> Do breed unnatural troubles; infected minds
> To their deaf pillows will discharge their secrets;
> More needs she the divine than the physician.

That dreams often betray obscure impulses is abundantly demonstrated. The offending element may be the motif of a symbolical dream. A young business man came to Dr. Brill to be cured of an obsession in the form of an abnormal interest in socialism.[1] "There isn't half an hour in the day when I am not thinking about the accursed thing," he said. "I wake up in the morning asking myself the question, 'Isn't socialism a correct theory?' Then I am compelled to get hold of all the books and pamphlets I can find and read what is said for and against it." The fixed idea persisted despite the fact that the patient was, if anything, opposed to socialism. The physician adopted the method of dream analysis to lay bare the cause of the disorder. One day Dr. Brill and the patient were discussing a dream of the latter, which involved a social event at which George Bernard Shaw and a man with a peculiar wig were guests. The dreamer recalled that on the previous day he had read a book to which the famous author had written an introduction. The patient told the physician that the wig of the other guest reminded him of the hair of his wife. Urged to continue the unburdening of his mind, the patient confessed

---

[1] Cited in Stolz, Karl R., *Psychology of Prayer*, pp. 189, 190 (New York: Abingdon Press, 1923).

that he had been jealous of his wife. Sensing a clue, Dr. Brill asked him to define socialism. "Socialism means collective ownership," was the reply. The truth had suddenly been brought to light. The malady was due to jealousy. Although the patient had tried to banish all doubt and jealousy, the half-controlled fear that there might be a "collective ownership" of his wife's affections haunted him subconsciously and expressed itself in the abnormal interest in socialism and wove itself into the fabric of his dreams. In possession of this knowledge, the physician soon freed the patient of his obsession.

The Word Association Device

Another fruitful device for the discovery of pernicious impulses or memories is known as the word association method. This instrument which was devised by Jung exploits the individual's responses to a list of words.[2] Jung has selected one hundred words which experience has demonstrated stimulate to activity the typical impressions which irritate persons. The subject is instructed to give the first word which occurs to him when each of the stimulus words is read to him. Hearing "water" he may say "drink." The reaction word is related to the stimulus word by some association. The principle of the association of ideas, i.e., that there is a connection between the states of mind which follow another, is laid under tribute by the experimenter.

As Jung maintains, the test is more than a kind of conversation between the subject and experimenter. Words represent condensed situations, things, and actions, and it is to such realities in verbal form that one is reacting in the word association experiment. The stimulus words impinge upon us much as the realities for which they stand. Maladjustments suggested by the words given to the subject are often disclosed by his verbal responses.

The reactions of the subject possess a twofold diagnostic significance. The nature of the reaction word is carefully scrutinized for any clue it may give to the originating cause of the subject's symptoms. If he says "burn" when he hears

---

[2] See his *Collected Papers on Analytical Psychology* (New York: Dodd, Mead & Co., 1916).

"love," the experimenter may suspect that a secret passion is at the base of the disturbance. Again, the interval of time which elapses between the stimulus and response, known as the reaction time, is of great importance. The interval may be the outcome of one or more of several conditions. Sometimes the reaction time is unduly extended because there is a paucity of ideas, sometimes because several ideas occur to the subject from which a selection must be made, and sometimes because the stimulus word disconcerts him and he tries to think of a reaction which will disguise his embarrassment. When stimulus words are repeated before they are reacted to, it is because the subject wants to grasp their meaning more fully or because he temporizes. When he gives two or more reaction words, although only one is requested, he betrays lack of control and adaptation. The experimenter is on the lookout for a convergence of responses. The several reaction words which by reason of their meaning and time factor may indicate internal friction are assembled by the experimenter and interpreted. The word association method is of course by no means infallible and magical in its effects, for many persons have through extensive practice and self-discipline learned to conceal the outward and verbal traces of their haunting repressions.

As experimenters in the psychological laboratory my fellow-students and I used to attempt to localize hidden articles by means of the association test. One of our number was delegated to conceal a given object, say a knife, anywhere in the building in which we were at work. A list of words designed to disclose the whereabouts of the article was compiled. The subject was given the test. The words significantly reacted to were grouped and deductions made. The experiment seldom failed. Sometimes a more complicated test was undertaken, a test which included the disclosure of the nature of the object secreted and of the identity of the person who hid it.

As a typical case of the word association method in operation in personality treatment the following supplied by Jung and Peterson may be cited:

Stimulus Word	Reaction Word	Reaction Time (in seconds)
1. Head	Hair	1.4
2. Green	Meadow	1.6
3. *Water*	*Deep*	5.0
4. Stick	Knife	1.6
5. Long	Table	1.2
6. *Ship*	*Sink*	3.4
7. Ask	Answer	1.6
8. Wool	Knit	1.6
9. Spiteful	Friendly	1.4
10. *Lake*	*Water*	4.0
11. Sick	Well	1.8
12. Ink	Black	1.2
13. *Swim*	*Can't swim*	3.8

One is not surprised to learn that the person whose reaction words are here quoted was the subject of moods of dejection and had recently contemplated suicide by drowning. His emotional tension and the impulse to end his life are revealed in the verbal responses and their respective reaction times. In this and other cases the results of the word association test serve as a point of departure for a more systematic and detailed diagnosis. The inference drawn from the subject's responses must be supported by other data, if the experimenter's procedure is to be scientifically valid.

Hypnosis as a Revealer

The skilled analyst, having failed by other means at his disposal to disinter the buried source of the disorganization of the personality may adopt the hypnotic method. So far from being occult and esoteric, the phenomena of hypnotism fall within the purview of natural sequences. The state of hypnosis is an induced subconscious condition in which the subject is under the control of the experimenter. The word hypnotism is derived from the Greek term meaning sleep. The state of hypnosis is subjective. The hypnotic condition is not produced by the transference of a physical substance or a mysterious psychic emanation from the operator to the subject. It is an extreme form of suggestibilty in which the subject is under the dominance of the experimenter. The aura of mystery and occult power with which the traveling hypnotist surrounds himself, his imposing appearance, the authoritative intonations of his commands, the passes of his hands, conspire to render his subject responsive, but they are not essential elements of hypnotism. The factor of central importance is the submission of the subject to the will of the operator.

Who can be hypnotized? Contrary to popular opinion, the strong-willed rather than the weak-willed can be most easily hypnotized. Young children, the intoxicated, and idiots cannot be hypnotized, for they are incapable of holding in mental focus and adopting the suggestions of the experimenter. It is impossible to hypnotize animals, although through patient and persistent manipulation sleep may be induced. A frog will usually go to sleep when his back has been gently stroked for a period of twenty minutes. A chicken can be put to sleep by repeatedly tucking its head under its wing until it is exhausted. Needless to remark, neither sleeping frog nor chicken will obey the commands of the experimenter. Rapport can be established only between the operator and the human subject. Only human beings can be hypnotized, and of these only those whose wills are strong enough to respond to the hypnotist and to obey his orders. No one can be hypnotized without his consent. The unbroken resistance which one may offer the efforts of the operator makes the experiment a failure. The hypnotist may be so persistent and insistent that ultimately opposition is overcome, but in any case the success of the experiment includes the co-operation of the subject.

The hypnotized person responds to the operator's orders in accordance with his previous knowledge and conceptions. The subject's performance does not transcend the limitations of his mental furnishings. When he is ignorant of the meaning of the commands of the hypnotist there is no definite reaction but merely a state of confusion. If the suggestion is made that he impersonate Julius Caesar and he has no knowledge of the character and accomplishments of that historic figure, the response is at best merely an indication of embarrassment. If he is told that he is a worthy with whose life he is conversant, say Abraham Lincoln, he will give an impersonation of his conception of that character. The reactions to the directions of the hyp-

notist are invariably constructed from the materials which the
subject has previously acquired.

Nor will the subject act contrary to his moral principles.
The ethical attribute is so deeply ingrained that it persists
throughout the duration of the hypnotic state and regulates the
conduct of the one who has in other respects surrendered his
will to another. If a hypnotized person in a public demonstra-
tion is commanded to descend the platform and to rob anyone
in the audience, he may go so far as to relieve a friend of his
of the contents of his purse, seemingly assuming that in due
time he will restore the amount taken and that his friend will
not object. If the subject is ordered to slay a person with a
dagger, he will in all probability refuse to obey; given a paper
dagger with which to perform the deed of violence, he may
approach another and simulate murder. When subjects do
respond to suggestions which are opposed to their moral professions, it is because at heart they are actually in accord with
the unethical demands.

Hypnotism does not infringe upon or suspend the laws of
the physical world. It is directly efficacious only within the
range of the personal. The hypnotized individual cannot sail
through space unsupported, nor walk, head downward, on the
ceiling like a fly. The wonders of the traveling hypnotist
are frequently a strange combination of fact and fake, of genuine hypnotic results and the use of mechanical aids and sleight
of hand. While many effects of hypnotism are startling, it is
not a power which transcends the limitations of the world of
natural law.

The power of recollection may be so intensified through hypnotism that what one is unable to recall in the normal state
can be remembered in the trance. The fact that the span of
memory is widened in the hypnotic condition is of value to the
analyst who is seeking a clue to the elusive source of an internal collision. Dreams which one fails to recall in the waking period will often be described in detail in the hypnotic
state. The hypnotized subject is able to reproduce experience
long forgotten but still subconsciously influential. An army
officer in Africa being hypnotized began to speak a strange lan-

guage. It developed that he was speaking in Welsh, a language
which he had learned as a young child and long since forgotten.
The skilled analyst in working with stubborn cases may take
advantage of the power of hypnotism to stimulate dormant
memory.

The use of hypnotism is not regarded as an unqualified benefit by experienced workers with deranged personalities. For
one thing, the subject is likely to become so dependent on the
experimenter that he is bereft of a will of his own and is helplessly subordinate. Any procedure which undermines the self-
reliance of the ego should be avoided except as a last and
desperate resort. Furthermore, the hypnotic suggestions are
likely to gloss over and thus obscure rather than reveal
the motivating impulse. A constructive program of re-education is to be preferred, for it places at the command of the individual all the available resources of personality. Hypnotism
robs the self of initiative and controls it from without.

Matured experience is a precondition of the successful application of the three diagnostic methods which have been here
introduced. Pastors will realize that the difficulties which one
encounters in dream analysis, word association, and hypnotic
suggestion are both serious and numerous. While it should be
conceded that many pastors will never acquire the requisite
skill to use these complicated and delicate procedures with
creative consequences, every worker with individuals should
be theoretically familiar with them and appreciate their application by specialists. The skilled pastor may apply the methods
of dream analysis and word association in his work with individuals who are disposed to co-operate with him, but only the
psychologically trained physician should venture to employ
hypnotism.

CHAPTER XV

RELIGION AND THE TALK CURE

ADVERSE criticism has been directed against psychoanalysis both as a comprehensive medical philosophy and as a complete theory of personality. No doubt much in the current theories and practices of it will be discredited by further experimentation and discarded, but beyond question there will be a permanent residuum. In fact, some of the basic principles of psychoanalysis have already been incorporated in respectable theories of human behavior.

Psychoanalysis as a clinical procedure is primarily a method of discovering and terminating certain morbid states of mind. It entails a process of delving into the depths of personality and bringing to the surface dominant subconscious forces and the past experiences which have created them. In the next place, it outlines a course of treatment called sublimation for cases in which the focus of mental infection is not eradicated through conscious exposure. At first the practice of psychoanalysis was restricted to the cure of mental disorders, but it has been extended to the interpretation of such things as works of art, fairy tales, folklore, mythology, dreams, wit, and religious experience.

Doubtless the theory and application of psychoanalysis have been excessively overweighted and extended by enthusiasts and extremists. As might be expected, researches in the field of mental analysis have led to variant interpretations and rival schools of theory and practice. To trace these divergent developments would carry us too far from the present task and purpose. It will suffice to introduce therapeutic methods and procedures of psychological analysis which appear to be scientifically justified and of service to the pastor.

Psychoanalytic Relief

It is only within comparatively recent times that the confession experience which is the core of the psychoanalytic treat-

196

ment has received scientific study, definition, and application. Freud's clinical investigations have convinced him that the cause of the neurotic disorder is invariably a repressed idea at variance with the social or aesthetic ideals of the patient. The irritating impression, together with the emotions that accompany it, as our previous discussion of the complex has indicated, lingers actively in the subconscious region of the mind and is inhibited whenever it seeks to emerge into clear consciousness. Within the domain of the subconscious the incompatible force creates a pathological disturbance. It affects the self somewhat as a focus of infection poisons the body. The perturbance manifests itself in the guise of symptoms which give to the patient no indication of their original associations. For example, the apparently unrelated mental or physical symptoms may be the expressions of a fear induced by a lack of understanding of a relatively simple morbid condition. The pathogenic increment is repressed because its character is painful. It is not fully suppressed because despite its unpleasant feeling tone it exercises a fascination. It attracts and repels the sufferer. He cannot utterly surrender himself to its fascinations nor completely expel it from his mind; hence it casts a diabolical spell upon him.

Once exposed and understood, the vexatious elements can be relieved of their power to distract the self. Socrates' dictum, "Know thyself," suggestively anticipates the modern mental analyst's creed. Not all complexes are readily exterminated. On the other hand, many disturbing memories or desires are recalled without much effort and disposed of at once. When a painful episode of the past, a distressing memory, is reinstated with its original emotional quality its pernicious spell may immediately be broken. The symptoms may perish and the balance of personality be restored. The very resolution to right a past wrong or to make restitution, if the revived memory makes such a course of action necessary to peace of mind, relieves conscience of an oppressive burden. If an unacceptable desire is released, it is scrutinized by the individual and made amenable to his will. Sexual desire, for example, once regarded as debasing, may now be recognized as natural and be given an outlet in agreement with ideals which control the personality.

Informal interviews of the distracted individual with a skilled analyst are often sufficient to bring to clear consciousness the disquieting experience. The consultant is encouraged to relieve his mind, to withhold nothing lurking in the fringes of consciousness, no matter how absurd, trivial, embarrassing, irrelevant, and disconnected his thoughts may seem to be. The analyst is alert to possible defense reactions and gives the consultant aid in penetrating the disguise which his disorder has assumed. A recital of intimate details of the person's private life may afford the analyst a clue. The motivating circumstance may emerge in the trend of the free associations. The root of the non-rational behavior is lifted into the area of recognition and control with all the emotional intensity which it originally excited. The reproduction of the emotional accompaniment, be it fear, disgust, horror, or any other form of unpleasantness, is of major importance in the relief of the disturbed personality. After all, the essence of most inward conflicts is emotional, and therefore the revival of the tension-inducing emotion is indispensable to the restoration of emotional stability.

On the other hand, there are sinister forces too deeply buried and too elusive in their ramifications to be excavated by the ordinary method of spontaneous verbal expression. They are apparently forgotten or securely hidden in the depths of the self. Technical diagnostic methods may be applied to obtuse and baffling cases by the specialist in mental derangements. The specialized diagnostic methods which are most frequently used are introduced elsewhere in this treatise. Not many pastors have the technical equipment and experience to warrant them in undertaking the treatment of pathological disorders.

It is said that Freud by chance discovered what has been called the talk cure. He had studied in Paris under great French neurologists who demonstrated that in the hypnotic state patients afflicted with certain types of nervous diseases could be induced to disclose the origin of their symptoms by rehearsing experiences which they did not remember in the waking state. The cure consisted in dispersing the symptoms through suggestion. At home in Vienna, Freud with his coworker, Dr. Breuer, proceeded to apply what he had learned in

Paris. One day a woman appealed for relief from a typical nervous disorder. The patient began to describe her symptoms and, being fluent and unchecked in her recital, occupied the alloted hour before completing her case history. She resumed the narrative the next day and brought it to a close two days later. When she had told her story in full her symptoms had vanished. She was well! In the course of her self-revelation the woman developed such an attitude of objectivity, confidence, and frankness that she told her physician things she had not realized she knew and had not suspected of being connected with her ailment. Further experimentation proved that this process, incredibly simple and devoid of the dramatic and mysterious paraphernalia of hypnotism as practiced at the time, afforded relief to many complex-driven patients.[1]

Some of the symptoms of neurosis which have been banished by the psychoanalytic treatment may be tabulated as follows: twitching of muscles, tic of eyelid, increase of asthma, dumbness, stuttering, writer's cramp, paralysis, swollen lips, skin eruptions, itching of scalp, buzzing in the ears, neuralgia, dimness of vision, deafness, pains in arms, legs, back, shoulders, and stomach, and visual, auditory, and tactile hallucinations. It is a matter of record that such manifestations often occur in connection with religious beliefs and practices.

Such types of faith cure as Christian Science and Couéism are repressive in their approach to the ailments to which humanity is subject. They focus the attention entirely upon the ideas of health. The consciousness of illness is excluded. "Day by day in every way I am getting better and better" is a formula which may be applied with positive effect to ailments which originate in the creative imagination of the sufferer rather than in a collision of attitudes. The core of faith cure is responsiveness to the suggestion of health. The suggestion of disability is equally potent. What had been induced by suggestion can be cured by suggestion. If a headache is the product of the

[1] On the other hand, Pierre Janet, world renowned psychologist, claims that Freud appropriated his method of clinical observation and therapeutic procedure, altered its terminology, and erected the whole into an inclusive medical philosophy.

imagination as such, it can be eliminated by the excluding conviction that it no longer exists.

Disabilities originating in internal conflicts cannot be cured by ignoring them or excluding them from the field of attention. In such cases the efficacious treatment centers in expression, not in repression. As we have had occasion to show, in order to be permanently cured of obsessional neurosis the patient must become clearly aware of the seat of the disorder, face it frankly, and come to terms with it in accordance with his standards of values. The application of a form of faith healing, with or without religious implications, may check the symptoms, gloss over the sufferings, and thus afford temporary relief, but the disorder itself is incurable by such a method. A relapse is inevitable.

The pastor can make use of some principles of psychoanalysis in his work with individuals distressed by the milder forms of internal conflicts. He is a worker in the area of anomalies rather than a specialist in the field of pathologies. The wise mental analyst will press into service the competent pastor when religious instruction, prayer, and confession of wrongdoing are indicated as remedial agencies in the treatment of severe nervous disorders. In his own field the pastor will make contact with people who are mentally or physically ill because they are morally diseased. He will labor with others who are theologically confused rather than morally defective. "Prove to me that God loves me and I will leave your study a well man," is a challenge that he may face. In his intimate associations with men harassed by ethical and religious collisions heavily charged with conflicting emotions the pastor has an opportunity which assumes the nature of a privilege to employ psychoanalytic means of relief.

John Wesley in an entry in his diary recounts a visit to a woman who had a severe abdominal pain. She had been given drug upon drug by her physician who did not in the least comprehend the cause of her indisposition. Wesley discovered that the woman was ill from grieving over the death of her son. What she needed was the comfort and consolation of the ministry of the Church, which Wesley promptly supplied to the im-

mediate relief of the sufferer. Wesley sagely remarks that a
man who has no religious life cannot be an expert physician.
He makes a plea for closer co-operation between the clergy
and the medical profession.

Dr. Harry Emerson Fosdick records the pertinent case of
a young girl who had been disappointed in love. When she
consulted him she was nervously broken and had been obliged
to leave college. She was experiencing ecstasies which she in-
terpretated as religious in origin and nature. She had derived
no appreciable benefit from the treatment which had been pre-
scribed by her physician. She did not respond positively to
medical care because her ailment was rooted in the realm of
religion. The physician did not understand the religious aspects of her case. Applying a combination of religion and
psychiatry, Dr. Fosdick was able to restore the disordered personality.

Mrs. Charles Henderson was prostrated by the death of her
little daughter. Her religious faith was undermined and she
no longer attended the public worship of the church. Her husband, an official of the church, influenced by her example, attended irregularly. Mrs. Henderson studiously avoided any
reference in social intercourse to the departed daughter. Feeling that she could not bear to be near anything that would remind her of the child she had so dearly loved, Mrs. Henderson
traveled extensively in foreign lands. After her return to her
home she continued her policy of silence. Once when a little
girl who lived in the neighborhood came to the door Mrs.
Henderson fled to her room, sobbing. The pastor suggested
to the husband and wife that they speak of the dead child and
do so in natural connections and often. The pastor urged
close and discriminating friends of the couple to refer to the
child when they called at the home. His efforts were effective.
Mrs. Henderson gradually adjusted herself to her bereavement.
Her attitude underwent a complete change. She was com-
forted and consoled. Gratitude for the privilege of having had
the child for a few precious years replaced her sense of irreparable loss. Her sorrow was given oral and emotional outlet,
and thankfulness, social sympathy, and renewed devotion to
the church followed.

The Therapeutic Value of a Protestant Confessional

Modern psychology throws a flood light upon the structure
and function of religious confession. That the New Testament
commends confession is evident from certain passages. James
in his epistle (5 : 16) exhorts the people to confess their sins to
one another and to pray for each other that they may be healed.
He senses a connection between religious confession and the
cure of disease. John in his first epistle (1 : 9) declares that
if we confess our sins God is faithful and righteous to forgive
us and to cleanse us from all unrighteousness.

In the undivided and pre-Reformation church the confessional was the product of a process of growth. At first the penitent
confessed his sins to the company of believers. In the course
of time the religious leaders acted as confessors. Secret auricu-
lar confession was not made a law of the Church, however, until
the early part of the thirteenth century.

The Roman Catholic is obliged to go to confession before
taking communion. The officiating priest gives the confessing
sinner two things: absolution and the obligation of penance.
Having heard the confession and being satisfied with it, the
priest affirms, "I absolve thee." Of course the Roman Church
teaches that the priest is vested with the power to forgive sin.
It is supposed from Matthew 16: 18, 19 that Jesus himself
conferred upon Peter the keys of human destiny. Peter's suc-
cessors are said to have inherited his unique power of absolution. It is assumed that also in John 20: 21-23 authority is
given the Roman priesthood to pardon iniquity. In this passage Jesus breathes upon his disciples and sends them forth,
declaring that those whose sins they remit are actually pardoned and those whose sins they retain are actually unforgiven.
That both passages are susceptible of a very different interpretation is, of course, strenuously denied by the Roman
Church. In the second place, the priest imposes penance.
Nevertheless, quite early in the history of the confessional the
payment of a sum of money came to be regarded as a satisfactory substitute for the appointed penalty.

We know to what abuses this practice led and how Luther
forcibly reacted against it. In fact, the entire system of in-

dulgences fell under Luther's condemnation. He controverted it for several reasons. The torture of conscience of the individual forced to lay bare his intimate sins further aroused Luther's disapproval. The conduct and demeanor of many confessors proved offensive to him. He did not reject the confessional itself. On the contrary, he recognized no one as a Christian who withdrew himself from it. But Luther seriously modified the fundamentals of the Roman doctrine. In the first place, while he used the formula, "I forgive thee," he did not contend that it was in him or in any other person to absolve men. He taught that God forgave the penitent sinner and merely announced His forgiveness through the lips of the confessor. In the second place, he rejected penance as a regulated series of penalties. Furthermore, he held that one could obtain absolution through a Christian lay brother as well as through a priest. Luther used the term confession in a rather wide sense, including in it the prayer for mercy and the humble confession to God. Later, toward the close of the seventeenth century, individual confession in the Lutheran Church was largely replaced by the general or congregational confession. The congregation as a whole confessed its sins before taking the communion.

In the light of psychoanalysis we can see that the more evangelical forms of Protestantism in their general reaction against institutionalized confession have been guilty of pouring out the child with the bath water. Modern Protestantism has yet much to learn about this means of grace. For centuries the confessional has survived and afforded the adherents of the Catholic Church a release from inner tension which has been held in contempt by Protestants. Protestants have held a position which has on the whole been shortsighted. They have sacrificed too much of positive religious worth. It is not necessary to accept the Catholic doctrine in detail in order to appreciate the function of the confessional. The Protestant Church may provide its constituency with a confessional without assuming all the powers and prerogatives which the Roman Church claims.

Not that the Catholic confessional is perfect. In some respects it is manifestly defective. As an ecclesiastical instrument it has a tendency to focus attention upon the guilt rather than upon the origin of the wrong confessed. Generally it is content with a cursory examination and does not probe to the source of the evil. Again, as a compulsory exercise it creates resistance to the disclosure of hidden but dynamic experiences. Nevertheless, in spite of its limitations, the Catholic confessional does untold good as a purifying and hygienic process. The Protestant Church conducting a confessional to which people may freely resort can conserve what is of value in the Catholic system and add to that other items from the wider field of psychoanalysis which have been sufficiently tested and found serviceable.

Unconfessed and unforgiven moral lapses, haunting questionable desires, and secret temptations create a breach in the personality which only confession and amendment can heal. The eruptive mental states may display themselves in distorted forms which to the untrained observer seem to have no connection whatever with the person's religious sentiments and behavior. Unburdening himself in confession, rehearsing vividly and with emotional excitement the details of the experience which has become a point of tension within him, the person finds relief. Conscience sits in judgment upon the discordant elements that become conscious and subject to the will through confession. Many evils confessed perish in the intense feeling of moral repugnance which accompanies the confession. Others require prayer for their complete eradication or for their transmutation into activities of higher ethical value. When the confessed experience is a mere memory, is a thing of the past with no connection with the present, its reinstatement is sufficient to purge the self and to restore its equilibrium.

The question may be raised, "Is it not possible to confess our shortcomings solely in order to resume sinning with impunity?" That confession is actually often a mere form, an exercise without moral meaning, cannot be denied without protest. The relief which an impenitent soul derives from confession is the relief which proceeds from the technical and formal compliance with an accepted requirement. It should be affirmed with all possible emphasis that insincerity effectively blocks the accomplishment of the fundamental purpose of the psychoanalytical process, which is the eradication of the confessed evil itself.

The general practice of psychoanalysis in the cure of disease demonstrates conclusively that the psychoanalytical treatment is of no avail in the cases of those who do not at heart desire a cure. A wife who is pampered as a patient and as such is relieved of burdensome duties; a man who derives an advantage from his neurotic incapacity for work, such as an insurance indemnity; a boy who would escape the routine of the schoolroom by the aid of a mentally induced pain—all these are outside the pale of successful psychoanalytic treatment. Similarly, a person who at heart clings to evil for some fancied advantage does not receive the full value of the confession. No confession is a true confession unless it is made by one overwhelmed by the consciousness of sin and guilt, by one truly penitent and broken-hearted and sincerely desirous of restoring severed relations with God and man. The shame and humiliation of revealing shortcomings and failings which should never have existed make it exceedingly difficult for the sensitive soul to regard confession as an easy escape from the consequences of misdeeds.

Confession which purges the personality of moral impurities must focus attention on specific wrongdoing which has created a conflict. Voluntary individual confession is therefore on the whole more effective than social or collective acknowledgment of failure or guilt. The public confession of the worshiping congregation may impart to the individual an aesthetic thrill rather than a sense of personal guilt and a desire for pardon and amendment. The prayer of confession recited by the congregation, being general in its statements of delinquency both of commission and omission, and phrased in choice diction and sonorous rhythmic periods, arouses in the worshiper a mild mood of penitence combined with a warm stimulating sense of well-being and an appreciation of literary values. Furthermore, one is exhilarated by participation in a dramatic religious attitude and act. The confession of an individual, in his closet or in the study of the pastor, tortured by an outraged conscience, so far from being an aesthetic and literary performance, is an excruciating episode. His oral confession is not a literary gem, but issues, charged with shame and compunction, haltingly and perhaps incoherently from the depths of a broken and contrite spirit.

Modern society allows the individual but few adequate opportunities to disclose his inmost worries. Our social code does not permit a man to complain of his failures or to parade his successes. He is at liberty to discuss his bodily ailments if he can find a willing listener, but frank discussion of spiritual anxiety is taboo. As it is, most members of the Protestant Church when they wish to unburden themselves, consult the lawyer or the physician. Indeed, some resort to the spiritualistic medium, the clairvoyant, or the fortune teller. Lawyers and physicians hear a multitude of confessions and, it should be gratefully acknowledged, are able to relieve many of their clients or patients. Ministers should regard it as an essential of their pastoral relations to display such an attitude of friendliness and concern that people of their own accord will confide in them. A procedure which combines an informal confessional and scientific values of psychiatry with that type of preaching which calls men to an immediacy of religious experience and arouses them from moral sloth is sorely needed.

CHAPTER XVI

ADJUSTMENT TO REALITY

INTEGRATION as the act of combining the elements of personality into a stabilized whole entails the rational meeting of all situations in which one is involved. Disintegration is patent evidence that crises or maladjustments have not been frankly faced and overcome. Defense responses carried to excess either arrest personality development or disorganize the self. Overcompensation is an indication of failure in integration. The emotional approach to problems betrays mental immaturity. In order to preserve the dynamic unity of the self in terms of accredited values life as an ongoing experience must be a sequence of adjustments.

The range of life-situations which demand personality reorganization is extensive. The sources of irritation and conflict are too numerous to be exhaustively catalogued. Any representative list would embrace such common perplexities as sickness, bereavement, bodily malformation, vocational maladjustment, loss of income, misunderstanding, frustrated love affairs, and domestic unhappiness. It would include a variegated assortment of moral defects. Inconsistencies, anomalies, and singularities as well as the more injurious emotional disabilities would be tabulated. The possible points of internal friction more or less critical are legion. Is there a comprehensive technique for their satisfactory disposition?

After all there is only one way in which personality defects and conflicts can be definitely and therefore satisfactorily corrected or resolved. Situations, regardless of their unpleasant character, must be recognized, analyzed, and disposed of in accordance with the dictates of wisdom. Other approaches are illusory or palliative and at best afford the distraught personality only temporary surcease. Self-deception, evasion, and subterfuge can only aggravate the focus of tension. Only when there is a firm determination to abide by the logic of the facts,

however disagreeable it may be, can an adequate adjustment
be made.

Facing the Facts

To face reality rather than to rationalize, pretend, daydream,
temporize, or transfer responsibility is the first step in deliverance from the thralldom of moral defect, personality crisis, or
environmental menace. Refusal to recognize unpleasant facts
is an indication of mental inferiority. Of the various subter-
fuges which the mentally immature adopt the most common and
perilous is wish-phantasy. Devotees of the Pollyanna philosophy flee from reality into a world of imaginary security and
bliss. When it is raining torrents, they exclaim, "What a
bright and beautiful day!" When they are really sick and
miserable they assure their solicitous friends that they are in the
pink of condition and feeling fit. They drug their minds into
the belief that disagreeable things are as pleasant as they prefer
them to be.

Each spring for several successive years little Arthur
Grant had been told by his mother that the Easter rabbit lays
colored eggs in the nests provided by children. The small boy
reveled in the dramatic fiction and supposed that the Easter
eggs he annually found were contributed by the dutiful rabbit.
When Arthur was seven years old his mother, persuaded that
he was old enough to adjust himself to reality, proceeded to
enlighten him just before Easter Sunday. The boy burst into
wild tears and protested against her statement that the Easter
rabbit was a myth. He was so agitated that his mother, heart-
stricken, hastened to retract the truth and to reassure him.
Arthur eagerly resumed his belief in the existence and benevo-
lence of the Easter rabbit. What might be pardoned in a child
is reprehensible in an adult. Individuals fifty years old see facts
where there are none, prefer phantasy to farsighted judgment,
and would live in a world of irresponsible optimism.

Workers with individuals experience difficulty in convincing
those who have sought refuge in vain imaginings of the peril
of their emotional attitudes. It takes courageous initiative,
insight, and perseverance to prove to a deluded person that his
house is built on shifting sand, and that sooner or later the

storms of reality will demolish it. Sometimes all that the worker can do is to let actual circumstances overtake and destroy the delusion, hoping that after the debacle the victim will be more amenable to the truth.

Mr. De Schweinitz records the pertinent case of Lydia Easton.[1] At twenty years of age Lydia was an unmarried mother. The child's father was prevented from becoming Lydia's husband by a previous marriage. Nevertheless, she wore a wedding ring and spoke of herself as a widow. She gave a social case worker a detailed account of her wedding and insisted that together they visit the clergyman who she alleged had performed the ceremony. The fact that the clergyman denied that he had officiated at a wedding of which she was a principal failed to relieve Lydia's mind of her self-deception. Lydia refused to recognize facts. She preferred to lead an existence of unreality the foundation of which was her intense desire for domestic life. She lived in imagination what circumstances had thus far withheld.

Less than two years after the birth of her first-born she bore another child, maintaining that in this case she had been assaulted. Although she had been intimate with other men, Lydia entered suit against the father of the second child. The social worker saw in the suit an opportunity to drive unreality from Lydia's mind. The preposterous case was permitted to come to trial. On the witness stand, Lydia, under merciless cross-examination, finally admitted that she had never been married. At last she realized that she had been living a lie and faced grim reality.

Later she accepted a position in a normal home as a mother's helper. She was made to feel that she had a real share in the family life. After serving a year in this congenial home Lydia met a man whom she later married. In her married life she actually realized what she had once possessed only in imagination. Be it noted that the first step in the reconstruction of her life was the recognition of an ugly and obstinate fact.

Not all disintegrated personalities can be brought before the tribunal of self-judgment. Some prefer to wear an invisible

[1] De Schweinitz, Karl, *The Art of Helping People Out of Trouble,* pp. 219 ff. (New York: Houghton, Mifflin Co., 1924).

but impenetrable mask. They are in need of a complete change in point of view and of radical adjustments, but they seem incapable of becoming brave and frank enough to undertake an honest inventory of themselves. They refuse to admit their real defects of character. They are too clever to become involved in a social situation which will demolish their defenses. Such a one is Miss Dora Calvin, college student. Several interviews with her netted such outstanding findings as unstable laughter, a rough and ready manner, flushing, easy tears, home and family fixation, dependency in her friendships, and a desire to escape responsibility. When her counselor asked her what she remembered of her childhood she retorted that it would be an act of disloyalty to her family to tell what she recalled of her early years. She is intelligent and possesses some qualities of leadership but is emotionally immature and unbalanced. She professed eagerness to accept an intensive academic assignment under the direction of one of her teachers, but when actually confronted by the task she felt inadequate and hedged. It is clear that Miss Calvin cannot register progress in the reorganization of her personality until she abandons her policy of resistance and her preoccupation with her own feelings. She orders her life so adroitly that no crisis emerges to confute her and to overthrow her barricades. How she can be motivated to apply constructive self-criticism is still problematic.

It is a truism, but one which cannot be reiterated too often that only when we recognize and face our weaknesses, failures and internal collisions can we control them. When evil desires are aroused we should not drive them underground where they will exercise a pernicious influence, but examine them. We should frankly concede that we have them, for only in acknowledging our possession of them can we subdue them. As has already been stated, to admit the existence of an unacceptable idea or impulse is in many cases to exterminate it. It may at once be consumed in the fires of moral indignation which the recognition of it kindles. If the disrupting element is a mere haunting memory, its emotional reinstatement may purge the personality at once and restore the harmony of the self. In fact, mental therapeutics calls attention to patients who have been cured by facing their morbid conditions. Hadfield refers to a case in point.[2] A woman while nursing in a contested area in France in the World War developed an anxiety neurosis. Suddenly she admitted to herself what she had hitherto denied —that she was afraid. Her state of anxiety was immediately dispersed and her fear, freely conceded, was easily conquered.

The identification of the source of a personality conflict is in itself not always sufficient to relieve the tension and restore the emotional equilibrium. The grasping of the painful situation is often diagnostic rather than remedial. The process of self-revelation is often merely preliminary to a prolonged and complicated process of reconditioning. In most cases a remedy must be discovered or devised, judgment exercised, alternatives weighed and balanced, and a program of action formulated and practically applied. Nothing short of a concrete adjustment in actual behavior will relieve the strain of active sinister associations. If progressively higher integrations of freedom and worth are to be attained the changed outlook must lead to alterations in conduct. Recognition of the disabling is the beginning of understanding and the conscious control of it is the end of wisdom.

There are at least five typical ways in which life-problems can be met—domination, sublimation, discrimination, accommodation, and submission. That the procedures overlap in actual practice will be evident as each is introduced and characterized. In some of these personality changes predominate, in others the environmental circumstances are chiefly affected, and in still others subjective and objective alterations are more nearly balanced.

Adjustment by Domination

When situations or defects are weaker than the combined resources of the personality they should be conquered. In direct proportion as opposing forces are overcome the personality becomes more potent. Personality is reintegrated in the subjugation of its obstacles. The feeling which accompanies the outrush of dominating energy, while at first unpleasant, becomes

[2] Hadfield, J. A., *Psychology and Morals*, p. 189 (New York: Robert McBride & Co., 1925).

increasingly pleasurable as the opposition yields. Victory is exhilarating.

To be sure, domination which leads to a higher form of personality organization must be in accord with the master sentiment. Domination must be constructive. In the conquest of his difficulties the emancipated individual is guided not by precedent or rule but by the anticipated effects both personal and social. His moral sanctions are grounded in the realities of experience. Face to face with the necessity of making an adjustment to reality, the wise man raises and answers these questions: How in all probability would the proposed action affect me? How would it presumably affect others? Is it in harmony with the ideal of creative living? The answers to such a series of questions determine his program of activities. His procedure is born of ethical love and directed by intelligence. It should be said in passing that the same evaluation should govern other methods of adjustment to fact as well as domination. It undergirds the good life in its various bearings and relations.

The subjective defects and outward obstacles which can and should be conquered are too numerous to be mentioned. One immediately lists such moral faults as lying and stealing, such morbid states as hypersensitiveness and paralyzing anxieties, such incompetencies as lack of education and social training, such physical disabilities as curable disease and removable bodily malformations. Poverty, social maladjustments, and vocational failure are somewhat more objective opposing circumstances which are often less powerful than the resources of a resolute personality. Great is the will to conquer both the world within and the world without!

The ramifications of solution by domination are endless. The method is effective even in some of the most perplexing and subtle emergencies. A college president, for example, has a brother who is a fruit peddler. For a long time the president was torn by the fear that the members of his faculty would learn that the man who sold fruit at their back doors was his brother. He was in constant terror lest the discovery of the personal relationship would humiliate and discredit him. He was advised to dominate the situation, to introduce his brother to his colleagues and friends, and to take the consequences both agreeable and otherwise. He took the advice, presented the fruit peddler to his associates and intimates. The president experienced a profound relief. Most of his friends respected him the more for his forthright attitude toward his brother of lowly status, and for the energy and ability that had carried him from poverty and meager early advantages to the presidency of the college.

Adjustment by Sublimation

The resolution of personality conflicts is frequently accomplished by a process of sublimation. When the subconscious disturbance is released it is disposed of in accordance with the person's governing sentiments. The irritating increment may not be wholly condemned nor entirely sanctioned, but refined, regulated, and given a higher form of discharge. The flow of the life force is not obstructed but deflected. A new channel of expression, a channel in harmony with obligatory social judgment, is opened. The ideal is not swept away by the current of contrary desire; desire is transformed by the ideal.

The impression has gained ground that restrictions imperil health and happiness. The discipline which sublimation implies is irksome. Many crave emancipation from restraint. They consider anything which curbs individual freedom a form of oppression and a possible source of conflict which should be stoutly resisted and speedily destroyed. They would continue only those moral practices and social customs which they suppose set personality free. Their watchword is "act according to nature."

Such persons, although they rightly subscribe to the doctrine that the most sacred if not the only sacred existences in the world are personalities, should pause long enough to raise the question, "How much personal liberty is possible in our complex social order?" None is in possession of unrestricted freedom of action. Our abilities and opportunities outline our possibilities. God himself cannot be absolutely independent; he must be limited by his own attributes and by whatever of initiative and creativity with which man is endowed. God

PASTORAL PSYCHOLOGY

cannot make us good against our wills. As soon as a man is forced to be good he, paradoxically, ceases to be good.

No one is free to do anything and everything. The enveloping social structure makes demands which we cannot ignore. As so many units of the social structure we are hedged about by restrictions which we are unable altogether to transcend. The leading character of the play *Old English,* written by John Galsworthy, adopted the motto, "Be independent at any cost." As the play unfolds Old English fails to live up to his motto. His motherless daughter who serves as his housekeeper attempts to order his daily life, and he yields somewhat to the pressure which she applies. As president of a navigation company Old English engages in reprehensible business ventures and becomes entangled in their consequences. At last worn out by his unsuccessful efforts to preserve his personal liberty at any cost, Old English commits suicide by an act of gastronomic overindulgence. Death by his own hand is his confession of failure to be absolutely independent. It is only by co-operating with others for the welfare of all that the individual achieves the measure of freedom to which he is justly entitled. The sooner we face this fact without blinking and the sooner we adjust ourselves to it the better for us and for others. Some one has remarked that goldfish in their glass jar are care-free, but they can hardly be called free.

The widespread belief that primitive peoples were free to do as they pleased is flatly contradicted by such knowledge of them as we possess. The lives of our early ancestors were to an amazing degree ordered by rigid tribal customs and ceremonies. Taboos were numerous and disregard of many of them punishable by death. The person who attempted to alter the traditions of the fathers felt the heavy hand of social disapproval and penalty. There was not much liberty of choice. Even today in central Australia marriage regulations are strictly enforced by the natives. A young man is not at liberty to choose his own mate, for there is one woman whom he is predestined by tribal arrangement to wed. The life of primitive man was so conventional and precedent-ridden that life in modern civilization, complex as it is, is comparatively flexible and independent.

The irresponsible tribal life of the savage is a later fiction of idle phantasy.

It is significant that in his teachings Jesus emphasizes decency, honesty, sincerity, compassion, sacrifice, and social justice rather than unrestrained personal liberty. He teaches a higher freedom through self-control, and emancipation through self-giving. "If the Son therefore shall make you free, ye shall be free indeed." Marcus Aurelius says: "Remember that to change thy mind and to follow him that sets thee right is to be none the less the free agent thou wast before." Millions have called Christ Master, and have found his yoke easy and his burden light. On the other hand, as he himself said, "He that committeth sin is the bond-servant of sin." The spirit which informed his precepts and example has been captured and disclosed in the verse of a familiar hymn, "There's a kindness in his justice, which is more than liberty."

Apart from its contribution to the dispersion of complexes the principle of sublimation has significant educational bearings. Attention has been directed to the value of transforming crude impulses for the development of emancipated personality.[3] The implications of the sublimation of pugnacity, hunger, fear, anger, and self-regard have been suggested. The list might be extended so as to include the refinement of the drives of acquisitiveness, curiosity, self-display, and kindred personality functions. A natural end of acquisitiveness is the securing of the necessities of life; the collecting of stamps, art treasures, and antiques may be regarded as sublimated expressions. Curiosity which tends to discharge itself in morbid and socially unapproved forms may be expended in scientific discovery and research. Self-display which in its undisciplined state manifests itself in an inordinate fondness for dress and desire for admiration may be subordinated to the appreciation of art, to the love of the beautiful for its own sake. The possibilities of sublimation as adjustment to the finer realities are too important not to be laid under tribute by parents, educators, pastors, and others who are charged with the responsibility of personality guidance.

[3] See Chapter III.

While some persons concede that the direct refinement of many impulses is both possible and obligatory they hold that the voluntary control of the sexual instinct is neither desirable nor necessary. They maintain that sexual inhibition is a menace to the health and well-being of personality. To say the least in reply, deliberate regulation of the sexual life is less detrimental than the disruption of idealism and the social and biological misfortunes which illicit relationships so frequently precipitate. Licentiousness in the name of mental hygiene is just as deleterious as licentiousness in the name of anything else.

Not that sexual desire is easily regulated. The sublimation of the sexual impulse admittedly demands the exercise of a rare quality of self-discipline. Civilization is thousands of years in advance of the fundamental urge of sexual appetite. Furthermore, the sublimation of the sexual instinct does not consist in the transference of the desire itself from one object to another, as is largely the case in the sublimation of such drives as pugnacity and curiosity. Sexual satisfaction itself is forfeited and the parental phases of personality are cultivated and given outlet. Only the more refined irradiations of the sexual impulse are expressed in protective and parental functions. Continence entails a gap which sublimation overleaps.

Nevertheless, the process of sexual sublimation has been accomplished with impressive frequency and wholesome effects. Many a woman the current of whose love-life has been checked by a faithless lover, or unrequited love or lack of opportunity to meet a prospective mate, has made an adjustment to reality through social work, teaching, or nursing which has afforded her a measure of tranquillity and self-realization. The second choice is often the only one that leads to a reasonable degree of serenity. The sublimation of the sexual impulse is of course not always permanent, for marriage often terminates it. Sublimation does not impair the natural functions of personality. A woman who has been a nurse or a teacher for a period of years will not on that account be a less congenial wife and tender mother.

Adjustment by Discrimination

There is a class of situations which include mixtures of good and bad elements. Such contingencies can best be met by a process of separation and selection. The good is discovered, lifted out of its uncongenial setting and positively reacted to, and the bad is simply discarded. Not all units of a classification are condemned and rejected, and not all are treasured. Discretion is exercised. A choice is made. The fruit grower does not throw away a barrel of apples because some of the apples are rotten; he separates the sound ones from the rotten, he casts out the bad ones and markets the good ones. Similarly, the discerning personality, so far from either accepting or rejecting a mixed situation as a whole, evaluates the units.

Professor Edwin B. Holt discusses the typical case of the young woman who comes to the city from the country home and pious family in order to earn her living.[4] At home she has been taught that the theater is the sum of all abominations. She is exhorted to shun it. From what she learns from the friends she makes in the city the moral tone of the theater as a whole is not altogether elevating. Her friends invite her to go to the theater with them. What should she do? Professor Holt refers to four possibilities. In the first place, she might flatly refuse to attend the theater. Would that be the wisest course? In the second place, she might go to the opposite extreme and thereby become a riotous pleasure lover. She might conceivably give herself to the garish night life of the metropolis. In the third place, she might compromise her ideals by observing the home teaching part of the time and by attending the theater now and then. She might lead a double life, and become a moral dual personality.

The wise young woman does not choose any one of these three possibilities. Instead, she reduces the situation to its constituent elements and consequently decides to go to the theater when there is sufficient reason to believe that the play is edifying. She resolves to prove the plays in advance, to reject the bad and to select only the good. The purpose of

[4] *The Freudian Wish,* pp. 118 ff. (New York: Henry Holt & Co., 1915).

parental teaching which is the safeguarding of her morals is respected in her refusal to see degrading plays. On the other hand, the wholesome plays seen afford recreation, social stimulation, aesthetic gratification, and a deeper understanding of life. The positive values of home training and of the theater are fused. Discrimination enlarges her life and leads to a higher integration of freedom and self-realization.

The young woman might venture a step or two beyond the point to which Professor Holt leads her. She might try to dissuade her friends who propose to see detrimental plays. She might devote energy to the improvement of the theater as a whole by identifying herself with a crusade for the suppression of bad plays and for the increased public support of good plays. On the other hand, many conditions, like apples in the state of decay, cannot be rectified; hence all that we can do is to avoid them ourselves and warn other people. At any rate, adjustment to cases of mixed quality can be indicated only by a discriminating sense of values.

Discrimination is not compromise. No concessions to evil are made. Conscience is not against but for constructive selectability. One is loyal to moral sentiment and at the same time gratifies desires for personality enrichment. As Bertrand Russell contends, the good life is the life inspired by love and guided by reason. One acts with a whole heart, for there is no conflict between conscience and the appropriation of the commendable elements in a mixed situation. The moral attribute is in undisputed possession of the field, and a new synthesis of the constituents of personality is attained.

Adjustment by Accommodation

Situations arise which one is powerless to subdue and to which one cannot possibly surrender with a clear conscience. The nature of many facts either social or psychological is as uncompromising as that of such physical phenomena as air, water, and fire. Adaptation of human behavior makes unrelenting circumstance tolerable or serviceable. When one looks across the room at the clock in order to see what time it is one is at first unable to discern clearly the hands and the numerals. One waits a moment for the complicated mechanism of vision to accommodate itself to the stimulus. Gradually the position of the hands on the dial become visible. It is the visual apparatus of the beholder and not the clock that makes the necessary adjustment. The weather, to suggest another analogy, is not subject to the human will, but we do not tamely submit to its extremes. Dress and diet are adapted to hot or cold weather. In like manner the alert individual accommodates his mode of action to unalterable environmental conditions in order that a need may be met.

Mrs. Theodore Dix states that while her husband is the kindest of men he is careless and untidy in his personal habits. He drops his clothes and other belongings on the floor as he goes from one room to another in the house. His lack of orderliness has been a grief of mind to his wife. Entreaties and threats are unavailing. Nothing could persuade him to act in accordance with the rule that there is a place for everything. The persistent nagging of Mrs. Dix finally almost drove him into the divorce court for relief. At last it occurred to Mrs. Dix that the domestic strain would be eased if she herself picked up his things and put them where they belong. The results have vindicated the accommodation. For one thing, her sense of neatness and orderliness is gratified. Furthermore, her changed attitude toward her husband has cleared the domestic atmosphere of the antagonism with which it was charged.

Accommodation to reality, like discrimination, is not compromise. The moral standard is not lowered. So long as both the means and the end are worthy conscience approves of the adjustment. The personality makes the adaptation with the sanction of social judgment. In fact, moral sentiment makes the serviceable accommodation to unconquerable situations imperative. It is not optional but obligatory. To refrain from such a profitable course of action is to be guilty of a moral defect of omission.

Adjustment by accommodation is a second best. It is well to bear in mind that first choices do not always permanently satisfy, for they may be the promptings of inexperience rather than of matured judgment. A wise man thanked God for unanswered prayer. The moon for which we sigh might, once in our possession, be green cheese and unpalatable, while the bread within our grasp is at least edible and nourishing. The woman a man feels he must take to wife or die of a broken heart may when seen with clearer eyes ten years later have lost her power to charm him. The woman he has married as a second choice may prove to be much more congenial and attractive. The promising and lucrative position for which one applied and to which another and much inferior man was invited may in the course of time reveal disadvantages one overlooked in the flush of eagerness. The position which one did accept as a second best may have given ample scope for all one's competencies. In fact, the kind of wife a man lives with and the kind of position he occupies depend much on his own ability to develop their latent capacities. Blessed is the man who can accommodate himself to the realities within the circle of his experience.

Adjustment by Submission

There are obstacles which cannot be dominated and to which accommodation is impossible. We defy them only to our own injury. There is peace under the flag of surrender to the inexorable. It is quite useless to expect miracles to be performed for our express benefit. Anguished expectations of doing or being the impossible inevitably end in disappointment, nervous exhaustion, and emotional conflict. When we firmly resolve to bear our invincible limitations the emotional relief is so great that we marvel why the sensible course was not previously pursued. The worst is over when we cease repining and exorcise the belief that impinging conditions will be agreeable just because we want them to be agreeable.

Young Mrs. James Richmond supposed that her husband was going to be prosperous. Although the couple married on a pittance and failed to prosper financially, they lived for years under the strain of keeping up appearances. They would do without meat for a month in order to give a dinner party. Mrs. Richmond would make over her old clothes hoping that her best friends would not know them. Bill collectors who crowded the doorsteps each month were the heralds of doom. Finally Mrs. Richmond sensibly faced the fact that her husband would never make a fortune, and that while he would always provide the necessities he would never afford luxurious living. The struggle to appear rich and fashionable was ended. Smart friends were given up and a new residence established among people of their own financial standing. All pretense was ruthlessly abandoned and the simplicities were cultivated. Accepting their lives as they are, the Richmonds are at peace with themselves and with the world.

Adjustment to tribulation centers in the attitude of submission. By nature we shrink from the abyss that threatens to engulf us and we do our utmost to escape impending doom, but a cosmic process like death is impartial and relentless. Resignation averts the peril and the blight of a despairing and disrupted personality. The Christian religion teaches a wise submission to the unavoidable, a firm faith in the persistence of the moral values, and an unfaltering trust in a good God. Prayer as a form of mental control furthers resignation. When petitional prayer, in the nature of events, cannot be answered, the prayer of surrender may be made with telling subjective effects. There is no disaster above which the religious attitude cannot rise.

A wife in a moving article records her adjustment to the imminent death of her brilliant twenty-eight-year-old husband.[5] He has been losing ground steadily, and his death is only a matter of weeks or months. He realizes his condition and is reconciled to it.[6] At first death cast a shadow upon the wife and filled her with gloom and dejection. After trying the fatalistic attitude, after agonizing over the preciousness of life, after uselessly crying out, "It isn't fair," she finally discovered how to meet the menacing lengthening shadow.

She writes that facing the death of a loved one is like facing other crises. It is chiefly a state of mind. When she adopted the right mental attitude she was prepared for the worst. When she ceased to struggle with the invincible, when she abandoned her efforts to escape grim reality, and admitted to

[5] *The Christian Century,* July 15, 1931, pp. 925 ff.

[6] For a statement of adjustment to a person's own imminent death, see Ozora Davis's address "Life-Giving Convictions," *Minutes of the National Council of Congregational Churches, 1929,* pp. 164 ff.

herself that she knew that death had marked her husband, she
absorbed the stern situation and began a process of reintegration.

Meanwhile she is leading a restricted business and social life.
She is wearing more becoming clothes than at any other time
of her life because of the tonic effect they have on both herself
and her husband. She goes to luncheons frequently, although
of course with her heart in her mouth. After a night of standing helplessly by while the loved one is in agony it seems strange
that her capacities to suffer and love are limitless. It is breath-
taking, she testifies, to find herself in communion with that
unquenchable love which fills her with strange strength, with
something that is far bigger than she is. Religion enables her
to tap the source.

She and her husband are living by days and not by years.
Each precious day is exploited. There is active delight in the
simplicities of life such as good food tastily prepared and a
clean house. The dog and the radio set are indispensable.
There is expression of inner thoughts and endearments, so
often withheld when one is careless of the passing days. Heart
meets heart in spiritual oneness as each day is freighted with
love and anticipation of separation.

We are not to become habituated to surrender but to learn
to accept overwhelming reality with dignity. The integrated
personality takes such gains as life holds and witnesses the
collapse of cherished prospects without being wounded beyond
recovery. The wise man cultivates a spirit of detachment which
makes him an interested spectator of the ebb and flow of his
personal fortunes. Although he does not cease to be a partici-
pant in whatever overtakes him, he views his situation and himself with a degree of objectivity that facilitates reconciliation.
He marvels how in the labyrinth of faulty judgment and uncontrollable events life acquires a significance which is beyond
compare. Above all he learns how to gather up the fragments
of a shattered dream and to weave them into a fresh pattern of
love and duty and service.

CHAPTER XVII

THE TECHNIQUE OF PRIVATE PRAYER AND WORSHIP

In order that we may live at our best we must have an adequate supply of energy. It is of the utmost importance that the sources of power for abundant living be discovered and exploited. Means for the release and canalization of surplus energy may be devised. Now prayer is a form of personality control, an act whereby vital power is made available and organized. As such, prayer reduces tension and furthers the integration of personality with idea values as the focus of reference.

We hear much about the structure and function of prayer, the intellectual and practical problems of prayer, but far too little about the technique of prayer and worship. To outline a prayer technique and to recommend it may seem to many devout persons an attempt to degrade prayer to a mechanical procedure, to a practice devoid of the spirit and quality of worship. A moment's reflection will show the fallacy of such a sweeping inference. That technique may destroy and displace the genius of prayer is an abundantly demonstrated fact. It is conceded that the source of a man's inspiration is of more importance than his method. On the other hand, we cannot do anything without the use of a method. Some methods are more profitable than others and when the remaining contributing factors are equal the best method will achieve the most. A technique is simply a refined means of accomplishing a purpose.

Method should be subordinated to and lost in the end which one has in view. When one is caught and stirred by the message and manner of an orator one is not conscious of the technique employed. When it is most effective the method is least in evidence. When one is captured and edified by an outpouring of prayer one is not disposed to segregate and analyze the technique of it. Nevertheless, in all such cases the technique is potently present. One of the fundamental contentions of the

223

religious educator is that instruction and training in the art of
praying should be given to every developing personality. It
would be hard if not impossible to cultivate an effective devotional life without establishing a prayer technique.

Professor Henry N. Wieman has suggested a technique of
prayer which is designed to disclose what is wrong with the
individual and how the defect can be remedied.[1] The five progressive steps which he outlines are here introduced with such
modifications and adaptations as seem justified.

Steps in Problem-Solving Prayer

The first act in private prayer or worship is complete relaxation and the calm and passive contemplation of the infinite
Power on which we are dependent for our every breath. One
is to achieve a state of poise and tranquillity, to celebrate the
sacrament of silence. Exertion is to be avoided. One is not to
make the mind a blank, nor to think of any specific thing
or problem. One is to be still and know that God is.

Experiments in relaxation performed under the direction of
Dr. Edmund Jacobson of the University of Chicago have
yielded a body of information useful to the pastor and religious
educator.[2] Dr. Jacobson's findings indicate that relaxation begins as a physiological process and gradually becomes mental.
Muscular tension induces or accompanies mental tension. The
objective evidences of advancing relaxation are limp appearance of the subject's body, flaccidity of the body, absence of
movement, cessation of speech, smoothing of facial muscles,
slow and regular breathing. If the subject is nervous, he is
not relaxing. The conscious state of nervousness consists of
varied sensations from muscular tension. The fact that one is
enjoying the process is an indication that one is actually relaxing. As the relaxation of the muscles progresses voluntary
attention diminishes. When relaxation is complete sleep overtakes one.

When muscular tension is reduced emotional excitement

[1] See his *Methods of Private Religious Living* (New York: The Macmillan Company, 1929).
[2] See his *Progressive Relaxation* (Chicago: Univeristy of Chicago Press,
1929).

evaporates. Proneness to anger, disgust, and resentment, all of which make a dispassionate view of an irritating situation impossible and are often subversive of morals, abate in direct proportion to the degree of relaxation attained. Relaxation is a precondition of effective muscular co-ordination. Such motor accomplishments as golfing, swimming, and dancing cannot be acquired apart from freedom from muscular and mental tension. Muscular tension accounts for many a topped golf ball, and consequent provocation only intensifies the causal factor and its deplorable outcome. Many a swimmer can testify that only when he had the courage to relax did he begin to swim with minimal effort and to have pleasure in aquatic sports. Only when the dancer is relaxed does he exhibit the grace and experience the exhilaration which characterize his art in its best estate.

The reader may determine for himself the validity and applicability of the principles which Dr. Jacobson's experimentation has yielded. Let him clench the fist, frown, close the eyes tightly, and note the degree of bodily and mental tension induced. In fact, one can sit still and hold one's self tensely motionless. Let the reader next lie down and systematically and progressively relax the arms, the legs, the trunk, the shoulders, the neck, the forearm, the eyes, the lips, the tongue, and the throat. Let him release whatever seems to be under physical strain and note the corresponding decrease of mental activity.

Periods of relaxation possess positive therapeutic value in cases of nervous hypertension, insomnia, anxiety, neurosis, stuttering, and other like disorders. In view of the fact that our conventional and artificial life overstimulates us and induces a brood of functional ailments which harass and hound their victims, relaxation both as a preventive and remedial agency should be understood and devotedly cultivated. A leading psychologist testifies that several times each day he systematically relaxes in the privacy of his office, his secretary having strict orders not to interrupt these balance-restoring periods.

The application of the principle of relaxation to the act of prayer is obvious. Before one can understand and estimate the problem which is agitating the mind, one must be set free from distorting and distracting conditions. Serenity and objectivity are necessary. Relief from tension prepares the mind for the effective approach to its own resources and to ultimate Reality.

The second step consists of a survey of the possibilities for aid and encouragement which reside in God. The mind is to overflow with the consciousness of God as a partner in our fortunes rather than as a Being whose function it is to preserve us from adversity or to rescue us from vicissitudes without our co operation. In taking this step the mind becomes more active. Passivity gives way to mental activity, but the resources of God and his good will rather than the specific problem which presses for solution are the objects of attention. In quiet contemplation one's faith in the potency and helpfulness of a divine Companion grows and fills one with hope and courage which are prerequisite to an adequate personality adjustment. Prayer is man's conscious intercourse with God. "He that cometh to God must believe that he is, and that he is the rewarder of them that seek after him." In all true prayer there is an inner attitude of humility and expectancy, a direct movement of the worshiper toward the heart of the Universe.

In the third step one comes to grips with the problem itself. The perplexing situation is frankly faced and reduced to its component elements. Self-deception, casuistry, and sophistry are avoided or discarded, and the attitude of the seeker of the facts in the case is adopted and maintained. Self-analysis, if that be called for, is vigorously and relentlessly made, and the findings, however unpalatable, are accepted. Stripped of pretense and disguise, one stands face to face with one's self as it actually is and not as one would prefer it to be. The obstruction which militates against a higher synthesis of the facts of experience is discovered, lifted into prominence, dissected, and evaluated. He who refuses to hale himself before the tribunal of his own intelligent judgment and to abide by the verdict derives no benefit from an act of prayer the object of which is personality reconstruction; on the contrary, the obtuse person degrades prayer to an exercise which entrenches the more firmly the defect. The conflicting factor must be exposed, the state of confusion banished, the issue clarified.

The fourth step is the logical continuation of the third. Diagnosis is followed by prescription. One seeks a remedy. One asks, "Is the adequate adjustment one by domination, or sublimation, or discrimination, or accommodation, or submission?" One inquires, "What changes in my program of living must I make in order to achieve the victory over the flaw in my personality of over crippling outward circumstance? What is the practical solution of my problem?" If the case involves a difficult decision, one raises the question, "Of the alternatives, which should be chosen?" A strenuous effort is made to think of or mentally devise fruitful courses of action and to anticipate the probable outcome of the practical application of each. The one that commends itself as the most expedient is selected for actual practice.

When no remedy can be forged on the anvil of prayer at once, later efforts at intervals may prove successful. A mind illuminated and sensitized by the religious attitude and sustained by faith and confidence functions at its best and releases its resources and makes them available for the end in view. The understanding person does not expect God to present him with a ready-made solution, but relies on divine love and wisdom to companion him in his energetic efforts to find the way in which he should go.

The fifth step centers in the verbal formulation of the rearrangement necessary for the actual solution of the personal problem. One states as definitely and clearly as possible the change in behavior which the correction of defect demands or the new principle which is to regulate life. The carefully considered and formulated statement is verbally repeated until it becomes a dynamic part of the personality. Vocalization is a means of directing the attention into the proper direction and tends to lead the mental functions into a single confined channel. Repetition makes the mental imagery of the object of attention increasingly vivid, realistic, and desirable. It generates an emotional tone which makes the formula personal and urgent. Since it is a law of our being, that we grow in the direction of exercise, the reiteration of a principle or program creates a new attitude and motivates conduct. That which was at first an external pressure becomes through personal acceptance and repetition an internal spur to action.

The Method of Jesus

The person who is living intensely is all the time struggling with emergencies. It is significant that the most rewarding acts of prayer occur at the turning points of our lives. When the course of life is even and uneventful, prayer, if engaged in at all, has its rise in a sense of religious obligation, is quite formal, and, aside from satisfying an accepted habitual requirement, is quite barren of practical results. The tendency of efficacious prayer is to vary directly with the crises in life. One recalls, for example, Christ's seasons of prayer in the critical hours that emerged in the trend of his mission. In framing the guiding principles of his progress Christ seems to have adopted a method similar to the one outlined above. One seems to glimpse in the extant records of his prayer relations the successive steps of relaxation, meditation, analysis, creative thinking, and internalization.

Consider the accounts of Christ's threefold temptation in the wilderness. In the baptismal experience the consciousness of his uniqueness was intensified. He retired to a region presumably uninhabited by human beings in order to formulate principles for the regulation of his career as a leader in the field of morals and religion. In the chosen environment there was an abundant opportunity for relaxation and the contemplation of the resources of God throughout the prolonged period of fasting. Three questions agitated the mind of Christ: What function of his ministry should under all circumstances have the precedence? By what method should he introduce himself to the people and do his work? What attitude should he take toward leaders whose outlook and objectives differed from his?

The temptations which assailed Christ were subtle and insidious. Faint with the pangs of hunger, he was tempted to secularize his gifts. The suggestion that he transform stones into bread might have been rationalized as a laudable prompting, not to be denied without sinning, to save his life in order that he might accomplish his mission. The temptation to cast himself down from the pinnacle of the temple, and thus to conform to a popular expectation of the coming of the Messiah from heaven in dramatic and miraculous fashion, might have been regarded as a zealous proposal to initiate his work by a method startling enough to produce immediate results. The temptation to fall down and worship Satan, to conciliate the opposing forces in the seats of ecclesiastical or political power by compromising his ideals, might have seemed like laudable strategy, like a friendly conspiracy to be all things to all men in order that he might win many. Christ was delivered from the insidiousness of each temptation by mental penetration; by a calm analysis of each proposal he exposed its fallacy and folly. In each case the discovery of the truth and his readiness to walk in its light set him free. In him the mystical and rational interacted with amazing consequences.

Three distinct principles emerged in the mind of Christ. He did not deny bread a place in the program of living but assigned it a subordinate status in the scale of values. Under no conditions would he disturb the proper balance between the eternal and the external. Self-preservation is by no means to be the paramount issue of his life. In the second place, he resolved to avoid sensational procedures in furthering his cause, and to rely on teaching, work with individuals, the contagion of personal contact, and the transforming power of fellowship with men. Finally, he determined not to lower his ideals in order to conquer, not to make concessions to the opposition, but to be true to his ideals at any cost. In possession of these fundamental principles Christ left the solitary place and began his work.

That these principles were internalized and became motive forces is evident from his decisions in subsequent crises. For example, in a desert place to which he had retired after his first works of healing performed in Capernaun he decided to make the cure of disease subsidiary, and accordingly left the city with his disciples to return only after the excitement created by the marvels of healing had had time to abate. Again, he refused to perform miracles at the request of those who were seeking a sign, referring rather to the sign of Jonah, which was preaching; and when he was enduring the agony of the crucifixion he ignored the taunting challenge to come down from the cross if he were the Son of God. At the zenith of his popularity with the multitudes he brushed aside the proffered crown, for his kingdom was a personal experience of divine love, and as such not in accord with the conception of the crowd. Furthermore, rather than win the favor of the hostile leadership of the nation through concessions, he cleansed the temple and challenged the scribes and priests either to accept or reject him, and thereby precipitated his martyrdom. Repeatedly and consistently Christ applied these fundamental principles to the exigencies which developed in the course of his public ministry. Time and again he withdrew from those who sought to thwart him in order that he might clarify his situation, keep life unified in terms of his sense of mission, and sensitize afresh his mind by response to the divine promptings. The place which problem-solving prayer occupied in his life is an inspiring example to every perplexed soul.

Method in Private Worship

Prayer does not always include an area of specific difficulty within the scope of its activity. Not every act of prayer has for its purpose the resolution of a definite conflict or the making of a delicate decision. Prayer may principally take the form of meditation, adoration, thanksgiving, aspiration, and identification with Reality. We call this type of prayer worship. Through worship we adapt ourselves to our environment as a whole so as to appropriate the inspiration and support of God. Using Wieman's suggestive terminology, the process of worship may be described as a time exposure of the spirit of man to cosmic Reality. It is a man's appreciation of the worth of God. In the attitude of worship the individual is carried out of himself by a power other and greater than himself.

The worship of the Protestant, whether it be public or private, is subjective. Worship for the benefit of God is out of the question among Protestants. To be sure, prayer, whether it be petitional or devotional, is directed to God, and in this respect is objective, but the purpose for which prayer is made is the satisfaction of the worshiper. God is the objective point of reference in a mood of worship in which the individual withdraws into himself, nourishes his religious sentiments, increases his faith state, fortifies his moral convictions, and accommodates himself to his destiny. It is through worship that the awareness of God as a Presence, more marvelous than anything one can imagine, is achieved.

The technique of private worship involves especially the elements of relaxation and contemplation; critical analysis, the solution of a special problem, and the formulation of a new program or principle of behavior are less prominent if not all but absent.

Many persons engender and deepen the attitude of worship through the reading of devotional literature and meditation on the concepts which it provides. Repeated affirmations of faith and confidence in God play an important part in devotional exercises. The individual may say to himself : "Faith in God is reasonable, intelligent, and good men have had it, it is right, it is rewarding; hence I too will exercise faith, I will trust in God in all of the varying circumstances of my life." Similarly one may cultivate a fear-relieving confidence. A single devotional thought in the literature of worship is frequently sufficient to kindle the flame of a reliance on God which consumes vague fears and nameless worries. When faith has been renewed and confidence has been restored and supported, courage, consecration to the highest, and joy emerge, and life in God's world is colored with a sense of infinite worth. It would be difficult to overestimate the tonic quality of worship.

I requested the members of a class in the psychology of religion to submit in writing, without signature if so preferred, responses to the question: "What circumstances do you find most conducive to satisfactory private worship?" The reactions are illuminating, and a few typical ones are here presented. A young mother says: "I experience a feeling of awe and reverence together with that of humility when in the quiet presence of the power and majesty of God as revealed in the beauty of nature, natural forces at work, and the mystery of life and death. When I attempt to explain these wonders and their Creator to my four-year-old daughter I feel a peculiar sense of His presence and my partnership with Him. I believe I really worship when planning a worship service for my church school class. I experience gratitude, remorse, humility, inspiration, a sense of divine guidance, and a desire to know, to be and to do better." A young minister of the gospel records his experience with refreshing candor: "The first essential in my case or at least of primary importance is a sense of physical well-being. If the digestive tract is not functioning properly, I might as well abandon the quest for God. There must be a sense of social adjustment; when I am able to meet my financial obligations and all my duty to society has been done, God is nearer to me. A cold stormy night seems to intensify the feeling of peace and security afforded by my home; sitting by the warm fireside in the congenial fellowship of books or music will lead me to contemplate the goodness of God and induce the worshipful mood. Standing on the summit of a mountain 'where the clouds have met the incense of the pine,' I have experienced the 'fascination' to which Professor Rudolf Otto refers." [3] Another testifies: "Worship is most satisfying when I can be alone in my study surrounded by familiar objects which to me have religious significance. I have found the quiet of a star-lit night helpful. I have also felt that physical posture is an aid to worship. I have a large easy-chair in which I completely relax and close my eyes."

The error is still too common that man is endowed with a special prayer instinct which functions without conscious control. The fact is that man has a capacity for prayer and worship, a capacity which must be carefully developed if he is to accomplish fullest self-realization. A capacity is quite different from an instinct. Prayer is not an inborn pattern reaction. It is not a biological reflex. Prayer in the face of a crisis is not an automatic performance like the winking of the eye when a foreign body approaches it. The prayer act is transmitted and acquired, however disposed one may be to learn it and however

[3] See his *The Idea of the Holy* (Oxford University Press, 1923).

habitual it may become. The effectiveness of prayer in an appropriate situation depends largely on the intelligence with which the nature and scope of prayer are grasped and the importance prayer has acquired in personal experience. A knowledge of the psychology and technique of prayer should banish both the biological and magical theory of the devotional life and disclose its underlying operating principles.

Instruction and training in what might well be called the science of prayer are imperative. One should learn what prayer really is, what to pray for, what not to pray for, and how to pray. A great many persons are like the woman who declared that she had no faith in God and in prayer because when she was a little girl her prayer that God mend a torn page in her geography was unanswered. No one brought up in a Christian environment should have such a distressing experience. Proper education in prayer and worship forestalls similar tragedies, and only a delicate process of reconditioning can restore a shattered religious attitude. It is much easier to slap a perplexed and anxious parishioner on the back and to tell him that he is "all right" and to "buck up" than it is to teach him the principles which support prayer and the methods which release and utilize moral and spiritual energies. The path of least resistance leads to futility if not to further conflict, but the path of understanding to adjustment and satisfaction.

CHAPTER XVIII

PASTORAL COUNSELING

As distinguished from preaching or lecturing or group teaching, the pastoral procedure is private, confidential, personal, and intimate. Not that pastoral care and any one of the other functions of the Christian ministry are mutually antagonistic. They are complementary; each supports the other.

The social situation which the congregation engaged in the act of public worship creates is unique and is freighted with potentialities for personality liberation and expansion which are not easily overestimated. The sermon which is a popular address on a religious theme, partly because it is general in its appeal, does generate hope, courage, self-dissatisfaction, moral resolution, comfort, and inspiration. The teaching situation enables one to impart to the small and homogenous group instruction and suggestions which do not easily lend themselves to homiletical treatment and presentation. Teaching which proceeds from pre-existing needs or interests and culminates in appropriate life adjustments is a mighty ally in personality building. One measure of good preaching or effective teaching is the number of individuals whom it moves to consult the pastor for additional and specific help. A normal fruition of preaching and teaching is the pastoral touch.

The Mental Health of the Pastor

The personality of the pastor himself is of primary importance in his work. A mature and wholesome outlook on life is essential to good pastoral service. Personal immaturity as reflected in timidity, preoccupation with self, and over-sensitiveness must be transcended before the pastor can make an effective approach to the problems which depress those who appeal to him for aid. When he himself is harassed by fears, torn by exasperation, and depressed by nervous fatigue he is unequal to the demands of the pastoral office.

When the blind lead the blind the outcome is disastrous to

both. The reproach, "Physician, heal thyself," is never more devastatingly caustic than when it falls from the lips of one who has discovered in his pastor the same personality defect from which he is seeking deliverance. Lack or loss of confidence in the pastor is calamitous. Only the adjusted and integrated personality inspires trust and co-operation in others. A prolific source of failure in pastoral relations is the entanglement of one's own difficulties with those of the persons who desire help.

On the other hand, sympathy with the undeveloped or disrupted personality the pastor is attempting to assist is a precondition of success. The worker who poses as a reformer feels superior and captious, and thereby antagonizes and repels the one in need. The word "reform" is excluded from the vocabulary of the wise pastor. He thinks in terms of re-education, rehabilitation, and development. He is a guide, not a stern judge or harsh critic. He is first of all a human being overflowing with good will and understanding.

Personal interest and scientific analysis are by no means incompatible. It is said that Sir William Osler, the great physician, tempered his professional relations with a measure of good cheer and sympathy that heartened his patients to meet the challenge of sickness and to battle for health. Playing goblin, he would convert the sickroom of a child into a fairyland. In fairy language he discussed the birds and flowers and talked to the dolls that shared the bed of a sick little girl. To be sure, the smiling eyes of the physician were the while observing the conditions which his instruments were signaling, and his brain was busy determining the proper course of treatment. Similarly the pastor should have a deep feeling for humanity as such and not as an assortment of cases, or networks of impulses, emotions, and weaknesses. Only when people like us can we do them good, and they will probably like us if we first like them.

Co-operative Counseling

The effective pastor functions as a counselor. Various aspects of the private personal service which he renders are included in counseling. At work as a counselor, the pastor detects the presence of a form of personality immaturity or maladjustment by its characteristic signs and symptoms. In the progress of counseling the appropriate treatment is outlined and recommended. The pastor does not prescribe drugs or perform surgical operations, but administers remedial and preventive means of his own calling, such as instruction, prayer, confession, persuasion, assurance, encouragement, and suggestion. The pastoral counselor may go a step beyond diagnosis and management; he may forecast the probable course and termination of the personality imperfection or defect. Counseling is the comprehensive procedure in pastoral care.

The counselor offers guidance in the acquisition of the ideals, knowledge, and skills which are essential to self-realization and social committal. Good pastoral work stimulates and aids persons to discover and define for themselves their needs, opportunities, and responsibilities, to face facts with intelligent courage, and to acquire the techniques for the mastery of the situations which emerge in the trend of their lives. It is the pastor's province to generate in men a discontent with their unnecessary limitations and to arouse their latent resources for personality rehabilitation or growth.

Counseling at its best is, then, a form of creative interaction. It is more than an exchange of experiences and opinions. It is not blind acceptance of the counselor's advice and the proposed course of treatment by the consultant. Not that the two are on a parity, for the one is the adviser and the other the advised. The pastor serves as confessor, instructor, and guide. Nevertheless, the interview as it progresses, unless it assumes the form of a monologue or private lecture, becomes a co-operative enterprise. The pastor does not take over the perplexity of another nor impose upon an immature or divided individual a set of pattern ideas and activities, but shares his life in such a way that the consultant makes the needful personal or social adjustment. Initiative and experience cannot be bestowed by the pastor, although he can often suggest or provide the opportunity for their development.

Counseling as the knowledge and application of certain definite psychological principles is a science. When it is the instrument of a pastor gifted with unusual insight, originality, and ability it becomes an art. The technique of counseling can be acquired by study, observation, and practice. Not every pastor can become an artist as a counselor, but all endowed with common sense, a desire to serve others, patience and the willingness to learn can become useful personal workers.

Suggesting the Interview

Who shall take the initiative in seeking the interview, the pastor or the person in distress? Generally speaking, the person who comes to the pastor of his own accord is more likely to co-operate than the one who is sought. Many pastors complain that about the only persons who do come to their studies on their own initiative are individuals who desire financial assistance or who want to sell them something. On the other hand, many a pastor reports that the members of his constituency are in increasing numbers requesting his services in the solution of their personality problems. The probabilities are that as Protestant pastors develop skill as counselors their services as such will be requisitioned by more and more persons.

The assumption that the pastor has discharged his obligations when he has ministered to those who have come to his study is false. Although the physician or the lawyer does not go from house to house inquiring whether there be any who need his professional services, and while indiscriminate pastoral visitation is hardly to be commended, the commission of the minister of Christ should send him forth to those who need him, but for reasons valid or otherwise do not come to his study for consultation. The pastor, unlike the lawyer or doctor, has no direct financial stake in his ministration to the individual. He is not restrained from taking the initiative in his work by the system of professional etiquette which governs the lawyer or the physician; in fact, the public rather assumes that the pastor of his own accord will be diligent in visiting those whom he can serve in the name of his Master.

The bed-fast, the infirm, and the shut-in cannot go to him. He must not ignore those whom despair has rendered indifferent, or those who are too ashamed to seek him, or those who are too bewildered to find their way to his study, or those to whom the sight of his face would be a rebuke for wrongdoing.

Many who of their own accord would not come to the pastor's study are deeply grateful to him for going to them and volunteering his services. It should be remarked parenthetically that the major objective of personal visitation is not to stimulate church attendance, however important that may be, but to minister to the needs of the individual.

The pastor who becomes known for his helpfulness both within and without his parish will be appealed to for counsel by persons whom he has not met and who do not personally know him. He will have mysterious telephone calls from those who insist on withholding their names and request interviews under conditions of the strictest secrecy. They will refuse to come to the pastor's study in the waiting room to which the appraising eyes of others may see them, or to his home where some member of the household may learn of their presence. They may prefer to come under the cover of night to some sequestered place, say a rear pew in an empty church. Such individuals seek protection and secluded helpfulness. The way to their own pastors seems too difficult, their conflicts appear too intimate and momentous to be bared to anyone whom they must frequently meet under other circumstances. Recognizing the call of human need, the pastor will not refuse to serve those who prefer to keep their identity secret. When such consultants are affiliated with denominations or forms of religion other than his own, the conscientious counselor does not try to estrange them from their habituated ways but encourages them to utilize the resources of their own faiths.

Young people, especially distracted by the inner turmoil and fever of adolescense, find it easier to consult one whom they do not know personally but whom they have reason to trust than to confide in those to whom they are bound by the ties of blood or friendship. When adolescent interests and problems arise the easy intercourse between parent and child gives way to constraint. Some of the new knowledge of the adolescent is tainted by a secretiveness which erects a barrier between father and son, mother and daughter. The personal ambitions and the secret dreams which color all the days of the boy cannot be shared by his father, lest they be misunderstood and treated with levity. Again, the boy is afraid that if he takes his father into his confidence, his father will be reminded of the occasion whenever they are together. The daughter does not want to disturb the peace of her mother with a revelation of foibles, failings, and strange longings. Young people do not want to live under the same roof with constant parental reminders of their inner conflicts and immaturities. Much adolescent reticence is induced by a fear that in a moment of anxiety the one parent would tell the secret to the other. For analogous reasons they may not consult their own pastors. The wise counselor whom they do actually approach will consent to serve them on their own terms of neutrality and anonymity.

The Setting of the Interview

Appropriateness of time and place makes important contributions to the work of the counselor. Privacy is, of course, a chief point of excellence in the setting. A stroll through the woods or park may open the heart of one who is responsive to the appeal of nature. It is not always easy to secure the necessary seclusion in a home or place of business. In such circumstances the pastor may not be able to do more than to indicate his willingness to aid and to extend an invitation to come to his study for consultation.

The setting of the interview in the pastor's study should be such as to put the consultant at ease and to arouse in him the attitude of confidence. The furniture of the room should be restful and the decorations informal and conducive to the mood of reconstructive activity. Hanging on the wall of the office of a college president is a painting of a peasant couple cooking dinner in a pot in a fireplace in the midst of the ruins of their cottage just consumed by fire, the dog crouching near and vultures hovering over the scene. The president explains that many a student or professor who has entered the office feeling that the world has been too much for him, has grasped the significance of the painting and taken courage. Some symbol or pictorial representation of man's ability to rise above adversity may well have a place in the pastor's study.

The consultant may prefer a seat not directly in front of the pastor, but at his side, and perhaps in the faint shadows rather than in the bright light. The interviewed does not like to feel that the spotlight has been flashed upon him. In the Catholic confessional a partition separates the priest from the penitent. The chair occupied by the visitor should be comfortable and enable him to relax the body.

There should be sufficient privacy and freedom from interruptions and distractions such as telephone calls. A door left slightly ajar when the pastor is being consulted by a woman may be a wise concession to social expediency. If the person has been admitted from a waiting room, he will be grateful if he may make his exit by another door. These and other details of the setting, which a sense of fitness will suggest, affording the consultant relaxed security, facilitate the delicate process of pastoral work to a degree which only the experienced counselor can appreciate.

A Variegated Class of Consultants

The good counselor is a patient listener. One man as soon as he has entered the pastor's study begins with emotional excitement to relieve his mind. Words pour forth from him like a river which has broken its dam. He has not come for advice but for the sole purpose of expressing himself freely in the presence of one who will listen to him. He may go so far as to declare that while he assumes that his pastor can give him no help he does crave the privilege of stating his case to an understanding listener. The pastor, once in possession of the facts, may to the surprise of the visitor offer pertinent advice. Whatever the outcome may be, the ear of the pastor is of importance to the troubled man, however much the latter's attitude reflects emotional immaturity.

Another consults the pastor with the expectation of obtaining specific aid. He comes because he has not been able to solve his problem himself and feels that his pastor will come to his rescue. He proceeds to set forth the details of his perplexity and to point out its various aspects and bearings. Suddenly he pauses, his face becomes radiant, and he announces with a note of victory that the solution has just occurred to him. The pastor has made no suggestions, asked no questions, volunteered no information, but only listened to the impassioned flood of speech. The consultant, gently stimulated by a friendly presence, has perhaps clearly formulated and analyzed his case, has attacked it with renewed vigor, and has himself done what he expected his pastor to do for him. To mention an alternative, perhaps a subconsciously elaborated solution was delivered to consciousness when the mood of confidence was induced. Although the part of the pastor in such instances, which are of frequent occurrence, is an humble one, it is a determining factor in the creative result.

Still another consultant is timid, fearful, and reticent. He is palpably burdened and visibly depressed, but of his own accord has but little to say. In such a case the pastor may find it expedient to stimulate the consultant in order to give the interview direction and point. To this end the counselor may ask a series of questions designed to culminate in a disclosure of the tension-inducing elements. The pastor should begin the process of diagnosis with questions which may be answered with a single monosyllable like Yes or No. When reluctance or hesitancy has been sufficiently overcome he may make inquiries the responses to which are more elaborate. It is necessary to obtain the social history of the consultant.

If the pastor suspects an emotional maladjustment, questions such as the following may possess diagnostic values: Did you get on well with your brothers and sisters? Do you love your mother more than you love your father? Which parent was dominant in the home? Do you alternately hate and love the members of the family? Did you sustain an emotional shock in childhood? Is your appetite good? Do you sleep well? What have you been dreaming about lately? What is your attitude toward the opposite sex? If married, is your mate congenial? Do you experience difficulty in making decisions? Do you avoid people? Are you easily embarrassed? Are you subject to periods of depression and loneliness? Do you prefer solitude? Do you lose your head easily in a dangerous situation? Are you easily enraged? Do you have unpleasant sensations now and then in some part of the body? Have you theological difficulties? Have you realized your vocational ambitions? Is adverse criticism extremely irritating?

Many points of tension have their origin in an ignored or forgotten experience. The originating impulse or event may or may not be recalled and recognized in the course of a series of informal interviews. In some cases it may be necessary to apply the more specialized technique of the clinical psychologist as described in a previous chapter. In fact, it will often be necessary and expedient to refer stubborn and obscure cases to the specialist in mental disorders.

Not seldom a person will come to the pastor's study with a preconceived conception of what ails him. The diagnosis of the consultant himself is not to be accepted at its face value by the pastor without further investigation and confirmation. The consultant may be disabled by a form of nervousness or worry the source and nature of which he himself does not completely understand. His interpretation of his difficulty may be warped and colored by prejudice, rationalization, and an incomplete knowledge of the relevant facts. He may allege in all sincerity that recent contact with modern science has destroyed his religious faith, whereas in reality his skepticism is the product of a shattered romance. The consultant's attitude and conceptions are not to be dismissed as entirely worthless, for they picture the world in which he lives. The rôle that a person plays in the world of his own imagination possesses a diagnostic significance which the counselor cannot afford to overlook.

Some people, especially the young, prefer to submit to the pastor written personal histories or informal letters. Many young people take delight in corresponding on subjects of crucial concern to themselves, such as home conflicts, perplexing sex attitudes, religious opinions and practices, and vocational problems. Although many are diffident and restrained in conversation, they do not hesitate to express themselves freely in writing. When they are not under the scrutiny of the watchful eye of another, they are more likely to share their difficulties and to liberate their emotional pressures. The composition of the letter impels the writer to dissect his situation, to evaluate his plans afresh, and to clarify his ideals, all of which is not always easily accomplished in an informal interview. Young people, especially when encouraged, will write the pastor letters in which no definite counsel is requested but which afford him an opportunity to make suggestions and to arouse additional thought. Much advice can be given in an indirect way by correspondence. The pastor becomes intimately acquainted with the background, the home life, the religious experience, and the secret ambitions of his correspondents, and, understanding their points of view and circumstances, is able to give them intelligent guidance in their life situations.

Critical Determination in Counseling

The wise counselor never loses sight of the importance of distinguishing symptoms from their causes. The treatment of symptoms rather than originating attitudes and experiences can at best afford the consultant only temporary relief or a false sense of security. An exhortation to have faith in the goodness and power of God, or an invitation to join the pastor in a word of prayer, however commendable as such, is no adequate substitute for an effort to bring to light the root of the consultant's difficulty. It is hard to overstress the fact that the removal of or adjustment to the causal factor is essential to personality rehabilitation or the recovery of emotional balance. The pastor in his work with individuals should consistently endeavor to correct disability rather than to alleviate symptoms.

The social worker applies the same principle. He no longer devotes the major portion of attention to wages, rental, and other items of the family budget, however important they may be, but occupies himself mainly with the problems of how to help those in need to develop better relations with their employers, their fellow-employees, and the members of their own families. In an emergency material relief must be given, but such a form of first aid is only preliminary to a longer and far more expert process of discovering and eliminating the underlying causes which have brought about distress. The causes are likely to be psychological; a sense of responsibility, self-development, and a mature conception of life may transform unfortunate outward circumstances and personal behavior. It is often far easier to give to one in material need the financial help he requests than to undertake the task of motivating and guiding a process of personality reconstruction to which he is indifferent or almost so.

To trace personality defects and social misbehavior to their sources is at times a project which requires exceptional diag-

nostic skill. The variety of possible originating impulses and
conditions is so extensive that at no stage in his experience can
the pastor suppose that he has nothing more to learn. Mr. and
Mrs. John Banks were having domestic difficulties. Friends
were unable to explain the friction, for the two were devoted to
one another and in most respects seemed compatible. Mis-
understandings and quarrels increased in frequency and intensity, and a separation seemed imminent. A psychologist, who
was a specialist in the human responses to color, became interested in the case. One evening the psychologist was a guest
in the home of the couple. He engaged Mr. Banks in a discussion of the importance of color in interior decorating. He discovered to which colors his host reacted with pleasure and to
which with displeasure. The psychologist observed that but
few of the favorite colors were present in the home and that
the disliked colors were supplied in profusion. He had discovered the origin of the unfortunate domestic conflict. Husband and wife responded differently to certain colors, colors
which were disturbingly present in the scheme of home decora-
tion. At an opportune time the psychologist suggested to Mrs.
Banks that alterations in the color plan be made. The young
wife adopted the suggestion but was frankly skeptical of the
predicted outcome. When the color changes had been made
marital misunderstanding and friction disappeared. The source
of the maladjustment and misbehavior was removed. The
case illustrates the subtle psychological processes which often
motivate reprehensible conduct. The simple is not to be complicated, but the complicated is not to be oversimplified. Easy
identifications are to be regarded with suspicion.

The disposition to reduce all personality disabilities to one
and the same source such as sexual frustration or the inferiority
complex should be resisted. Clinical psychologists have in
several conspicuous instances given exhibitions of such a restricted tendency. One marvels at the rich powers of the
imagination which by hook or crook subsume all mental ailments under a single category. No one concept can interpret
with sufficient sharpness of detail the infinite varieties of human
limitations. There is more than one arrow in the quiver of
personality. No one principle underlying personality problems

should be overweighted, although it is indisputable that a few sources of disorders are more frequently active than all others.

For example, excessive, not to say obsessive, bodily cleanliness is by some invariably regarded as symptomatic of an effort to rid the self of a sense of guilt. In this connection one recalls that washings and lavings play a prominent part in Jewish religious rites of purification. In order to symbolize his belief in the innocency of Jesus on trial Pilate washed his hands. One remembers Lady Macbeth's nocturnal attempts to remove the homicidal spot from her hand. Do we not say, "I wash my hands of the affair," when we disclaim further responsibility? The case of a young man who washed his hands an unusual number of times throughout each day was thoroughly investigated. So far from discovering that the obsession was motivated by a subconscious memory of a reprehensible deed or desire, the investigator learned that the young man had recently made an intensive study of disease germs and that the frequent washing of his hands was prompted by his fear of the microorganisms.

When a problem is attributed to an extraneous or irrelevant cause the consultant is plunged into greater confusion and misery. Miss Gertrude St. John is a college student. Her academic rating was below the level of minimal graduation requirements. She was regarded as a problem student by her teachers. She was depressed, discouraged, and undertalkative. The faculty adviser was positive that she was the victim of an erotic escapade or desire. Registering no improvement in either her personal behavior or her studies, she was formally notified by the committee on admissions at the close of her sophomore year that she was dismissed from the college. The dean was dissatisfied with the disposition of the case. He invited Miss St. John to his study. When she was admitted she was visibly on the defensive. The dean told her that he had a daughter of the same age who was also a student, and that fortunately he had been able to help her in several crises. Could he be of any assistance to Miss St. John? Sensing that it was not assumed that she was morally delinquent or unfortunate, that the dean had no psychological theories to support, and that he was understandingly sympathetic, she disclosed the root of her attitude. She had misinterpreted a periodic physiological irregularity. The dean referred her to a physician for appropriate treatment. Miss St. John was permitted to return to college the following school year, and her wholesome personality and the rare quality of her academic work have abundantly vindicated the confidence reposed in her. In order to be valid the counselor's diagnosis must be a scientific determination proceeding from critical perception.

Allies of the Pastoral Counselor

The judicious supplementing of counseling with the use of books is recommended. A well chosen book will give the consultant a wider and perhaps more systematic knowledge of the nature of his perplexity and how to overcome it or adjust himself to it. It is well to bear in mind that some persons derive more benefit from the contact with and advice from the counselor himself than they do from books. The personal touch is paramount. On the other hand, since most neurotic persons are introverts, many consultants will appreciate articles or books which meet their needs. To be sure, the emotional and suggestible reader may indulge in morbid introspection and imagination and thereby exaggerate or intensify his condition. Taking such possibilities into account the pastor will exercise due caution in his book recommendations.

Only rarely will it be expedient to advise the reading of the technical and in part controversial volumes of Freud, Jung, and Adler. Fortunately treatises on personality adjustment written in popular style and balanced in the discussion of the subject matter are available. A consultant who is emotionally disordered may find Professor English Bagby's *Psychology of Personality* illuminating and practically suggestive. The woman suffering from some type of nervous exhaustion may derive light and leading from Dr. A. Myerson's *The Nervous Housewife*. Dr. Joseph Jastrow's *Keeping Mentally Fit* may acceptably serve those whose interests and problems are in the field of mental hygiene. Dr. William S. Sadler's *The Mind at Mischief* may with clarity and force reveal the hidden spurs to a variety of aberrations. Conflicts between early acquired religious beliefs and the teachings of modern science may be resolved by the study of a constructive treatise. A young woman who is unable to reconcile the doctrine of evolution with accepted religious teaching, taking the advice of a pastor, read Henry Drummond's *The Ascent of Man* and pronounced this not recent but still valuable volume the most helpful book she had ever read. Books setting forth with transparent simplicity the origin, purpose, message, and permanent significance of the several documents of the Bible, books which are on the library shelves of the alert pastor, will be a godsend to a person who has found the inherited conception of the Scriptures untenable but has not yet been oriented to the historical method of Bible study and its results. Using discretion, the pastor makes books his allies in his personal service.

In the course of his work with individuals the pastor may have occasion to refer consultants to either the psychiatrist or the social welfare worker. In order to co-operate most effectively with these specialists the pastor must have a clear understanding of their objectives, resources, and methods. He must realize that, like himself, the social worker and the psychiatrist are concerned with the promotion of mental health, the improvement of social relations and circumstances, and the cultivation of adjusted and integrated personalities. All three apply remedial as well as preventive measures and work with almost every age group.

Not only do the three workers have much in common, but each is a specialist who can contribute something to the constituency of the others. The pastor's own resources will often be supported or supplemented by the ampler stores, economic and otherwise, of the social agencies of the community. When the consultant is in need of exactly what the social worker can supply the duty of the pastor is evident. The psychiatrist devotes his professional energies not only to the insane, to those afflicted by the major forms of psychosis, but also to persons suffering from the comparatively minor emotional and social maladjustments and to so-called problem children. Although the pastor makes considerable use of the knowledge and technique which the psychiatrist has developed and tested, he will not attempt to supplant the psychiatrist, especially in the field of serious mental disorders. He will refer the hysterical and psychotic consultant to the psychiatrist for more expert care and treatment. In such a case the psychiatrist takes complete charge and outlines the course of treatment. The pastor places himself at the service of the psychiatrist. There are circumstances in which the best turn a pastor can do a consultant is to advise him to appeal to the social worker or psychiatrist for the specialized type of aid needed.

A SELECTED BIBLIOGRAPHY

ADLER, ALFRED, *Education of Children.* New York: Greenberg, Inc., 1930.

——, *Understanding Human Nature.* New York: Greenberg, Inc., 1927.

——, *A Study of Organic Inferiority and Its Psychical Compensation.* Washington, D. C.: Nervous and Mental Disease Publishing Co., 1917.

——, *The Neurotic Constitution.* New York: Moffat, Yard & Co., 1917.

BAGBY, ENGLISH, *The Psychology of Personality.* New York: Henry Holt & Co., 1928.

BAUDOUIN, CHARLES, *Suggestion and Autosuggestion.* London: George Allen & Unwin, Ltd., 1920.

BEERS, CLIFFORD W., *A Mind That Found Itself.* Garden City, N. Y.: Doubleday, Page & Co., 1923.

BERMAN, LOUIS, *Glands Regulating Personality.* New York: The Macmillan Company, 1921.

BOORMAN, WILLIAM RYLAND, *Developing Personality in Boys.* New York: The Macmillan Company, 1929.

——, *Personality in the Teens.* New York: The Macmillan Company, 1931.

BRILL, ABRAHAM A., *Psychoanalysis.* Philadelphia: W. B. Saunders Company, 1922.

BROWN, WILLIAM, *Mind and Personality.* New York: G. P. Putnam's Sons, 1927.

——, *Science and Personality.* New Haven: Yale University Press, 1929.

CAMERON, W. A., *The Clinic of a Cleric.* New York: R. R. Smith, 1932.

CAMPBELL, CHARLES A., *A Present-Day Conception of Mental Disorders.* Cambridge: Harvard University Press, 1924.

CANNON, WALTER B., *Bodily Changes in Pain, Hunger, Fear, and Rage.* New York: D. Appleton & Co., 1920.

COE, GEORGE A., *The Spiritual Life.* Chicago: Fleming H. Revell Company, 1900.

——, *Motives of Men.* New York: Charles Scribner's Sons, 1928.

COLLINS, JOSEPH, *The Doctor Looks at Love and Life.* New York: Garden City Publishing Co., Inc., 1926.

DASHIELL, JOHN F., *Fundamentals of Objective Psychology.* Boston: Houghton Mifflin Company, 1928.

DE SCHWEINITZ, KARL, *The Art of Helping People Out of Trouble.* Boston: Houghton Mifflin Company, 1924.

ELLIS, HAVELOCK, *Man and Woman.* New York: The Macmillan Company, 1927.

ELLWOOD, CHARLES A., *Introduction to Social Psychology.* New York: D. Appleton & Co., 1917.

FISHBEIN, MORRIS, AND WHITE, WILLIAM A., *Why Men Fail.* New York: The Century Company, 1928.

FREUD, SIGMUND, *Wit and Its Relation to the Unconscious.* New York: Dodd, Mead & Co., 1916.

——, *Psychopathology of Everyday Life.* New York: The Macmillan Co., 1917.

——, *The History of the Psychoanalytic Movement.* Washington, D. C.: Nervous and Mental Disease Publishing Company, 1917.

——, *A General Introduction to Psychoanalysis.* New York: Boni & Liveright, 1920.

FRINK, HORACE W., *Morbid Fears and Compulsions.* New York: Moffat, Yard & Co., 1921.

GRAY, ARTHUR HERBERT, *Men, Women, and God.* New York: George H. Doran Company, 1922.

HART, BERNARD, *Psychology of Insanity.* New York: The Macmillan Company, 1912.

HEALY, WILLIAM, AND HEALY, M. T., *Pathological Lying, Accusation, and Swindling.* Boston: Little, Brown & Co., 1915.

HINKLE, BEATRICE M., *The Re-Creating of the Individual.* New York: Harcourt, Brace & Co., 1923.

HOLT, EDWIN B., *The Freudian Wish and Its Place in Ethics.* New York: Henry Holt & Co., 1915.

JACKSON, JOSEPHINE AGNES, AND SALISBURG, HELEN M., *Outwitting Our Nerves.* New York: The Century Company, 1922.

JACOBSON, EDMUND, *Progressive Relaxation.* Chicago: University of Chicago Press, 1929.

JAMES, WILLIAM, *The Varieties of Religious Experience.* New York: Longmans, Green & Co., 1917.

JANET, PIERRE M. F., *Principles of Psychotherapy.* New York: The Macmillan Company, 1924.

JASTROW, JACOB, *Keeping Mentally Fit.* New York: Greenberg, Inc., 1928.

JONES, ERNEST, *Treatment of the Neuroses.* New York: William Wood & Co., 1920.

——, *Papers on Psychoanalysis.* New York: William Wood & Co., 1923.

JUNG, CARL GUSTAV, *Psychological Types.* New York: Harcourt, Brace & Co., 1923.

——, *Collected Papers on Analytical Psychology.* New York: Dodd, Mead & Co., 1916.

——, *Psychology of the Unconscious.* New York: Dodd, Mead & Co., 1916.

KING, BASIL, *The Conquest of Fear.* Garden City, N. Y.: Doubleday, Page & Co., 1921.

LEE, PORTER P., AND KENWORTHY, M. E., *Mental Hygiene and Social Work.* New York: Commonwealth Fund, Division of Publications, 1929.

MACKENZIE, JOHN GRANT, *Souls in the Making.* New York: The Macmillan Company, 1929.

McDOUGALL, WILLIAM, *The Group Mind.* New York: G. P. Putnam's Sons, 1920.

MENNINGER, KARL AUGUSTUS, *The Human Mind.* New York: A. A. Knopf, 1930.

MILLER, HUGH CRICHTON, *The New Psychology and the Preacher.* New York: Albert and Charles Boni, 1924.

MORGAN, JOHN JACOB BROOKE, *Psychology of Abnormal People with Educational Applications.* New York: Longmans, Green & Co., 1928.

MYERSON, ABRAMAM, *The Nervous Housewife.* Boston: Little, Brown & Co., 1920.

OLIVER, JOHN RATHBONE, *Fear.* New York: The Macmillan Company, 1927.

OVERSTREET, HARRY A., *Influencing Human Behavior.* New York: W. W. Norton & Co., 1925.

——, *About Ourselves.* New York: W. W. Norton & Co., 1927.

PFISTER, OSKAR ROBERT, *Psychoanalytic Method.* New York: Moffat, Yard & Co., 1917.

PIERCE, FREDERICK, *Our Unconscious Mind and How to Use It.* New York: E. P. Dutton & Co., 1922.

PRINCE, MORTON, *The Unconscious, the Fundamentals of Human Personality, Normal and Abnormal.* New York: The Macmillan Company, 1929.

——, *The Dissociation of a Personality.* New York: Longmans, Green & Co., 1913.

RIBOT, THEODULE A., *Psychology of the Emotions.* New York: Charles Scribner's Sons, 1912.

RIVERS, WILLIAM H., *Conflict and Dream.* New York: Harcourt, Brace & Co., 1923.

ROBINSON, WILLIAM J., *The Menopause.* New York: Eugenics Publishing Company, 1930.

SADLER, WILLIAM S., *Mind at Mischief.* New York: Funk & Wagnalls Co., 1929.

SANGER, MARGARET H., *Happiness in Marriage.* New York: Brentano's, 1926.

SIDIS, BORIS, AND GOODHART, S. P., *Multiple Personality.* New York: D. Appleton & Co., 1909.

SPERRY, WILLARD L., *Reality in Worship.* New York: The Macmillan Company, 1925.

STRECKER, EDWARD A., AND APPEL, KENNETH E., *Discovering Ourselves.* New York: The Macmillan Company, 1931.

STOLZ, KARL R., *Psychology of Prayer.* New York: The Abingdon Press, 1923.

SWIFT, EDGAR JAMES, *Psychology and the Day's Work.* New York: Charles Scribner's Sons, 1918.

TERMAN, LEWIS, *Measurement of Intelligence.* Boston: Houghton Mifflin Company, 1916.

THOMAS, WILLIAM, *The Unadjusted Girl.* Boston: Little, Brown & Co., 1923.

THORNDIKE, EDWARD L., *Adult Learning.* New York: The Macmillan Company, 1928.

VALENTINE, PERCY F., *Psychology of Personality.* New York: D. Appleton & Co., 1927.

WATSON, JOHN B., *Psychology from the Standpoint of Behaviorism.* Philadelphia: J. B. Lippincott & Co., 1924.

WEATHERHEAD, LESLIE D., *Psychology in Service of the Soul.* New York: The Macmillan Company, 1930.

WHITE, WILLIAM A., *Outlines of Psychiatry.* Washington, D. C.: Nervous and Mental Disease Publishing Company, 1926.

——, *The Principles of Mental Hygiene.* New York: The Macmillan Company, 1917.

———, AND JELLIFFE, S. E., *Modern Treatment of Nervous and Mental Diseases.* Philadelphia: Lea & Febiger, 1913.

WIEMAN, HENRY N., *Methods of Private Religious Living.* New York: The Macmillan Company, 1929.

WORCESTER, ELWOOD, AND McCOMB, SAMUEL, *Body, Mind, and Spirit.* New York: Charles Scribner's Sons, 1932.

WRIGHT, HELENA, *Sex Factor in Marriage.* New York: Vanguard Press, 1931.

INDEX

Adler, A.
  educational theory of, 35 f.
  psychic nutritional activities, 134
  reference to technical writings of, 246
Adolescence
  character of, 48
  constraints of, 238 f.
  conventional attitudes of, 60
  desire for recognition, 57 f.
  emotional tension of, 49 f.
  fears of, 151
  idealism of, 59
  independence of, 58
  occupational problems of, 54 ff.
  physical energy of, 50 ff.
  self-consciousness of, 50
  sex qualities of, 52 ff.
Alcoholism
  escape mechanism for inferiority, 140 f.
Ambiversion
  nature of, 65
  relation of to religious experience, 72 ff.
Aurelius, Marcus
  quoted, 215
Authority
  dominated child as the product of, 41

Bagby, E.
  cases of fear compulsions cited, 145, 154
  volume of recommended, 246
Beecher, H. W.
  as a worker with adults, 92
Benet, S. V.
  example of narcissism, 170
Berman, L.
  glandular classification of personalities, 70
Blair, J. H.
  experiment in adult learning, 85
Boorman, W. R.
  example of suggestion, 31
Breuer, J.
  co-worker of Freud, 198
Brill, A. A.
  case of dream analysis, 189 f.
  cases of subconscious motivation, 128
Burgess, E. W.
  case of sublimation of pugnacity, 45

Bushnell, H.
  as a worker with adults, 92
  theory of Christian conversion, 39
Byrd, R.
  hero of the boy, 180

Caesar, Julius
  hypnotic impersonation of, 193
Christ
  as an educator of adults, 90
  development of, 89
  loyalty to and ethical love, 104
  method of in prayer relations, 228 ff.
  ministering in the name of, 237
  portrayal of as the dying Savior, 103
  prophetic quality of, 77
  quoted, 20, 215
  rallying center of, 107 f.
  reference to life and teaching of, 63
  tolerance of, 76
  trial of, 188
Christian Science
  limitation of, 199
Coe, G. A.
  case of social suggestion, 32
  relation of temperament to religious experience, 77 ff.
Compensation
  description and examples of, 176 ff.
Confessional, The
  modification of by Luther, 203
  moral and mental values of, 204
  place and form of in Protestantism, 206
  Roman Catholic form of, 202
Corporal Punishment
  failure of, 45
Counseling
  appropriateness of time and place, 239
  as a form of creative interaction, 236
  danger of bias in, 244 ff.
  diagnostic questions in, 241
Darwin, C.
  recording incompatible data, 129
Davis, O.
  adjustment of to death, 221
Daydreaming
  example of, 94

255

Daydreaming—(*Continued*)
  outcome of frustration, 34
  relation of to degeneracy of the
    will, 138 f.
Deland, M.
  citation from a story of, 173
DeSchweinitz, K.
  case of self-deception, 209
Domination
  adjustment by, 211 f.
Dreams
  anxiety variety of, 187
  as unfulfilled wishes, 186
  reasoning of, 188
  sensory origins of, 186
Drummond, H.
  volume of recommended, 247
Ductless Glands
  relation of to personality, 71
Durant, W.
  reference to book of, 88

Edwards, J.
  as a worker with adults, 92
Emotion
  conflict of, 37, 49 f.
  dangerous upheavals of, 175
  motivating power of, 101
  persuasiveness of to piety, 103
  reconstitution of, 142 f.
  relation of to complexes, 121
  relation of to failure in integration,
    207
  relation of to feeling, 121 f.
  transference of, 182
Evangelism
  rôle of, 17
  the future of, 20
Extroversion
  nature of, 65 f.
  relation of to religious experience,
    77 ff.
  relation of to temperament, 66 ff.

Faris, E.
  classification of wishes, 33
Fear
  as a form of inferiority, 145
  cast out by love, 104
  consciousness of, 146
  definition of object of, 152
  doctrinal origins of, 149 f.
  excavation of hidden origin of, 153
    f.
  non-rational forms of, 147 ff., 150
  physiological accompaniments of,
    146
  transformation of by religion, 16 f.

Fosdick, H. E.
  application of religion in psychia-
    try, 201
Freud, S.
  appropriation of Janet's method,
    199
  contribution of to dream psychol-
    ogy, 186
  discovery of the talk cure, 198 f.
  reference to controversial writings
    of, 246
  theory of neurotic behavior, 39
  theory of origin of complexes, 120
    f., 197
Galen, C.
  temperamental classification of, 65
Galsworthy, J.
  reference to Old English, 214
Gladden, W.
  exponent of social religion, 18
Gray, W. N.
  study of reading interests of adults,
    88
Gray, Z.
  popularity of novels of, 88
Habit
  dependence of on motivation, 95
Hadfield, J. A.
  conquest of fear by definition of
    object, 210 f.
Hall, G. S.
  fears of children and young people,
    151
Hankey, D.
  conception of religion, 107
Hart, B.
  case of subconscious conflict, 130
Hero Worship
  as a form of compensation, 180
  identification with hero, 31
  rôle of in adolescence, 59
Hilprecht, H. V.
  reference to dream of, 188
Holt, E. B.
  case of adjustment by discrimina-
    tion, 217 f.
Home Training
  purpose of, 41 ff.
Hyperthyroidism
  relation of to personality problems,
    72
Hypnosis
  nature of, 192 f.
  limitations of, 193 f.
  who can be hypnotized? 193
Ibsen, H.
  reference to drama *Ghosts*, 174